The Canadian
FAMILY IN CRISIS

John F. Conway

James Lorimer & Company, Publishers

Cover photograph: kids at playground in Hope, British Columbia. Photo credit: Brian Milne, Firstlight.

Canadian Cataloguing in Publication Data

Conway, John Frederick
   The Canadian Family in Crisis
   Includes bibliographical references.
   ISBN 1-55028-286-7 (bound) ISBN 1-55028-284 (pbk.)
   1. Family Canada. I. Title.
HQ560.C66 1990 306.8'5'0971 C-89-094960-3

James Lorimer & Company, Publishers
35 Britain Street
Toronto, Ontario M5A 1R7

Printed and bound in Canada

6 5 4 3 2 1 89 90 91 92 93 94

Contents

Acknowledgements

All or portions of the manuscript were read by Curtis Fahey and Virginia Smith of James Lorimer and Company and by Margaret and Sally Mahood. Their suggestions helped immeasurably. And copy editor Jane Fredeman often rescued my prose from itself. It is impossible to list all my friends and colleagues who contributed over the years to shaping my ideas on the topic, but I thank them all. And I thank all those scholars cited in the footnotes whose work made this attempt at an overview possible. Leanne Osborne typed the manuscript, including my interminable revisions and insertions. Grants from the University of Regina President's Fund and from the office of the Dean of Graduate Studies helped defray some of the xeroxing and typing costs.

Finally, I have to acknowledge the help of my spouse, Sally Mahood, my three sons, Liam, Aidan, and Kieran, and my daughter, Meara. Writing this book posed many mini–crises for our family, and their tolerance and good humour over the months were vital to seeing the task through to completion.

This book is dedicated to:

Geneviève Bergeron, 21,

Hélène Colgan, 23,

Natalie Croteau, 23,

Barbara Daigneault, 22,

Anne–Marie Edward, 21,

Maude Haviernick, 29,

Barbara Maria Klueznick, 31,

Maryse Lagonière, 25,

Maryse Leclaire, 23,

Anne–Marie Lemay, 27,

Sonia Pelletier, 28,

Michèle Richard, 21,

Annie Saint–Arneault, 23, and

Annie Turcotte, 21,

who were brutally murdered on 6 December 1989 at the École polytechnique de Montréal.

May this book serve as a small candle to help illuminate the darkness of our understanding.

Preface

The crisis of the family in Canada is one of monumental proportions, and it touches us all.

The figures are astonishing. In this decade about one marriage in two will likely end in divorce.[1] Between 1966 and 1986 the divorce rate increased by about eight times, and the duration of marriage before divorce fell dramatically.[2] More and more of us are declining to take the emotional risk of marriage. Single parent and common–law families are growing faster than traditional "husband–wife" families.[3] Wife beating and child abuse, physical and sexual, are the fastest growing crimes in the country. Each year tens of thousands of Canadian children suffer through a marriage breakdown. More and more families are childless, and the Canadian fertility rate is dangerously below replacement levels. Between 60,000 and 100,000 children, aged 10 to 16, run away each year. Reports of homelessness, hunger, and poverty afflicting our children can be read daily in our newspapers.

What these facts tell us is that the traditional family no longer delivers emotional solace to growing numbers of Canadian men and women. The family has also increasingly failed to provide many children with the minimal emotional and physical security necessary for shaping confident and emotionally healthy adults.

If the family serves any purpose in advanced industrial society, it is to provide emotional gratification for its members, while ensuring the birth, early care, and socialization of children. The crisis of the family has called into question these obligations. The traditional family is dying and new alternatives are emerging, but the transition involves pain, anguish, and uncertainty. While the sanctuary, the traditional family, is being dismantled around us, the new alternatives to deliver love and comfort and to socialize children have yet to receive the recognition and support so vital to their successful emergence.

This crisis is increasingly at the centre of political debate and public concern. During the 1984 federal election campaign the leaders of the three major parties participated in a special debate on issues related to women and the family. Yet in 1988 Prime Minister Brian Mulroney refused a similar debate, no doubt sensitive to the fact that most of the promises delivered in 1984 had not been honoured.

Meanwhile, conservative politicians use the crisis of the family to polish their images. Saskatchewan Premier Grant Devine worries that urban lifestyles, allegedly characterized by drugs and promiscuity, undermine the traditional family. Alberta Premier Don Getty declares that the family is "Canada's hope for the future."[4] The 1988 Premiers' meeting calls for a national conference on family values, which is held in Regina in 1989.[5] Former federal Health and Welfare Minister Jake Epp declares, "I'm trying to preserve as much as possible the traditional family."[6] Quebec Premier Robert Bourassa offers cash incentives to encourage women to have more babies,[7] and Alberta Premier Don Getty offers payments to keep women at home to care for their children.[8] Such efforts to turn Canadians back to the traditional family cannot hope to succeed. But by focussing on such measures, governments appear to act, while the painful transformation of the family moves inexorably onward.

Some of these politicians genuinely believe that by resisting the new family forms and supporting the traditional family, they are doing the right thing. Others are convinced that only support for the old–fashioned family will sell on Main Street. Still others wonder how much such intervention in the family, however beneficent, the public will accept. And the potential cost implications of effective family policies are enormous in the short term.

And this poorly directed concern is understandable. As the crisis deepens, the ideological positions on the family harden. This is particularly true of the right wing. REAL Women (Realistic, Equal, Active and for Life) complains that the Supreme Court, the Charter of Rights and Freedoms, gay rights, abortion rights, and universal day care are destroying the family and insist that more support must be forthcoming for the role of women as wives and mothers in the home. A new federal political party, The Family Coalition Party, is created based on opposition to abortion and support for the traditional family unit.[9] A central theme of the anti–choice movement is that the traditional family is being destroyed by the freedom of reproductive choice among women. Such attitudes are buttressed by more official opinions such as those expressed in *The Family: Preserving America's Future*, a task force report presented to former President Ronald Reagan in 1986, which argued seriously that the crisis of the family has resulted from 20 years of "liberal social experiments, from no–fault divorce to permissive sex to the easy availability of welfare."[10]

On the other side, feminist groups ranging from the National Action Committee on the Status of Women to various pro–choice groups, joined by groups of trade unionists, social workers, social scientists, mental health workers, and day care advocates, have mounted a convincing lobby that insists that the crisis of the family must be confronted. The price of avoiding the issue is just too high: homeless and hungry children; child and teen suicide; battered women and abused children; enforced pregnancy and unwanted babies; and increasing economic injustice for growing numbers of women and children. The crisis of the family, they argue, has become a general social crisis and must be confronted with effective family policies.

The structural transformation of the family continues irresistibly, and those in power take half or quarter measures. And as the debate rages, the victims of the crisis of the family continue to grow in number.

Many years ago the famous American sociologist Robert S. Lynd wrote a provocative little book, *Knowledge for What?*[11] Lynd enjoined social scientists to accept as part of their scientific obligation to the community the urgent clarification and communication of the pressing problems of an epoch to the people. Some years later C. Wright Mills wrote *The Sociological Imagination*.[12] He appealed to social scientists to endeavour to make "personal troubles of milieu," where people try as best they can to adjust to crises individually, into "public issues of social structure," where the community, alerted to a problem that is in fact centrally social, can mobilize its collective resources to adjust to the problem while endeavouring to solve it. This book is inspired by these two imperatives.

In the past 25 years there has been an enormous amount of research in Canada on the problems of women and of the family. This present book is deeply indebted to that work. One thing has been made crystal clear — the crisis of the family and the problems of women in achieving equality are intimately linked and cannot be solved separately.

PART I

The Changing Nature of the Family

Therefore shall a man leave his father and his mother, and shall cleave unto his wife and they shall be one flesh ...

And the Lord God said unto the woman ... I will greatly multiply thy sorrow and thy conception; in sorrow thou shalt bring forth children; and thy desire shall be subject to thy husband, and he shall rule over thee ...

And unto Adam he said ... cursed is the ground for thy sake; in sorrow shalt thou eat of it all the days of thy life ... In the sweat of thy face shalt thou eat bread ...

Therefore the Lord God sent him forth from the garden of Eden, to till the ground from whence he was taken.

Genesis

Introduction

Social scientists often get carried away with a definition of terms, discussing fine distinctions between "statistical families," "economic families," and "extended families." But the family in our experience is clear. It is the coming together of a man and a woman, usually but not always legally married, to express their mutual love and commitment. If the relationship lasts, children are often produced, and then the family is made of mother, father, and children living together under one roof, developing a long–term economic, social, and emotional unit. Sometimes, as the years advance, the family expands to include aging grandparents. *nuclear*

The big things are commitment, obligation, responsibility. Recognizing that we all must age and that our sexual currency on the love market must decline, physical love is replaced by deeper bases of understanding and support and, often most importantly, the shared love and excitement of raising children. The establishment of the family is an effort to find assured meaning and solace, as well as to express our emotional selves in more fundamental and lasting ways. That was "the family." That is the family. And that will be the family in the future. The human species has not yet produced an alternative as fulfilling or as rewarding. *the prob. wt arg.*

That fundamental marriage, or common–law, relationship that brings two adults together sets the stage for the bearing and raising of children, for the care and comfort of the old and dying, and for emotional and financial support in our declining years. In the distant past marriage and the family were *the* social structure of the species. And today they remain *the* central social experience of our day to day lives.

The family in this sense is in crisis. It has been in crisis before — when feudalism declined and collapsed; when industrial capitalism emerged; when war, famine, and plague swept a land. But the crisis today, just like previous crises, is specific and needs focussed attention, if only because new embryonic family forms are emerging and urgently appealing for midwives.

1 / Families Past

The Origin of the Family

We will probably never know for certain when, where, and how the human family emerged. Freud suggested that, prior to civilization, the human species probably lived in hordes much like those of our present primate relatives.[1] These hordes were characterized by a dominant male who enjoyed sexual access to all the females and denied sexual gratification to the younger, subordinate males. But, inevitably, the younger males conspired against the dominant male (father), rose up against him, and slew him. There followed a wanton sexual debauch with the females. Extending his metaphor, Freud speculated that the younger males were overcome by guilt for having slain the father, for their incestuous liaisons with the females, their mothers, and for the aggression it led to among themselves. Ultimately, the young males erected taboos against incest and aggression and realized that human social life, on which their collective survival depended, had to be rooted in the suppression of instinctual gratification.[2] The seeds of the human family were thereby sown: the suppression of sexuality within the group, controls on sexual gratification, the prescription to go outside the immediate group for sexual partners, and the subordination of the sexual and aggressive instincts to the tasks of survival and civilization.

While Marx might have conceded the outlines of Freud's metaphor, he argued not that our animal natures were merely repressed, therefore always threatening to burst through the fetters of civilization, but that as the human species emerged our very nature was transformed. Thus, members of the human species became human in the fullest sense, rather than just intelligent animals wisely controlling their more bestial tendencies in the interests of co–operation and survival. Marx never specifically wrote at length on the emergence of the family, but Engels did.

Taking off from Morgan's nineteenth–century classic *Ancient Society*, Engels attempted to relate forms of the emerging human family to Morgan's main stages in the history of human development.[3] Thus during the period of "savagery," when the human species took its survival directly from nature through hunting and gathering, the dominant family form was "group marriage," which was characterized by informal pairing and a simple division of labour based on age and sex. Dependence was mutual, as the food–gathering activities of women and children were as vital as the hunting activities of the men. During the period of "barbarism," after the invention of agriculture and the domestication of animals led to complex systems of food production and storage, the dominant family form was "pairing marriage." It required a more permanent household organization, but the division of labour remained mutual. There was still no clear dependence of women and children on men. As barbarism evolved into more complex forms of "civilization," a more strictly monogamous marriage emerged, laying the basis for the modern nuclear family. With civilization came private property and the state, as well as the more rigid patriarchal family based on male domination and the subordination and dependence of women and children. Monogamy was enforced on women (but not on men) in order to assure paternity and the orderly inheritance of property by the progeny of the dominant male. The modern nuclear family form's emergence lies, therefore, for Engels, at the cradle of women's oppression with the establishment of a rigid patriarchy and a system of male privilege.

Certain themes are clear. How did forms of sexual regulation emerge? How did patriarchy reach ascendancy? How did the relationships of mutuality and reciprocity get transformed into relationships of domination and dependence? And these are important questions. Even today biological determinists continue to assert that male domination and female subordination are "natural" and biologically inevitable. It is important therefore to understand how the human family came into being and developed if only to remind ourselves of its *social construction* — that is to say, to remind ourselves that the species and its circumstances, not Nature, decreed the character and form of the human family.

It has been suggested that there appears to be a gradual move from sexual promiscuity to increasing exclusivity in moving from lower to higher non–human primates.[4] Some lower primates practise extreme sexual promiscuity when the female is in estrus. At the next stage there is a degree of exclusivity since mating occurs mainly between estrus females and dominant males. Finally there's the gibbon, one of two anthropoid apes most closely related to the human species, whose social organization closely parallels a human, monogamous, nuclear family.

By and large, however, there are few clear indications of a nascent human family among the primates. Like humans, infants of non–human primates are dependent on their mothers for a long period of time. Unlike humans, non–human primate sexuality is clearly directed hormonally. Like humans, non–human primates live in groups and engage in complex social interaction. Unlike humans, non–human primates neither co–operate nor engage in systematic food sharing. The social life of non–human primates may be a step towards human social life, but only a very small step.

A number of crucial things evidently happened in the transition of the human species from its primate roots. Co–operation had to replace conflict. Year–round sexual interest had to establish itself. Systems of kinship had to replace hierarchies based on brute strength. More complex patterns of social life, including a division of labour, mutuality, and reciprocity, had to replace the simple primate social life of competitive sexual activity, grooming, random play, and protection from predators. Territorial hostility had to be replaced by mechanisms to assure harmony and mutual aid.

Early Families

All this and more was achieved by the remarkable human invention of the family." With the family came a division of labour, food sharing, long–term relationships of reciprocity and obligation, the regulation of sexual activity, harmony, and co–operation, elaborate kinship relationships binding disparate groups together,

= camp

and the assurance (more or less) of survival for all members of the family group from birth to death. The human family was clearly the watershed that separated the human species from all others. The species could not have survived without it.

When they compare the highest non–human primate hordes and the simplest hunting and gathering human groups, cultural anthropologists point to the enormous discontinuous chasm that separates the two. Freed from the rigidity of biological adaptation, the human species has been able to survive in virtually every environment presented to it. Through cultural and technological innovations, humans can live under water and in outer space, fly through the air, and race at dizzying speeds along the ground. Today that is so self–evident as to be hardly worth noting. But if we return to the contrast between our nearest primate cousins and our simplest human ancestors, what is most striking is just what was at first distinctively human.

There were three specifically human adaptations that marked the species off clearly from all other animals. These were the division of labour, food sharing, and the establishment of a new social role, that of "husband–father."[5] These three phenomena assured the species' survival and success. The division of labour — women gathering food and men hunting — provided the species with a more secure and balanced supply of food. The change from the anarchy of individual feeding to the systematic, reciprocal sharing of food characteristic of the human species in all times and places occurred. What was required was the establishment of the husband–father social role, "in which specific males relate to specific females and their young, taking on special responsibility for their welfare."[6] And this new social formation was cemented by emotional attachments resulting from continuous "year–round *sexual interest* under conscious control in both partners," made possible by "the suppression of estrus and the concealment of ovulation."

This more or less universal early human family form, defined by Gough as "a married couple or other group of adult kinfolk who co–operate economically and in the upbringing of children, and all or most of whom share a common dwelling,"[7] dominated and defined the experience of the species from perhaps two million years ago to 10 or 15,000 years ago, when agriculture and the domestication of animals began. If the life of the human species to this moment in time were 24 hours, this "primitive" family form existed for 23 hours and 46 minutes. The more modern family form, which culminates in today's nuclear family, emerged only 14 minutes ago. The specific content of the family form varied, but there were certain universals: some degree of taboo against incest; a sexual division of labour; group security; and forms of marriage defined as "a socially recognized, durable (although not necessarily life–long) relationship between individual men and women." From this marriage relationship "springs social fatherhood, some kind of special bond between a man and the child of his wife, whether or not they are his own children physiologically."[8] And, finally, men generally enjoyed higher status and greater authority than women.

Perhaps this last point needs further attention. Women may not have had as much status or authority as men in hunting and gathering societies, but neither were they oppressed, nor were there elaborate systems of male privilege. If women's lesser status had any biological root it was because they bore and suckled children, and women in such societies would probably be pregnant or suckling an infant throughout their fertile years. Indeed, given life expectancy, it is doubtful many women lived beyond their fertile years. This fundamental biological fact meant that it was not practical for women to hunt and that it made more sense for them to gather food and carry out household tasks, things that could be easily reconciled with pregnancy and infant care. The practicality of the situation provides an explanation — we need not hypothesize some hormonal or instinctual basis for what was an eminently practical sexual division of labour.

Men's superior strength may also provide some explanation for their higher status as well as their possession of and knowledge of weapons. But the status differences between the sexes were not particularly marked. Women's food gathering activities were vital to survival as were their child bearing and rearing functions, since children were the group's future. Children were the old age pension for those few to live to an old age. Furthermore, women performed crucial domestic tasks — food preparation and crafts of various kinds. Indeed, women probably invented agriculture and domesticated the first animals. Therefore, women were highly regarded in the family as a system of survival and social life between the sexes went forward on a roughly egalitarian basis. Proponents of the subordination of women can find no support in hunting and gathering families. Life for women, as for men, may have been short, but it was neither nasty nor brutish.

Ironically, woman's greatest contribution to the species became the source of her enslavement to male patriarchy and male privilege. Agriculture and animal husbandry led to the need for more permanent settlements — the need for developed property and its defence — as well as to the emergence of the first fairly regular economic surpluses. Such property had to be defended, and the surplus had to be controlled and distributed. As more complex social systems were elaborated on the more secure bases of wealth and survival, production and politics became increasingly separated from the household. Women's sphere — child care and domestic work, supplemented always by labour in the fields — became increasingly private and centred in the immediate nuclear family. Men's sphere — hunting, now warfare and politics, and the supervision of property, production, and surplus — became more and more part of an enlarged public sphere from which women were more or less systematically excluded. As civilization became ever more complex, women became chattels, dominated by, and subordinated to, men. Children, previously the assured collective future of the small group, became private possessions of the father. Marriage became increasingly an enforced and continuing monogamy on women, as men strove to assure their paternity and the future of their property and their "line." As property, politics, and production became the public sphere in which men exercised their expanding options and powers; home, hearth, and heart became the private sphere in which women exercised their narrowing options and powers under the diligent, paternal supervision of father and then husband.

While women's work was still recognized as vital, it was locked up in a narrow definition of womanhood, which idolized the domestic virtues overlaid with obedience, and participation of women in the public sphere was constricted if not outright forbidden. A woman could still have influence and find fulfillment, but only if she accepted the narrow confines of the womanly virtues and if she were blessed with a kind and loving father and a gentle and loving husband. Otherwise, her life could be one of unrelieved suffering, hard work, and degradation.

The Industrial Nuclear Family

If in our 24 hour life of the species, the monogamous, patriarchal family emerged 14 minutes ago, the Industrial Revolution, which ushered in the modern industrial nuclear family, occurred less than two minutes ago. The Industrial Revolution, which set in motion the social, political, and economic changes that were to lead to the beginnings of women's emancipation, at first more deeply enslaved them. Further, the Industrial Revolution, which was to transform the family into its modern form, at first threatened to destroy all vestiges of significant family life, at least for the industrial working class. The pre–industrial patriarchal family of rural cultivators was still a unit that combined production and consumption, life in the public sphere and life in the private sphere. The division of labour based on sex remained rigid, and women remained largely consigned to the hearth. But the distance between hearth and field was not that great, and though it occurred in the context of patriarchy and male privilege, social and economic life between the sexes, and between adults and children, continued to be importantly mutual and reciprocal. As the capitalist market emerged and commercial agriculture took hold, the separation between domestic life and production for the market increased. As capitalism and the market triumphed, the separation between the two areas became greater and greater, resulting in the public sphere dominated by men becoming increasingly central in importance, and the domestic sphere, increasingly secondary.

The Industrial Revolution completed the process of separation between spheres of production external to the family and the spheres of consumption and reproduction internal to it. Work became something done outside the home to earn a wage to provide for the family's subsistence. The family's economic importance declined sharply as it was stripped of its productive economic functions. For the first generation or two of the Industrial Revolution, the family almost ceased to exist for many among the new working class as every member — husband, wife, and children — was forced into the factory system to toil for subsistence. As the revolution continued to consume this industrial fodder at an alarming rate through accident, illness, and exhaustion, working class organizations, middle class reformers, and enlightened capitalists began to present a compelling case for reform. For the working class, reform became a matter of life and death. For middle class reformers, humanitarian reform was the only way of preventing a disastrous decline in the collective morality, health, and vitality of the society. For enlightened capitalists, reform became essential to ensure that labour continue to be productive, healthy, and somewhat contented.

In this context the modern version of the industrial nuclear family emerged, a universal but poorer expression of a model of family life only the middle and upper classes could hope to afford to enjoy with any degree of security. The notion of motherhood emerged: the sacred and primary vocation of women, consigned to and subordinated in the domestic sphere while enjoying the benign and devoted economic support of men. The notion of fatherhood, and of the providing husband, was also born: a man must work out in the cruel world, but he did so in order to support a devoted wife and obedient children, who in turn waited to soothe, comfort, and refresh him for the next day's effort. So too emerged our romantic notion of childhood as an age of innocence, during which the necessary skills for adulthood would be lovingly if somewhat sternly imparted. Family life was private, and the home was the place where love, fulfillment and emotional meaning were sought. In many ways, it was a cruel vision that few could live in reality. Women and children continued to work in the wage labour force, in factory or in field, usually out of necessity, sometimes out of choice. But that vision of the family became the ideal to which many aspired, a dream of a heaven, or at least a haven, on earth. And as reforms were instituted, as real wages climbed, it became the reality for increasing numbers of ordinary people.

But this vision was based on the subjugation of women under the autocratic control, benign or otherwise, of men. Women could not vote. Women could not own property. Women could not keep their wages. It was legal for a husband to beat his wife and take his sexual pleasure from her regardless of her consent. Women were, legally speaking, non–persons with few rights, no privileges, and only indirect power. A woman who could not, or would not, embrace her allotted place in the scheme of things was either outcast or sentenced to a life of enormous difficulty.

By the mid–nineteenth century the industrial nuclear family had become the norm for virtually all Canadians regardless of class, including farmers producing for the market.[9] The husband/father worked outside the home to bring home a wage or salary (or profits, if he were a small or large capitalist). The wife/mother worked in the home, doing domestic labour (or supervising others doing it for her), bearing and raising children, and providing for the emotional needs of family members. No longer important in the social production process, the family had become the site for consumption and for the emotional fulfillment of its members. Sex roles were clearly defined and the lives of the sexes were separated clearly in the two spheres — private and public. The ideological glorification of the family, of childhood, of husband–fatherhood, and of wife–motherhood, ensured that the industrial nuclear family was the way all good, normal people lived. Men eventually became husbands and fathers, devoting their labouring time to securing the economic survival needs of wives and children. Women eventually became wives and mothers, devoting their lives to hearth, home, and husband. Good, normal men and women raised obedient, respectful children who would themselves leave the home of their family of birth and find fulfilment by establishing their own homes and families. This notion of the family, and indeed the reality of the family for most, was to continue until the post–World War II period when fundamental economic changes began undermining the traditional industrial nuclear family and transforming it extremely rapidly.

The Industrial Revolution, though initially enslaving women more completely, had also set in motion a series of intellectual and economic changes that established the conditions necessary for the increasing emancipation of women. The great democratic agitations, most clearly epitomized by the American and French Revolutions in the eighteenth century, and the revolutions of the 1830s and 1840s in the nineteenth century, inevitably provoked a debate about the rights of women. The arguments in favour of rights for women were given their best articulation in Mary Wollstonecraft's *Vindication of the Rights of Women* in 1792, in William Thompson's *Appeal of One Half the Human Race against the Pretensions of the Other Half* in 1825, and in John Stuart Mill's *On the Subjection of Women* in 1869. The 1882 Married Women's Property Act in the United Kingdom was one of the first victories of this agitation for women's rights. With the turn of the century, the debate over women's suffrage dominated pre–World War I politics. Except in New Zealand and Finland, where the vote was won for women in 1893 and 1907 respectively, what finally won women the vote in places like Canada, Great Britain, and the United States was the role they played in the war effort during World War I. The contributions women made in factory, field, and the armed services gave irresistible material force to the intellectual, political, and philosophical arguments which had long since been won by the advocates of women's rights.

Two industrial developments, accelerated as a consequence of World War I, continued the process of women's material emancipation and the transformation of the nature of the family. If the early phase of the Industrial Revolution had more completely subjugated women by more clearly consigning them to the hearth, the later phases began to pull women away from the home into the paid industrial labour force. The modern industrial economy needed women's labour, and women increasingly needed to, and wanted to, work. Women may have remained low paid, segregated into "women's work," and treated as a reserve army of labour; nevertheless their labour became increasingly necessary to the expanding industrial capitalist economy. At the turn of the century the female participation rate in the labour force was just under 20 per cent, after World War I it rose to just over 20 per cent, and thereafter it began a slow but steady climb to just over 30 per cent in 1961. Most of these women were single. Even as late as 1951 only just over 11 per cent of married women were working.[10] But the stage was set.

The other industrial development had to do with the industrialization of housework, as more and more labour– and time–saving inventions lightened the burdens of domestic labour. Until some technical alternatives to labour–intensive domestic drudgery were available and affordable, it was simply not feasible for a married woman with children to contemplate a significant commitment to work outside the home. Therefore, although members of the family of the 1940s and 1950s didn't realize it, the family as an institution was on the threshold of a dramatic transformation in its nature, a change that was to be so rapid as to create "a crisis of the family."

The Decline of the Industrial Nuclear Family

The traditional industrial nuclear family reached its apotheosis in the 1940s and 1950s. This was the era of the glorification of *the* family — dad at work and mom at home with the kids — imposed as the norm on the general society. And it *was* the norm. It was the family depicted in Dick and Jane readers and on television shows like *Father Knows Best*, *Life with Riley*, *Leave It to Beaver*, and *The Adventures of Ozzie and Harriet*. It was the family of the Dagwood and Blondie comic strip and movie series. This was the way people expected to live and the way they were taught to want to live.

This traditional family indeed existed for the overwhelming majority of Canadians in the 1940s and 1950s. In 1941 only 4.5 per cent of married women held a job outside the home.[11] The impact of World War II was evident in the 1951 rate when 11 per cent of married women were in the paid workforce. This changing reality of married women was the inevitable consequence of a general rise in overall female participation in the labour force. In 1941 21 per cent of females over 15 years of age were in the labour force, by 1945 this grew to 33 per cent, falling back to 25 per cent the following year and further shrinking to 24 per cent in 1951.[12] But this post–war decline was short term.

Working women in 1951 were overwhelmingly single — 62 per cent, while 30 per cent were married, 7 per cent were widowed, and just over 1 per cent divorced. Most of these women worked in areas like services (personal, recreational, food, and lodging), health and welfare, education, and in certain types of factories, manufacturing textiles, foods and beverages, and leather and rubber products.[13] On a weekly basis, working women could expect to earn about 55 per cent of what men earned.[14] The pattern was clear; women who worked in the labour force did so until marriage, when most withdrew, re–entering it typically only under the compulsion of loss of husband through death or divorce. In fact, only a bare majority of single women 15 years of age and older worked in 1951 — 58 per cent. Men worked outside the home. Women — even 42 per cent of single women — did not, except, one suspects, out of the most extreme necessity.

And what of the home and the family of 1951? There were about 3.3 million families comprising over 87 per cent of Canada's 14 million people. Over nine in 10 were headed by married men and enjoyed a husband and wife at home. Such a family had in fact been dubbed the "normal" family in the 1941 Census. Only just over 10,000 families were headed by a divorced person, overwhelmingly a woman. Divorce was so unusual that there were a scant 32,000 divorced people at the time the Census was taken, but it was twice the number in 1941, a taste of things yet to come.

And what of children? The average family in 1951 had two children, but averages can often be deceiving, as in this case. In 1945 Gallup reported that 60 per cent of Canadians thought the ideal family should have four or more children.[15] By 1951, few had reached that goal: 32 per cent of families had no children, 24 per cent had one, 20 per cent had two, and another 24 per cent had three or more. Fertility rates among women remained high from 15 to 44 years of age.[16] Having babies, for many women in 1951, spanned a lifetime.

Childbirth was still a risky business in 1951; more than one mother of every 1000 infants died in childbirth. Further, 39 out of every 1000 infants died before reaching one year of age, and over 18 of every 1000 births were stillbirths.[17] Women wanting to control their reproductive function faced the criminal law and unforgiving public attitudes. Birth control and abortion were illegal; and a woman risked sterility or death if she sought an underground abortion.

The large, stable family of the 1940s and 1950s, in which I grew up, is in the minds of most conservative politicians today when they design family policies. It sounds idyllic. That semblance of serenity and security was purchased at the enormous cost of consigning half our population to a life of domestic isolation and hard labour. On Mondays, laundry day in our house, my mother would spend 10 to 12 hours feeding the wash for eight people through a wringer washer and hanging it on the line to dry. The price for that appearance of stability was borne, usually silently, by women. Juxtaposed with the smell of freshly baked bread in my memory is my mother's quiet weeping some nights after she thought we were long asleep.

For women who wanted a choice, there was none, and the socialization process ensured that few wanted to be anything other than wives and mothers. Low wages, restricted jobs, no career future, hostile attitudes, and blatant sexual discrimination made the paid labour force an option of only very last resort. Today wife beating and child abuse are major public issues, but we have no reason to suspect these atrocities were any less epidemic in 1951. Indeed, they may have been more commonplace, if only because they were more hidden, and women in 1951 did not have even the few legal protections available today.

In other words, this traditional nuclear family was premised on the oppression and exploitation of women. And for every wife and mother who successfully practised her wiles on her husband in the television world, there were probably many others in the real world whose efforts were met with verbal abuse at best, or fists and boots at worst. Remember *Life with Riley*, the comedy television serial? Riley was a big, friendly buffoon, who was always successfully conned and manipulated by his wife and children. But the message was clear: buffoon or not, Riley was the head of the house, and his real power had to be dealt with.

When my mother re–entered the labour force at the age of 46 in 1957, a whole new world that had nothing to do with her motherly or wifely status opened up for her. At first she went out to work because the family needed the money, but she never wanted to return to live in domestic bliss. When she re–entered the work force, she didn't realize that her new–found sense of self was a small part of a larger social transformation that was to rumble throughout the 1960s and erupt into an earthquake in the 1970s and 1980s.

Women's Liberation and the Decline of Patriarchy

The women's liberation movement of the 1960s again inserted feminism into our political, social, and economic discourse, something that had been largely absent since the suffrage movement of the turn of the century. Despite early efforts to dismiss the movement, the feminist agenda quickly established itself. Although it emerged hand in hand with movements for civil rights, peace, an end to the Vietnam war, student power, and a sensible approach to the environment, the movement has persisted to the present day, scoring a series of major victories.

The new feminism was new precisely because it was so thoroughgoing in its critique of the place of women in society. Whereas the suffragists had largely accepted that women were to be wives and mothers first, the new movement criticized these orthodoxies and the subordination of women they enforced. The movement criticized the place of women in marriage and the family, in factory and office, in field and parliament — indeed, in all the private and public spheres where women were confined by the old notions.

Two publishing events of the early 1960s epitomized the new feminism. One was the publication of Parshley's translation of Simone de Beauvoir's *The Second Sex* in 1961.[18] The other was the appearance of Betty Friedan's *The Feminine Mystique* in 1963.[19] Despite the obvious differences between the perspectives of the two authors, these books struck a chord among women of the 1960s and provoked many men to begin a critical reassessment of relations between the sexes. Friedan's question "Is this all?" and de Beauvoir's call for an equal brotherhood with men both reflected and helped to clarify a deep dissatisfaction among women.

In Canada the women's movement won some significant victories. In 1968 a new Divorce Act established more lenient grounds for divorce, including physical and/or mental cruelty and a three–year separation (changed to one year in 1985). In 1969 birth control was legalized and limited access to safe, legal abortions granted. In 1967 a Royal Commission on the Status of Women in Canada was set up. Mandated to examine women's status in Canada with the widest possible latitude, the Commission reported in 1970.[20] Although a decade later the Canadian Advisory Council on the Status of Women complained that the *Report* and those recommendations ultimately implemented "had very little effect,"[21] the *Report* was in fact a monumental indictment of the second class situation faced by women in the society and the economy. Subsequently, laws were passed forbidding sexual or marital discrimination, improving women's legal status and granting women somewhat stronger rights to shares of property in the event of a marriage breakdown. Programs of affirmative action were begun to help overcome the legacy of inequality. It became very quickly clear that Canada, like other Western industrialized countries, had entered a new era.

What impact did this have on the family? Inevitably the family began to change more rapidly. But we have to be careful here lest we join the chorus on the far–right, which claims that the women's liberation movement somehow caused the good old family to change. Structural changes in the society and the economy affecting the family had already begun in the post–World War II period — more women were working, more married women were working, more women with children were working, the number of children per family was going down, divorces were increasing. What happened in the 1960s was the coming together of a set of material and ideological circumstances that made women's emancipation increasingly possible. Certainly some of this had to do with women's changing attitudes about themselves and their purpose in life. But choices can only be contemplated when they are available. The economy was changing so that women could more and more conceive of a life and an identity outside the home, since more and more jobs became available. Advances in household technology and declines in the birthrate meant less time each day and fewer years of a woman's lifetime had to be devoted to domestic labour and child rearing. The inability of a single wage to provide a family with all that it increasingly wanted and expected added a further pressure on women to seek remuneration outside the home.

Between 1966 and 1976, therefore, the family changed dramatically. In 1966 92 per cent of families were still husband/wife families, and only 8 per cent were single parent families. By 1976, 90 per cent were husband/wife families while 10 per cent were single parent. Families were smaller and less stable. In 1966, there were 1.9 children per family; by 1976 this had fallen to 1.6 children. The fertility rate had fallen well below the replacement level of 2.1 children per woman. In 1970 Gallup reported that 34 per cent of Canadians believed the ideal family had only one or two children; by 1974 52 per cent felt that way. In 1966, 29 per cent of families had no kids, 40 per cent had one or two, and 31 per cent had three or more. By 1976, 30 per cent had no kids, 48 per cent had one or two, and only 22 per cent had three or more. In 1966 only 2 per cent of families were headed by a separated spouse, while not half of 1 per cent were headed by a divorced spouse. By 1976 these figures had become 3 per cent and 2 per cent respectively. In 1966 less than half of 1 per cent of Canadians over 15 were divorced; in 1976 about 2 per cent were divorced.[22] In 1966 the divorce rate was 235 per 100,000 married women; by 1976 the rate was just over 1000, an increase of almost five times.[23]

More and more married women were working outside the home. In 1966 27 per cent of married women were working.[24] In 1976, 44 per cent of married women held down a job, including 37 per cent of those with children under the age of six. And the rate was highest among younger wives. Practice and attitudes were changing rapidly. For example, in 1960 Gallup found that only 5 per cent of Canadians approved of married women with young children working outside the home. By 1975, 18 per cent approved.[25]

Let's pause here to present a "snap–shot" of the Canadian family at the end of the 1970s and the beginning of the 1980s.[26] Most families, 89 per cent, were still husband/wife families, and 57 per cent of them had children still at home. But 51 per cent of wives worked outside the home, including 45 per cent of those whose youngest child was under age three, 52 per cent of those whose youngest child was between the ages of three and five, and 61 per cent of those whose youngest child was between the ages of six and 15. Altogether, 55 per cent of wives with children under 16 years of age worked. These working wives and mothers could expect to earn, on the average, 64 per cent of what men earned and brought home 28 per cent of total family income. These husband/wife families had an average of 1.3 children. Not surprisingly, in 1981 52 per cent of Canadian children were supervised, for part of the day, by a nursery school or kindergarten, a day care centre, or a babysitter inside or outside the home. Only 48 per cent of children were cared for exclusively by parents in their own home.

The other 11 per cent of families were single parent, 83 per cent headed by women.[27] Almost one–third of these families headed by women resulted from bereavement, while 55 per cent resulted from divorce or separation, and 11 per cent were headed by women who had never married. These families had an average of 1.7 children. Families headed by women could expect to receive only 52 per cent of the family income enjoyed by families headed by men. Now the fastest growing family category, single parent families headed by women increased 59 per cent from 1971 to 1981, while husband/wife families increased by only 22 per cent. But there was another rapidly growing "family" formation, that of the non–family household. In 1971, only 18 per cent of households were non–family; in 1981 this was true of one in four households. In 1971, only just over 6 per cent of women, and 4 per cent of men, lived alone. In 1981, over 10 per cent of women and almost 8 per cent of men lived alone. For many, then, marriage and the family were ceasing to be the centre of their existences, either as a result of circumstances or choice.

By the end of the 1970s and the beginning of the 1980s, it was clear that a variety of types of family formations was emerging;

some of them had always characterized a minority of families in former times, some were quite new. Excluding childless couples and those living alone (two growing categories of households with great significance for our population figures in the future), there were at least six major categories or types of families as we entered the 1980s. There was the traditional family, with dad out at work and mom at home with the 1.3 kids. There was the dual–income family, with both spouses in the workforce. There was a "transitional" family in which the mother temporarily left the labour force for a child's younger years and then returned to work. There was the single parent family headed by either a man or a woman. Such families would have to be further categorized as to the reasons for their formation — separation, divorce, death of spouse, or single (i.e., never married). Then there was the "blended" family, one of increasing consequence, in which divorced partners with children remarry, sometimes someone with children from a previous marriage, sometimes someone childless.[28]

The family of our myths, rooted in the isolated domestic enslavement of women, had ceased to exist. And there was no hope of going back since the trends so clear at the end of the 1970s began to accelerate even more rapidly in the 1980s. But these new emerging family forms brought with them, for women, a new kind of enslavement, for men, a new sense of unease, and for children, a new vulnerability and uncertainty. Families were in crisis as the problem of transition and adjustment remained largely unaddressed and completely unsolved.

2 / Families Present

Let's survey the diversity of family forms in Canada as we enter the last decade of the 20th century. All the developments noted throughout the 1960s and 1970s have continued and accelerated.

The Husband/Wife Family

In 1986, 84 per cent of Canada's more than 25 million people lived in 6.7 million families. Of these, 5.4 million families, or 80 per cent, were husband/wife families.[1] There was an average of 3.1 people in each family, including an average of 1.3 children. This is the only family type to have declined in its share of total families since 1981. There are now four significant variations of husband/wife families in Canada.

The husband/wife family with both spouses working

If there is a "typical" family in Canada, it is now what Statistics Canada calls the "dual–earner family."[2] In 1986, 62 per cent of all husband/wife families enjoyed two earners; over one–half of all families in Canada are now of this type (3.4 million). This reality is reflected in the enormous growth in labour force participation throughout the 1980s among married women with children.[3] By 1988, 57 per cent of married women with children under six years of age were working, as were 70 per cent of those with children aged six to 15. Overall, in 1988 54 per cent of all married women held jobs. The rates were highest among younger and better educated women. For example, 74 per cent of women married to husbands under the age of 45 worked, while only 48 per cent of married women whose husbands were over 45 did so. This burst in job holding by married women with children resulted primarily from the serious declines in real family income that have characterized the 1980s[4] and that hit youngest families hardest.[5]

Married women therefore increased their importance in maintaining family income, bringing in a record high of 29 per cent of total family income of dual–earner families. As well, dual–income families were better off on the whole, with average incomes of $50,000, compared to an average family income of $40,000 for families dependent solely on a husband's income.

Such families were almost as likely to have children as traditional husband–income families. But they tended to postpone having children: only 32 per cent of dual–income families with wives under the age of 25 had children, compared to 77 per cent of traditional families. For the ages of 25 to 34, 70 per cent of dual–income family wives had children, compared to 95 per cent of traditional family wives.

Although dual–earner families are the most economically successful family type, they have serious stresses.[6] Adequate and affordable day care, balancing two jobs and family obligations, reconciling conflicts in parental and career demands on husbands and wives, and meeting the rocketing costs of raising children all provoke what sometimes appear to be an endless series of daily crises.

The husband/wife family with only the husband working

The traditional nuclear family of the 1940s and 1950s now constitutes only 27 per cent of all husband/wife families in Canada. Only 22 per cent of the total (1.5 million) are of this traditional sort. Husband/wife families with only the husband working tend to have lower incomes and a higher risk of experiencing poverty. Both spouses tend to be older than the spouses of dual–earner families and less well–educated. Such families tend to have more children, and wives in such families tend to have had children at a younger age than their dual–earner counterparts.

Analyses of the problems faced by women in such families constitute a major portion of the vast literature generated on woman in the last three decades. Such women are typically economically dependent and socially and emotionally isolated. They strive to realize themselves largely through the traditional roles of wife and mother. Therefore, they tend to subordinate themselves to the needs of husband and children and face severe limitations on their personal growth. They often feel their role is devalued by society.

Men in such families face significant stresses as well. Since they tend to have a strong commitment to the traditional role of husband/provider, the increasing economic stress of maintaining family income weighs heavily on them, and they have more difficulty adapting to the threat of female competition for jobs and promotions. Like the traditional wife, such a man is experiencing the distressing disintegration of a way of life around him as he struggles to seek confirmation of the intrinsic value of the traditional sex roles.

The husband/wife family with only the wife working and the husband/wife family with no earner

These two groups of families, together, constitute 11 per cent of husband/wife families in Canada. In 4 per cent of cases, the wife is the sole earner, and in 7 per cent of cases, neither the husband nor the wife is an earner. While clearly most of these families can be explained by retirement, early or otherwise, or by unemployment cycles, there are some other significant trends. In 1967 only 1 per cent of husband/wife families depended on the wife as the sole earner. Thus the 1986 figure represents a four–fold increase in such families. The most significant feature of both these family groups is that, while the majority of both spouses is over 55, the proportion of husbands over 55 years is much greater. The explanation for the growth in these types of family, particularly the family in which the wife is sole earner, can be partly found in the decline in the employment of men from ages 55 to 64 that occurred between 1975 and 1985.[7] In 1975, 24 per cent of this group were not employed, while in 1985 the figure reached 36 per cent and the trend appears to be long–term and upward. While much of the increase is explained by early retirement and a sustained absence from the labour force (never worked, or a five–year absence), 40 per cent of this increase is the result of a loss of job or lay–off. Obviously, one of the consequences of the growth in female participation in the labour force is this emerging long–term trend to higher rates of unemployment among older men. Evidently they are bearing the brunt of the trend since the 1960s to lower rates of participation in the labour force for all men 15 and over, while female rates have increased dramatically.[8]

The Single Parent Family

In 1986, 13 per cent of Canada's families were single parent families, making it the third largest family type and reflecting a startling growth rate of 20 per cent since 1981. About 82 per cent of such families are headed by women, including 94 per cent of single parent families with heads between the ages of 15 and 24, and 85 per cent of such heads between the ages of 25 and 44.[9] Over 1.2 million, or 14 per cent, of Canada's children live in single parent families, and it is estimated that about one in two Canadian children will live part of their lives in a single parent family.[10]

The female single parent family

The reasons for the formation of this family type have changed dramatically. In the 1960s the overwhelming majority of female single parent families resulted from the death of a spouse (63 per cent), the next largest group resulted from separation or divorce (35 per cent), and only 2 per cent were headed by single (never married) mothers. By 1986, 57 per cent of such families resulted from separation or divorce, 28 per cent from death of spouse, while 15 per cent were headed by single mothers. In the case of marriage breakdown, mothers get custody of the children in about 85 per cent of cases.[11] In addition to the growth in marriage breakdown, the most dramatic change in the basis for the formation of female single parent families is the growing trend among single women to have and keep babies born outside of a permanent relationship. This trend began in the 1970s and has continued to advance in the 1980s when, for example, over 86 per cent of unmarried mothers in Alberta and over 88 per cent in Ontario kept their babies.[12] The increase has been supplemented by a rise in the number of older single mothers, often professionals, aged 30 to 39, seeking to become mothers without being wives, and sometimes doing so through artificial insemination.[13]

Female single parent families are in the most difficulty economically. In 1985, 60 per cent of them were below the official poverty line, and such families received less than half the family income of husband/wife families, while remaining the most dependent on forms of government assistance. This can partly be explained by female single parents' lower participation rate in the labour force. Only 42 per cent of those with a child under six worked outside the home, while 63 per cent with children aged six to 15 did so. The figures for married women with children were 57 per cent and 70 per cent, respectively. Female job ghettoes, low incomes, the lack of affordable day care, and the absence of a spouse obviously make it more difficult for single parent mothers to bring home incomes that make that work worthwhile. As a result, single parent families headed by women languish in poverty. In 1985, 1.1 million children in Canada, representing over 19 per cent of all children under 16, lived in families below the official poverty line. About 68 per cent of them lived in families headed by female single parents.[14]

There are those who argue that these families are going through a brief episode in their life cycles and that most will eventually return to a family based upon a husband/wife relationship. But the trend for this type of family formation continues to go upward — that is, at each Census the group is larger and represents a larger share of the total number of families. This means that many Canadians, especially women, will experience episodes of single parenthood. The 1984 Statistics Canada Family History Survey studied 1.4 million women aged 18 to 65 who were or had been single parents, representing 18 per cent of all women in that age group and 26 per cent of all those who had borne children.[15] The end of the single parent episode was defined as when the woman entered a new relationship or when parenting ceased as children left home. The study found that the average age of single mothers when the episode began was about 21 years with a duration of over four years, while the average age of divorced or separated mothers when the episode began was 32 years with a duration of almost six years. Average durations of such length are not brief, and 12 per cent of the women surveyed endured a second experience of single parenthood.

Female single parents are beset by problems. There are the obvious economic problems of low incomes, poverty, poor housing, and constant stress and insecurity. There are the emotional and psychological problems of endeavouring to raise young children without the support of a spouse. There are the loneliness and lack of emotional and sexual fulfillment resulting from the absence of a stable love relationship. Furthermore single parent mothers face more sexual harassment, at work and socially, since many men view single parent women as "fair game." As well, single parent mothers still face discrimination in society. And separated or divorced single parent mothers are often the targets of physical abuse by former spouses, experiencing a much higher rate of wife abuse than married women.[16]

The male single parent family

The reasons for the formation of this family type have also changed dramatically. In the 1960s the overwhelming majority of male single parent families resulted from the death of a spouse, followed distantly by marriage breakdown. By the 1980s, marriage breakdown accounted for the formation of 67 per cent of such families, and bereavement for about 30 per cent (interestingly, almost 4 per cent were never–married fathers).[17] About 18 per cent of Canada's 854,000 single parent families are headed by men. Significantly, Statistics Canada projects that male single parent families will grow rapidly between now and 2001.[18]

Single parent fathers tend to be older than single parent mothers and to be parenting older children.[19] Only 6 per cent of single parent family heads between the ages of 15 and 24 and 14 per cent between the ages of 25 and 44 are male, while 23 per cent are 45 or older. Single parent fathers have a higher probability of remarrying, and the duration of divorce tends to be about one–half of that faced by single parent mothers.

Male single parent families are considerably better off economically than female single parent families. A study by Richardson revealed that only 10 per cent of divorced men, compared to 58 per cent of divorced women and their children, were below the poverty line. Canada–wide figures are less generous. About 20 per cent of male single parent families, including 35 per cent of children in such families, are officially poor.[20] This is significantly above national averages, but well ahead of the situation of female single parent families. Male single parents receive 142 per cent of the incomes received by female single parents and 88 per cent of the incomes enjoyed by husband/wife families with children.

Contrary to popular stereotypes, studies of single parent fathers suggest they are quite successful at parenting, and they express more satisfaction than single parent mothers.[21] This doubtless has something to do with their greater economic security. It might also have something to do with the fact that single parent fathers tend to be raising older children. But they do share with all parents Canada's crisis in day care. And, in common with single parent women, they face the problems of loneliness, social isolation, a lack of satisfying sexual outlets, and the dilemmas of reconciling the conflicting demands of work, domestic labour, and child care. Then, too, since their remarriage rate is higher, and the duration of divorce much shorter, on the average, single parent fathers face fewer years of being alone. Furthermore, such men express greater happiness and higher levels of satisfaction after remarriage.

The Common–Law Family

Although it has long existed, the common–law family came into official being only in 1981.[22] Prior to 1981, the Census counted common–law marriages in the single category of "married or living as married." In 1981 the Census began collecting such data, supplemented by Statistics Canada's 1984 Family History Survey. In 1986, almost a million Canadians were living in 487,000 common–law families, representing over 7 per cent of total families, and the common–law family was one of the fastest growing family types.

The Family History Survey found that common–law marriages were quite commonplace, particularly among the young. Seventeen per cent of adults between the ages of 18 and 65 had lived common–law at one time in their lives, including 22 per cent of those in the 20 to 24 year age group, but only 1 per cent of those in their forties. Among total marriages in 1986, common–law unions accounted for 60 per cent of marriages among the 15 to 19 year age group, 30 per cent of those among those 20 to 24, and 20 per cent among those 25 to 29. In 1981, these figures were 49 per cent, 23 per cent and 11 per cent, respectively.

Common–law marriages are most typically a one–time event; 63 per cent end in legal marriage after an average duration of 2.3 years. Usually, but not always, partners in common–law liaisons married each other. Common–law families have an average of 0.6 children each, and about 38 per cent of such families have children. (Families based on legal marriage have an average of 1.3 children, and 65 per cent of such marriages have children at home.) Common–law families, since they are so young, share all the economic problems of young families in general, like declines in real family income and declining real wages for younger workers.

The growing rate of common–law marriage has to do with the overall crisis of the traditional family since young men and women are increasingly reticent about taking the step to formal marriage, at least until after a trial period. Perhaps it reflects a growing determination on the part of younger women to ensure that they avoid the burdens of a long–term commitment until they see if their partners can adjust to women's growing sense of freedom and independence. Perhaps, too, it reflects a growing willingness among young men to seek relationships that are more egalitarian and flexible.

The problems with traditional patterns of courtship are obvious. Both men and women are on their best behaviour, especially men, who compartmentalize their social selves between who they are and what they do with male friends, with women from whom they are seeking casual sexual gratification, and with women they have decided are desirable for marriage.

The 1989 case of Chantal Daigle and Jean–Guy Tremblay provides an excellent example. Tremblay began pursuing Daigle in November 1988, and within weeks the couple were cohabiting. Two months into the union Tremblay suggested marriage and urged Daigle to stop using birth control; by March 1989 she was pregnant. Daigle says that Tremblay then became physically and verbally abusive. Tremblay insists that he never hit her "hard enough to leave marks." In early July 1989 Daigle left Tremblay and decided to have an abortion. Tremblay successfully sought a court injunction forbidding the abortion, a decision upheld by the Quebec Court of Appeal. First he told the press that he himself would care for the baby, then decided his father would, and then he suggested he would allow Daigle to keep and care for the child. In an interview, Tremblay revealed his dream — a traditional family with him out at work and Daigle at home with the child. Daigle's response was simple, "I don't even want to see that guy again."[23] Happily, the Supreme Court of Canada unanimously found in her favour.

A period of common–law marriage is no absolute insurance for a woman, or for a man, but it provides more insurance than traditional courtship ending in idyllic marriage to be followed by capital "R" reality. In the context of today's emotional uncertainty, it will doubtless continue to be an important testing period for growing numbers of young Canadians.

Table 1: Canadian family forms in the 1980s				
	Number	% of Husband/ Wife Families	% of All Families	% Poor
1. Husband/Wife Families	5.4 million	--	80	11
Both spouses working	3.4 million	62	51	4
Husband only working	1.5 million	27	22	13
Wife only working	216,000	4	3	?
Neither working	378,000	7	4	?
2. Single Parent Families	854,000	n.a.	13	52
Female single parent	700,000	82*	11	60
Male single parent	154,000	18*	2	20
3. Common-Law Families	487,000	n.a.	7	?
All families	6.7 million	--	100	13

Source: *Canadian Social Trends*, Statistics Canada, Summer 1986 to Summer 1989. All figures are approximate and rounded. Poverty percentages reflect trends at different times in the 1980s and should be viewed as ballpark estimates, given significant year to year fluctuations during the 1980s.
* percentage of all single parent families.

Other Significant Family Trends

Transitional families

This term has been selected to refer to those families in which the wife works until the birth of a child, stays home for a portion of the child's younger years, and then returns to work. The figures show that this is probably the family of choice for many Canadians, an effort to combine for both women and the family the benefits of work outside the home with the benefits and fulfillment to be found, for child and mother, in a period of full–time parenting. There are also a growing, though exceptional, number of men who enjoy taking on a full–time parenting role for a time.

In 1981, 52 per cent of all married women with children stayed at home. By 1986, 62 per cent were in the work force. With the modest improvement in the economy after 1986, the participation rate of married women with children under six dropped to 57 per cent in 1988. The fall in the percentage of women with children under six working suggests that many of them were reluctantly in the work force out of economic necessity.

The fact is that increasingly women and their families simply have no choice but to shorten a mother's absence from the labour force. The transitional family is increasingly beyond the grasp of even middle class families, and women who wish to take time out from work for babies are aware of the tremendous financial burden involved.

The days are largely over when a working woman had to make an almost total economic sacrifice in order to leave work to have a baby. Formerly, women typically lost their income as well as seniority and often the job itself. And a return to the labour force often meant starting over at the bottom job rung. Today, working women enjoy, through collective agreements and labour laws, the right to maternity leave and some guarantee of a later return to work without loss of seniority or job. Still, they cannot expect anywhere near reasonable compensation for foregone income. All that women in Canada receive is the maternity benefit under UIC, which entitles them to a 60 per cent benefit level for 15 weeks maternity leave with a weekly maximum of $363. There is a certain irony that we have used our unemployment plan to grant maternity benefits to women: they are unemployed!

A 1984 study by economist Monica Townsend reported that Canada ranked 22 out of a group of 23 industrialized nations surveyed on maternity leave benefit policies.[24] Most countries paid higher percentages of the woman's former earnings and allowed the leave to extend longer.[25] If, as a society, we want sufficient babies to be born to renew our population, while at the same time allowing existing families to retain some degree of economic security and supporting women in their desire to work outside the home, then we will have to do much better than we are doing.

The blended family

The blended family (also called the reconstituted, melded or remarriage family) is increasingly common. In 1961 only 9 per cent of all marriages were remarriages, while in 1985 30 per cent were remarriages.[26] With rates like these, it will not be long before a majority of families in Canada are based on remarriage. Since it is such a recent phenomenon, we as yet know very little in detail about this family type.[27] But we do know that accelerating divorce rates have not led to the widely heralded death of the family; rather, high rates of divorce and remarriage indicate that divorce simply leads to the reorganization of the family.

Neumann reports that the biggest problem faced by a blended family is that it must face "inheriting leftovers," particularly ongoing emotional relationships.[28] The blended family feels a lot of pressure to succeed. The stress of the sense of competing with the previous spouse, particularly in relationships with the children from the first marriage, requires a great deal of concerted effort.

Indeed, most research suggests that the biggest problems concern the children of the former marriage, especially if they are early adolescents aged 11 to 14.[29] Stepfathers seem to provoke the most problems, particularly with stepdaughters, and there is a greater risk of incest. What Nett refers to as the "discrepancy between parental and spousal roles" is greater in such families. The reason is self-evident: each spouse may be the biological parent of some children and the stepparent of others. The com-

plexities of the problems faced by all families with children —
sibling rivalry, competition for love and attention, emotional
manipulation, maintaining discipline, enforcing rules, and ensuring a minimum of order — can become overwhelming. Indeed,
there is also evidence that in some cases children over 10 years
of age set out to "sabotage" the remarriage.[30] Hence such families
are somewhat less stable, and the adjustment period can be rather
long. One Vancouver psychologist and family counsellor reports
that it takes four to seven years for a blended family to begin to
feel in their hearts like a "real" family. And he claims that 40 per
cent of remarriage families fail within the first four years if there
are children involved.[31]

Fewer children
More families in the 1980s are having no children, and those
which do, have fewer. One in three families in 1986 were childless, up from 29 per cent in 1961. Each Canadian woman in the
1980s will, on average, have 1.4 children, down from about four
in 1960, and childlessness is rising. In the 1980s well over one–
half of women aged 20 to 24, almost one in three women aged 25
to 29, and around 15 per cent of women aged 30 to 34 are
childless. The slight rise in the number of women aged 35 to 39
who are having children will not make a dent in this decline in
the numbers of children in the population. In 1961 34 per cent of
Canada's population was under the age in 15; in the 1980s the
figure is 21 per cent.

These demographics have ominous portents for the future. In
the 1980s those over the age of 65 constituted the fastest growing
population group, while those under 15, and those between 15 and
24, are the slowest growing groups. When those now in the 35 to
44 age group, the baby boom bulge, hit 65, the distortion in the
society will be very serious. Canada's population will peak at 28
million in 2011 and begin an absolute decline if present trends
continue. With declining numbers of young people in the labour
force and a growing army of the elderly, the economic and
emotional strains will be potentially phenomenal. Will we be able
to honour our pension plans? Will we be able to afford the rising

costs of health care in general, and chronic care for the elderly in particular?

As demographer Karol Krotki put it, "there is no doubt that our society is dying out in a statistical sense ... What we need is another baby boom."[32] Other experts agree, and there have been some political responses by governments. Quebec's 1988 budget offered cash incentives to encourage child–bearing: $500 for each of the first two children and $3,000 for each subsequent child. There were further inducements: larger tax deductions for child care costs, a special tax deduction for working parents, an interest free loan for the first family home, and a promise of 60,000 more day care spaces.[33] Quebec, of course, has an even lower fertility rate than the rest of Canada. Ottawa has also responded by financing 26 population studies commencing in May 1986. One of these studies, by Quebec economist Georges Mathews, recommended a child allowance of $200 per month for every child after the first two, payable until the child is five years old. Improved maternity leave benefits and more subsidized day care spaces would also help people decide to have more children, he argued.[34]

The point is that the new family forms have proven themselves incapable of renewing the population. The issue therefore affects the whole society. Simplistic solutions cannot deal with the problem in the long run. Women don't decide not to have children solely on the basis of economic considerations, though those are of critical importance. Certainly, if having children were economically easier for women and their families, then probably more children would be born. But, as well, we have to ensure that the bearing of children does not entail unacceptable social and psychological costs for women and for their spouses.

Rise in non–family households
As the young postpone marriage and as the proportion of the elderly in the population increases, there has been an amazing growth in non–family households. Although most of this increase is the result of the growth in one–person households, as such households are typically counted, it also reflects a growth in flexible living arrangements in general. In 1961 only 4 per cent of Canadians 15 and older lived alone, rising to 9 per cent in 1981

and increasing to 10 per cent, or 1.9 million Canadians, in 1986. The two largest groups in this category are elderly widowed women and younger people who are either single, divorced, or separated. If we take only the population under 65, the trend to single person households grows as age advances. Among 15 to 24 years olds, only 4 per cent live in such households, 96 per cent of whom are single. In the 25 to 44 year age group, 8 per cent live in single person households, 70 per cent of whom are single. In the 45 to 64 age category, 10 per cent of Canadians live alone, 43 per cent of whom are divorced or separated, 29 per cent of whom are single, and 28 per cent of whom are bereaved. Such figures suggest that many younger Canadians are postponing family formation and that the experience of family living for many may be episodic as it is interrupted by divorce, separation or death. Finally, as more and more gay people affirm their sexual orientation publicly, the figures on non–family and single households also conceal a rise in a new family form, the gay family, which will continue to be a source of policy controversy as such families demand recognition and access to state family programs and benefits, as well as to the many family benefits in collective agreements.[35]

The growing diversity of family forms is self–evident. New, "unorthodox" family forms — especially dual–earner and single parent families — will become the orthodox family forms of the future as they characterize the experience of a growing majority of Canadians. Families are smaller and less stable, and family life is more episodic as we marry later, as divorce and separation rates grow, and as remarriage touches more and more of our lives. Many more Canadians are opting for single lifestyles, and fewer are feeling it obligatory to have children. More women are choosing to have children as single mothers and to remain single for significant portions of their lives. Materially, people have more choices, and, ideologically, people are more willing to exercise them.

3 / Families Future

After the Industrial Revolution the family became primarily a psychological institution. It now has no productive economic functions, and domestic family labour is no longer important in the facilitation of consumption. Certainly the consumption entailed in the acquisition of the technology and services to diminish domestic labour is tremendously important to the economy. But, still, a man does not *need* a wife to do domestic labour. Nor does a woman *need* a husband to bring home a wage. The sexual division of labour is no longer essential to survival. Many of the family's child care obligations are also gone. Today, a family can assign a major portion of what child care responsibilities are left to it to public schools, day care centres, and babysitters. In other words, a family does not *need* a full–time parent in the house.

What are left are the family's emotional functions: love, renewal, meaning, identity, confirmation, support, recognition, belongingness. Marriage and the family still provide some degree of regulation of sexual intercourse and the procreation of children. But again, one no longer *needs* a spouse for sexual gratification, nor to have and raise children (though here women obviously have more options than men).

Marriage and the family, therefore, have become more and more matters of choice and decision. The family long ago ceased to be an economic necessity, though the dual–income family of today has certainly become an economic convenience. But we are increasingly unwilling to give up merely for convenience what we were formerly compelled to give up out of necessity. Wives and husbands have long since ceased being necessities to each other in the brutal material sense. Fewer and fewer people, men and women, are willing to compromise too extensively if a marriage or family relationship is fundamentally dissatisfying and unhappy.

This is certainly more true of women. Two in three divorces are initiated by wives, and an Ontario study found that 36 per cent of such divorces involved violence and/or alcohol abuse by the husbands.[1] That's one extreme. Clearly women are less willing to put up with violence and drunkenness, but more and more of them are also leaving what many around them considered to be happy, stable, and successful marriages. Brenda Rabkin's study found that such women simply wanted more from the relationship.[2] They wanted a greater degree of emotional intimacy, a more equal partnership, and greater control over their lives. They were willing to "trade down" economically to leave what they saw as dead–end relationships. A clear pattern emerged: their husbands resisted their efforts to greater independence and refused to do a just share of domestic and child–care work. This trend is inescapable. No institution that relies on the exploitation and oppression of a particular group can hope to survive when that group begins to resist. The traditional family depended on the domestic enslavement of women. Women have not only decisively rejected that, but they are also increasingly refusing to tolerate lingering traditional male attitudes and behaviours in the new family forms. As Rabkin points out, women are increasingly willing to exercise their new options. For different reasons, the same pattern is emerging among men. Growing numbers are avoiding marriage and the family, instead choosing to live for an extended period as single men, unfettered by marital and parental obligations. As a result, there is a complementary phenomenon among men and women. Women are unwilling to put up with the constraints traditional marriage entails, and many men are postponing the commitment of becoming husbands and fathers.[3]

But the increasing choices available to men and women will not make the changes go forward naturally, spontaneously, and exultantly. In such a fundamental transformation of as central an aspect of our social structure as the family, the individuals swept up in the changes, whether through choice or circumstance, or a combination of both, must make basic readjustments. Old behaviours, attitudes, and core identities must change as people strive to live in a new social world which requires the adoption of new behaviours and attitudes and the establishment of new core identities.

When technology wipes out industrial or craft skills that people have spent a life–time acquiring and perfecting, they feel bereft, without confirmation of who they are, as they seek a new niche in the work world. Similarly, when agricultural crises force farm families off the land, they must repair the bruised social and economic roots of their identities as they seek another, far different way of life. All such large social structural transformations exact a certain social and psychological cost from those experiencing them. Old identities, and their daily material and social confirmation, are torn apart, and new identities must be rebuilt. And it is never easy.

Structural Transformation

The same can be said of the current structural transformation of the family. However, since the family touches us all so intimately, the social and psychological costs exacted from this transition are far larger and the pain of readjustment far greater. As we are socialized to take our expected place in our culture, we acquire what one sociologist has called a "social–structural map."[4] It becomes a central part of our core identity, guiding us from "one social–emotional place to another." It tells us to whom we can go for love, in whom we can confide, how to behave appropriately in different interpersonal and social situations. Most importantly, the social–structural map provides us with a set of "problem–solving responses." It pinpoints how we are to deal with the problems that beset us and to whom we can turn for help, guidance, and support. By identifying our emotional connections, the map gives us a sense of rootedness, of place, of confidence in, and predictability about, the world around us. It links us to the social world through a web of relationships that constitutes our sense of identity and place and daily provides us with repeated confirmations of who we are. When those relationships are disrupted or poorly developed, our adjustment and functioning become impaired. Clearly our families form the central part of our social–structural maps. Therefore, disruptions of, and readjustments in, family relationships can be enormously difficult or even damaging.

This basic axiom has been repeatedly confirmed. Virtually all epidemiological studies of mental and emotional disturbance have consistently found a clear inverse relationship between poverty and low socioeconomic status and the risk of such disturbance.[5] But such studies have also found a clear relationship between disruptions in family relationships and mental disturbance. Sometimes the underlying factor for disruptions in family relationships is economic, such as poverty or unemployment. Sometimes the disruptions in family relationships, particularly in the case of women, lead to poverty, resulting in a double jeopardy: distress as a result of family breakdown, followed by stress as a result of poverty and economic insecurity.

The Midtown Manhattan study found an association between psychological impairment and divorce or separation. The Stirling County study in Nova Scotia found a relationship between levels of community disintegration, and attendant personal difficulties, including marital and family problems and the risk of psychiatric difficulty. The Camberwell study of depression among women found that "traumatic life events or major ongoing difficulties" preceded the onset of depression in women. Among the provoking events were "separation from a key person," such as divorce or separation. The researchers further found that among the factors that increase a woman's vulnerability to depression was "the lack of an intimate relationship with someone in whom she could trust or confide, especially a husband or boyfriend." Fourteen studies of the relationship between marital status and rates of mental disturbance found that rates were higher among single, separated, divorced and widowed people than among married people. In 1986 a nine year study of 7,000 Californians reported that people who lack supportive social relationships exhibit higher rates of mortality, depression, suicide, and failure to cope effectively with life stress.[6] The consensus in the literature is that single men have higher rates of mental illness than married men. Furthermore, those who are separated or divorced have higher rates of suicide and mental disturbance than both single and married populations.

Finally, the escalating incidence of mental illness among children has been correlated to the growing rate of family breakdown.[7]

Clearly family breakdown exacts an astonishing emotional toll from those affected. But does this mean we should act to save the traditional family and to reverse the trends that appear to afflict us so grievously? The traditional family itself is implicated in a great deal of emotional and psychological disturbance. In other words, the changes in the family are causing a great deal of distress. But so too do efforts to resist those changes.

For example, the Camberwell study found that one of the major ongoing causes of depression in women was a poor marriage, and included among the vulnerability factors were having three or more children under 14 and no job outside the home. Other studies have found that the risk of psychiatric disorder in women is increased when they are caring for small children in social isolation. As well, high rates of depression occur among traditional wives when the children grow up and leave home.[8] And some studies have found that, in general, rates of mental illness are higher in married than in unmarried women. In a study of the relationships between mental illness and the economy, it was found that in times of economic difficulty middle–aged married men are more at risk of mental illness than other groups of men.[9] There is thus clear evidence that negative psychological effects can result for both men and women if they cling desperately to traditional marriage and sex roles in an effort to find meaning, happiness and security.[10]

Yet remaining single appears to be an unsatisfying solution for most. A 1987 Toronto study found that single men and women are more likely to feel that life is worse than they had expected, to exhibit twice the rate of depression, to experience four times the rate of loneliness, and to be less sexually gratified than married men and women.[11] And it appears that economic limitations are a key source of frustration for single men and women, especially single women. Understandably, therefore, 73 per cent of single men and women in the study believed that being happily married was important. But, surprisingly, the study found that 70 per cent would rather stay single than lower their expectations of marriage.

It appears, then, both that the social structural changes involved in the changing nature of the family are causing stress and provoking emotional difficulty and that trying to return to the traditional family would cause just as many problems. The obvious solution is to support the new emerging family forms at both personal and policy levels. These changes will lead to the more complete emancipation of women, free men from the burden of traditional male role models, and provide children with a more enriched life. Still, the costs will be great, and some groups will be at higher risk. Can we make a painful transition less painful? Can we make a deeply disorienting experience less disorienting? Admitting that we have a crisis of the family on our collective hands and agreeing to move decisively to meet it requires a more complete accounting of the costs being exacted from the victims. First, the children.

PART II

Victims of the Crisis: Children

"Why can't the system help kids?"
Kay, a Toronto run–away,
Globe and Mail, 4
March 1988.

Introduction:
Who Cares for the Children?

In 1959 the General Assembly of the United Nations adopted *The U.N. Declaration of the Rights of the Child*, enumerating eleven specific principles as well as affirming a child's right to enjoy the fundamental rights and freedoms "specified in the Universal Declaration of Human Rights ... to the end that he may have a happy childhood and be enabled to grow up."[1] As we watch television reports of children damaged and destroyed by famine in Africa or by civil war in Beirut, as we read reports of the sexual enslavement of children in Bangkok or of the shooting and imprisonment of children in Soweto and in the West Bank and Gaza, we are moved and outraged. Less dramatically, certainly, but here in Canada too, growing numbers of children suffer from our society's incapacity to deliver adequate protection from physical harm, sufficient calories to fend off malnutrition, and the minimal emotional support and security necessary to ensure psychological health and happiness. For thousands of Canadian children, Canadian society has failed to honour principles of the U.N. Declaration, including

2. The child shall be given the means necessary to enable him to develop physically, mentally, morally, spiritually and socially, in a healthy and normal manner and in conditions of freedom and dignity.

3. The child shall enjoy special protection by law and by other means ...

8. The child shall in all circumstances be the first to receive protection and relief ...

10. The child shall be protected against all forms of neglect, cruelty and exploitation ...

Well, you could respond, no society can be perfect and we can't hold the whole society to account for the failures of individual fathers and mothers to live up to their responsibilities. Perhaps that argument would be comforting if we could be assured that the victimization of children in Canada were caused by the actions of irresponsible individuals. Unfortunately, the evidence is otherwise and provides no such comfort. Much, perhaps most, of the victimization of children can be traced directly to the structural failure of the changing family to fulfill its obligations as an institution. And while it may be true that in particular tragic instances individual blame can be assigned, it is incumbent on us to try to understand the social context and the stresses and strains that may have increased the risk of such tragedies. In that way we can move from simply dealing with casualties and symptoms to dealing with causes and prevention.

The vital importance of childhood experiences in shaping the adult personality is widely known, and it has been estimated that about one–half of a child's full cognitive development is reached by the age of three or four.[2] The core self–concept and basic social–structural map are established primarily through interaction with parents and other adult care–givers in the child's immediate experience, and the amount of time a child enjoys with them, their educational level, and the economic affluence of the household have positive associations with the child's development.[3] It is from these "significant others," as Mead put it, that the child acquires his or her sense of self and place, and anything that disrupts the security, stability, and quality of a child's early interactions with parents can have not only immediate negative consequences, but also long–term deleterious effects on later adjustment.

Our society expresses deeply ambivalent attitudes regarding children. One sociologist has suggested that children today are seen largely as "emotional assets" of parents.[4] Children bring no economic rewards to the family; indeed, they are a source of constant financial drain. Yet people continue to have children for the emotional gratification they bring. As families have fewer children, parents can indulge their children more than ever before. Designer clothes, expensive high–tech toys and the latest computers all appeal to a growing market among affluent parents. Yet at the other end we can see children lining up at food banks and school meal programs. Most of us love and protect our children diligently, yet daily we read reports of abused children who die at the hands of those we expect to love them most. The prime minister can promise a $4 billion day care program just before an election and then renege on it with apparent impunity.[5] As a society we want and need mothers of children to work, yet we pay minimal wages to our day care workers.[6] There is something deeply wrong with a society that remains incapable of providing adequate quality care for all its children, where some children enjoy love and security and others are beaten to death.

Canada's day care crisis well reflects this deep ambivalence toward children. Canadians are seriously divided on the question of increased government spending to provide subsidized day care centres. In an August 1989 Gallup poll, 49 per cent favoured such increased spending while 43 per cent opposed it.[7] Predictably opinion follows age on the question. Those most likely to have young children heavily favour increased government spending for day care, while those less likely to have young children tend to oppose it strongly.

As a result the crisis of care for young children of working parents remains chronic and worsens. In 1990, it is estimated that 75 per cent of women of child–bearing age are working.[8] Over 50 per cent of the total Canadian work force consists of families in which both parents work, and another 6 per cent of the work force is comprised of working single parents.[9] In other words, over one–half of Canada's total work force requires day care. Among women with children at home, those most likely to work are separated or divorced women between the ages of 35 and 44 years.[10] Clearly their need for subsidized care is greatest.

Estimates vary about the number of children who require day care and the number of available licensed spaces, but all studies agree that spaces lag far behind need.[11] The 1987 Special House of Commons Committee on day care provided comprehensive figures based on 1986 data.[12] Fifty–six per cent of women with children under three, 62 per cent of women with children between three and five, and 68 per cent of women with children between six and 15 were in the labour force. This involved over 1.2 million pre–school age children. There were only just over 197,000 licensed day care spaces available in that year. Among pre–schoolers cared for in non–parental arrangements, and requiring care, only 7 per cent of those aged up to 17 months, 14 per cent of those aged from 18 to 35 months, and 34 per cent of those from three to five years were served. The committee's report also provided estimates on the number of children aged six to 12 who were either unsupervised "latchkey" kids or received care from an older sibling — there were 360,000 such children in 1986, representing about 15 per cent of all Canadian children in that age group.

Day care, even poor day care, is expensive. The average annual cost ranges between $3,600 and $4,800, though very high quality care can cost as much as $9,000. Clearly these costs represent an enormous drain on the incomes of working parents. Even so, a 1987 Decima poll found that 59 per cent of parents rated day care quality as either fair or poor. The House of Commons committee's researchers found that even those administering and monitoring provincial systems believed that one in six licensed day care centres across the country were "poor" or "very poor," actually *below* minimal licensing standards. What about the conditions in unlicensed "family" day care homes?

In 1987 then Health and Welfare Minister Jake Epp commented that parents, not day care workers, are better qualified to raise children.[13] In response the day care lobby accused the minister of endangering children in unregulated, unlicensed day care.[14] If working parents can't get good quality, regulated, licensed day care, they will take what they can get. Nor does the minister's response provide solace to the estimated 6 per cent of young children who are left completely unattended by desperate working parents.

The importance of adequate quality child care for working parents cannot be overstated. One major U.S. study of 30,000 employees in 30 corporations found that 40 per cent of women and 25 per cent of men with babies and toddlers claim that worries about child care reduce their productivity, and more than 50 per cent of both men and women felt stress as a result of work/family conflicts centring on child care problems. Those suffering such stress were more likely to be absent from work, to have trouble getting up in the morning, to believe their work performance suffered, and to have more health problems.[15] Another study found that the effect of working on a mother's sense of psychological well–being had most to do with the ease or difficulty of child care arrangements. It found extremely high depression levels among employed mothers who had problems in arranging child care and who had the sole responsibility for child care.[16] The availability of adequate child care also clearly has a great deal to do with the decision of working parents to have children. Access to quality day care for working parents increases psychological well–being, improves morale, increases productivity, and reduces absenteeism.

For the children of working parents the importance of adequate, quality day care is self–evident. Low child/staff ratios, qualified staff, a low rate of staff turnover, and adequate resources for programming enhance a child's development, and the reverse has potentially negative effects.

The care issue is even more vital for children who are left unsupervised or supervised by an older sibling. American estimates vary on the number of such children: the U.S. Census estimated that 2.1 million children under 13 are regularly left unsupervised by working parents before and after school. Others put the figure at between five and seven million children. In comparison, Canada has an estimated 360,000 such children. Market researchers have found that these children in many cases become the "brand managers" of the family and take on many household tasks: 37 per cent of children between six and 11 shop or do chores before dinner, 13 per cent of children aged six to 15 make dinner for themselves most of the time, and 8 per cent actually make dinner for the family. In response, marketing consultants have targeted for special attention syndicated children's television programs between three and five p.m. Spending on advertising in such shows has gone from nil in 1982 to $107 million in 1988 as more and more of the major consumer products manufacturers and their advertising agencies add "latchkey kids to the overall consumer mix."[17]

The evidence is, then, overwhelming. The new family forms no longer provide adequate care for a growing number of our children.

Such families require a community response in the form of a system of universally available quality child care. Perhaps the community has not acted because children are seen as the private "emotional assets" of their parents. Perhaps the public is reluctant to contemplate the levels of public spending necessary. Perhaps there remains nostalgia for the traditional family. An adequate system of publicly provided, universal child care would be an open admission that the traditional family is dead and that the increasingly dominant family forms require new community responses. Perhaps some are haunted by the obvious question: Just how many of the wives and mothers in Canada's traditional families would continue to embrace that role if quality child care were easily accessible and affordable?

Inadequate care is only one of the costs being exacted from our children as a result of the changing nature of the family, and perhaps it's the least important. Most working parents manage to muddle through their child care problems. And who is to say it is a bad thing for an 11– or 12–year–old to care for herself or himself after school or to prepare supper for the family? Indeed, as Mandell suggests, perhaps we are witnessing a transformation in our very notion of childhood as children contribute more and more to sustaining the household.

> [C]hildren are socially constructed as robust, independent and helpful individuals who are more involved in family economics … Given then that couples are likely to continue to want and to bear children, it also follows that the role of children within families will alter to minimize parents' financial costs and maximize parents' emotional gains … Rather than signalling a loss of childhood or a demise in children's innocence, these changes indicate the closer integration of children and women in a more egalitarian and interdependent family.[18]

While this argument has considerable merit, such a reconstruction of our notion of childhood, just like the reconstruction of the nature of the family itself, does not come easily. The transition costs, socially and psychologically, remain high. It is to these that we now turn.

4 / The Economic Insecurity of Children

Canada's distribution of income shares has been remarkably stable over time.[1] Attempts at income redistribution through an allegedly progressive income tax policy and a variety of income security policies designed to ensure a fairer access to income for lower income Canadians have failed. The shares of total income, including social benefit payments, going to the poorest 20 per cent of Canadians in 1951 was 4 per cent, while the richest 20 per cent received 43 per cent. Thirty years later the figures were unchanged: the poorest 20 per cent still received 4 per cent; the richest received 42 per cent. The real incomes of all Canadians have advanced considerably, and Canada remains an extremely privileged society even for the poor when compared to the lot of many in the Third World. But income levels and notions of poverty are relative to time and place. Though Canadians as an aggregate have improved their real levels of income, their shares of the pie have stayed static. More than that, Canadians' expectations of a continuing advance in levels of real income, encouraged by the progress achieved in the 1960s and the 1970s, have been dramatically dashed in the 1980s, a decade characterized by declines in real incomes.

Though shares of income have remained static for more than three decades, the nature of the income Canadians obtain has changed quite dramatically. In the 1980s more than 60 per cent of families had two or more earners, and almost 65 per cent of wives worked. In the 1950s, 60 per cent of families relied on one earner, and less than 15 per cent of wives worked. There has therefore been a dramatic rise in the real incomes of working married couples with young children, and the two–income family has become the dominant characteristic of high–earner families.

There has been another major change in the nature of the incomes of Canadians: their growing dependence on social benefits (including old age pensions, income supplements, family allowances, unemployment insurance, and social assistance payments). In the 1950s, the lowest income group received 29 per cent of its income from social benefits. In the early 1980s, that proportion had about doubled to 57 per cent. (Middle income families over the same period also about doubled the proportion of their incomes coming from social benefits: 5 per cent to 9 per cent). Therefore, although the share of income received by the lowest income families has not changed, increasingly that income is made up of social benefits. In 1951, 56 per cent of the income obtained by the poorest fifth of Canadians was *earned* income. By 1981, only 30 per cent was earned. What this means is that those who are most economically insecure today are those most dependent on state aid, rendering them even more vulnerable to the whims of politicians. These social programs were necessary not to *redistribute* income but to ensure that the distribution remained about the same. In their absence, the poorest 20 per cent of Canadians would today be receiving less than 2 per cent of total income. As for the income tax system, the effects are marginal at best. In 1981 the highest income quintile saw its income share fall from 42 per cent before taxes to 40 per cent after taxes, while the two lowest quintiles gained a 1 per cent share each.

Not surprisingly, Canada's poverty rates track rises and falls in real income levels. Poverty is controversial in a society like ours that affirms egalitarian ideals. As a result, politicians in power tend to minimize the extent of poverty, while those in opposition tend to maximize it in order to attack the government's economic policies. Therefore, the level that is chosen to define official poverty is a source of considerable disagreement. Statistics Canada, for example, from time to time assesses what an average family spends, as a percentage of income, on such basic necessities as food, clothing, and shelter and then sets the official poverty line at 20 percentage points above that level.[2] In the 1970s, the Statistics Canada poverty line was set at 62 per cent — that is, families or individuals spending 62 per cent or more of their incomes on the basic necessities were deemed to be officially poor. This poverty line was revised in the 1980s and set at 58.5 per cent.[3] The Canadian Council on Social Development (CCSD) argues that the poverty line ought to be set to include all families who earn 50 per cent or less of the average family income, and the 1971 Special Senate Committee on Poverty set the poverty level at about 56 per cent or less of the average family income. All poverty lines make adjustments to account for size of family, region, and rural/urban differences. In terms of the politics of poverty, it is important to realize that official poverty figures always understate its real extent. Most published data use the Statistics Canada poverty line, the one used in the formulation of government policy.

A related issue is the question of a poverty line, or a low–income cut–off, to measure poverty. For example, in 1988 Statistics Canada declared that in communities with populations of 500,000 or more, all families of three with incomes at $20,411 or less were "poor." Those who earned $20,412 were officially "not poor." Obviously, this declaration makes no social or economic sense. When we talk therefore of the official "poor," we exclude a significant group of the "near poor," who face the same problems as the "official poor." Only once, in 1969, did Statistics Canada study this group, concluding that they were more similar in many ways to the official "poor" than to the official "non–poor."

There is a third issue in the politics of poverty. Many of the poor are very poor, falling far below the official poverty line. One Montreal study found that about one–half of the official poor receive 60 per cent or less of the Statistics Canada poverty line income.[4] We know that the one million Canadians on welfare in 1987 received benefits ranging from 59 to 84 per cent of the official poverty line, depending on the generosity of the province of residence.[5] Furthermore, workers at the minimum wage cannot expect to earn much more than 68 per cent of the poverty line.[6] And things have been getting worse very quickly. In 1975 a worker at the minimum wage could earn a poverty line income with 50 hours of work each week. In 1986, a worker on the minimum wage had to put in 87 hours to reach the poverty line.[7]

That helps explains why in 1967 62 per cent of the poorest Canadians still managed to own their own homes, no matter how modest. That figure fell to 43 per cent by the early 1980s.[8] It also explains why the heads of most poor families (56 per cent) are active in the labour force, yet remain officially poor.

With these three *caveats* in mind — official figures tend to understate the real extent of poverty, arbitrary official poverty lines ignore an almost equal number of "near poor," and many of the official poor are very, very poor — we can examine the extent of poverty among Canada's children.

Child Poverty

Child poverty is deeply unsettling. As John Sargo said in *The Bitter Cry of the Children* in 1906,

> Poverty ... is always ugly, repellent and terrible either to see or to experience; but when it assails the cradle, it assumes its most hideous form.[9]

Even for the roughest minded, children are not seen as the authors of their own misfortune. When a Tory backbencher recently commented that many people were "poor by choice," many probably agreed, but it cannot be argued that children make that choice. Their deprivation closes a lifetime of doors of opportunity. The "feminization" of poverty, which I will address in Chapter 8, is acknowledged but there is also a "juvenescence" of poverty — a larger and larger portion of the poor in Canada are children, many of whom are young children in families headed by young parents.

In 1971, 1.7 million of Canada's 6.8 million children were poor — one in four,[10] and children accounted for about 39 per cent of all poor Canadians.[11] Over the next decade Canada scored some considerable success in its commitment to reduce poverty. By 1980, 896,000 of Canada's 5.9 million children were poor, representing 15 per cent of all children, or about 26 per cent of all poor Canadians. Therefore, in a decade, the absolute number of poor children had been cut in half, and the proportion of poor Canadians under the age of 16 had been dramatically reduced. This was part of the more general success story in reducing Canada's official poverty. Indeed, in 1980 the poverty rates for all Canadians, and for children, were the same at 15 per cent. But the recession of the early 1980s changed all that. Poverty rates began to move upward again. But the poverty rate among children went up much more dramatically. In 1986, Canadian children made up over 27 per cent of the poor; one child in six was officially poor, and as many as half of these were "very poor." There were perhaps another million "near poor."

There has, in fact, been a clear trend in the last 20 years — the greatest risk of poverty has shifted from the old to children and young families.[12] In 1969 elderly families (head over 65) suffered a poverty rate of over 42 per cent. In 1986, that rate was under 10 per cent. On the other hand, in 1972 families headed by persons under 25 years suffered a 16 per cent poverty rate. In 1986, that had almost doubled to over 30 per cent. Now the risk of poverty in Canada is greatest for families with children, for single parent families, and for families with only one earner.[13] That was clearly partly the result of the trend towards poorly paid jobs for young workers from 1981 to 1986. For example, in 1981 16 per cent of workers aged 16 to 24 earned the lowest wages, this figure more than doubled to 33 per cent in 1986.[14] Even as we move towards a marginal economic recovery, women and children remain the most likely to be left out.[15]

As a result, in the 1980s Canada has witnessed levels of hunger and homelessness unprecedented since the Great Depression. In Atlantic Canada, 150,000 people routinely rely on food banks,[16] as do 60,000 in Toronto alone.[17] In B.C. there are over 50 food banks, the most in any province.[18] In 1986 over 1.2 million meals were served in soup kitchens and homeless shelters.[19] In 1987 the CCSD estimated there were anywhere from 130,000 to 250,000 homeless in Canada,[20] including many children as the "new homeless" made up of whole families began to grow.[21] Hungry children, including, for example, hundreds in Vancouver's 17 inner city schools,[22] have become commonplace across the country. One can view this deterioration as symptomatic of a growing general social crisis resulting from the erosion of the social welfare system, as Graham Riches argues in his book, *Food Banks and the Welfare*

Crisis.[23] Or, with B.C. Premier Vander Zalm one can believe that hungry children exist only because they do not have parents who love them enough, lazing in bed rather than preparing school lunches for their children.[24]

The negative impact of poverty is well–documented. A massive health survey carried out jointly by Statistics Canada and Health and Welfare Canada found that low–income Canadians tend to be less educated and less happy and to have poorer health and shorter lives than more prosperous Canadians.[25] There was a clear inverse relationship between mortality rates and social class that remained "durable" over time. These findings were confirmed by an Ontario health survey in 1986: those with higher incomes lived longer and healthier lives than those with lower incomes.[26] If the lowest income and highest income quintiles are compared, the lowest had almost three times the rate of mental disorders, more than twice the rate of negative feelings, and seven times the rate of anxiety and depression. Men at the top of the income scale live 6.3 years longer and enjoy 14 more years of good health than men at the bottom. Another study found that poor women suffer three times the frequency of depression of middle class women.[27]

The 1975 National Council of Welfare report *Poor Kids*[28] pointed out that poor kids are more likely to be sick and to suffer retarded development, more at risk to fail or drop out of school, more likely to live in crowded and unhealthy homes, and more likely to be labelled delinquent than better–off children. The 1986 Ontario health survey found that children in lower socioeconomic groups are more likely to suffer from chronic health problems, more at risk to develop psychiatric disorders, and more prone to poor school performance than more affluent children. Indeed, a more recent study found that poor children have twice the school drop–out rate of non–poor children.[29] A Statistics Canada study found that poor children in urban Canada are much more likely to die than the children of the better–off.[30] This pattern was found to be the case for child deaths as a result of accidents among older children and for child deaths as a result of illness among infants. The poorest 20 per cent of Canadians in urban Canada had a child death rate up to the age of 19 years of 90.6 per 100,000, while the wealthiest 20 per cent had a rate of 58.1 per 100,000.

Children raised in poverty are more likely to be poor later in life and in turn to raise children in poverty. They very quickly lose any hope for the future. June Callwood captures well the downward spiral in the psyches of poor children.

> Until about the age of 8, children born to someone poor do not believe that the bad times will last ... Ten–year olds already are wiser and know that being poor will be endless. They protest unbecomingly, some with rage, some with cunning, some by with-drawing.[31]

Imagine that you are one of Canada's more than one million officially poor children. You live in a tiny house that is cold in spring, autumn, and winter. You share a double bed with three siblings, and during the winter it is pushed so close to the space heater there's a constant risk of fire. When the cold comes, the rats come in. You are almost always hungry; three mornings there is a hot breakfast at school, and near the end of the month you go with your mother to the food bank. Some days you take food from your schoolroom's "sharing shelves." You miss a lot of school because you are often sick, and sometimes there are no clean clothes to wear. Often there's no place at home to do homework. Your parents can't afford the extra charges for many of the school's programs. Every now and then on payday dad doesn't come right home and mom gets worried and then angry. Finally, dad comes home, and there's a big argument. Sometimes they hit you after they've quarrelled if you get in their way. You feel things will never get better and that there must be something terribly wrong with you and your parents because you are so poor. Though this portrait is fictionalized; it was drawn from the *Poor Kids* report and accurately records child poverty.

Child Poverty and the Family Crisis

To what extent is child poverty in Canada a result of the crisis of the family? Divorce typically leads to a precipitous fall in the material standards of living for women and a dramatically higher poverty rate for women and children. The transition to new family forms has thus increased the poverty, and general economic insecurity, of many children (see Table 2).[32]

Table 2: Poor children under 16 by family status, 1971 and 1986				
	1971		1986	
	Number	%	Number	%
All poor children	1,657,017	100	1,016,000	100
Husband/wife families	1,314,576	79	610,400	60
Female single parents	296,298	18	361,000	36
Male single parents	46,028	3	44,600	4
Estimate of number affected by marriage breakdown	147,000	9	235,000	23

Sources: National Council of Welfare, *Poverty Profile, 1988* (Ottawa: Supply and Services, 1988); National Council of Welfare, *Poor Kids* (Ottawa, 1975); Mary Anne Burke "Diversity the New Norm," Statistics Canada, *Canadian Social Trends* (Summer 1986).

In 1971 there were about 1.7 million officially poor children, representing almost 25 per cent of all children under 16 in Canada. Over 79 per cent of these children lived in husband/wife families, just about 18 per cent lived in single parent families headed by women, and just under 3 per cent lived in single parent families headed by men. If we look at it another way, over 69 per cent of children in single parent families headed by women and almost 34 per cent of children in those headed by men were officially poor. Thus, children in single parent families headed by women faced over *three times* the risk of being poor compared to children in husband/wife families, while children in single parent families headed by men faced almost *one–and–one–half times* the risk. Clearly, these 1971 figures tell us that the absence of a husband/wife family was a significant factor in poverty for over one in five poor children.

By the 1986 Census things had changed dramatically. About one million children, about 18 per cent of all children, were poor. That improvement, however, involved a significant redistribution of poverty as children were negatively affected by changes in the family. In 1986, just over 60 per cent of all poor children lived in husband/wife families, a sharp decrease from 1971. Only a little more than 12 per cent of all children in husband/wife families were poor that year, a considerable improvement over the 21 per cent figure of 1971. Children in single parent families headed by women accounted for almost 36 per cent of all poor children in 1986, more than twice the share in 1971. And children in single parent families headed by men accounted for over 4 per cent, again a substantial rise. By 1986 children in female single parent families faced *five times* the risk of poverty compared to children in husband/wife families, while children in male single parent families faced about *twice* the risk.

In 1986, 57 per cent of female single parent families, and 67 per cent of male single parent families, resulted from divorce or separation. These figures suggest that for as many of 235,000, or over 23 per cent, of all officially poor children in Canada, marriage breakdown was a factor of some significance in precipitating a fall below the poverty line. A similar estimate for 1971 suggests that was true for only about 147,000, or about 9 per cent, of all poor children. In other words, even as the total number of poor children declined, the proportion of all poor children for whom family breakdown was a significant factor in precipitating poverty increased *by over two–and–one–half times*. In 1986 18 per cent of all children in Canada were poor, and for about one in four of them marriage breakdown was implicated in the fall into poverty.

This brings us to a fourth issue — the duration of episodes of poverty. The statistics reported above describe the occurrence and distribution of poverty and identify those groups which experience a higher risk. But they tell us nothing about how persistent poverty is for a particular individual over time. Some will argue that episodes of poverty are brief in an individual's or family's total life experience. Many university students, for example, are officially poor for a time, but go on to comfortable incomes after graduation. And, if children, and their parent or parents, suffer only brief episodes of poverty, the problem is hardly as pressing as the statistical snapshot suggests. But if, on the other hand, poverty remains a chronic condition for large numbers of people over a number of years, then the consequences are much more disastrous.

Just as Statistics Canada has not devoted much attention to the "near poor," so it has neglected the *persistence* of poverty over time. Ross reports three Canadian studies on the question.[33] The 1969 Statistics Canada survey reported that three in four of poor unattached individuals and two in three poor families were poor in 1968 and in 1969, suggesting a high level of persistence. A similar survey done by Canada Health and Welfare for 1972 and 1973 found that three in four of the poorest households remained poor, while over one in two of the "near poor" did so. A third study done by the Institute of Public Affairs at Dalhousie University studied a sample of "welfare households" that went on to find employment between 1973 and 1976. Most jobs hovered at the minimum wage level, and three in four lasted six months or less, suggesting a high degree of persistence of poverty. All three studies suggest, therefore, a significant degree of persistence of poverty episodes over some considerable time. As Ross says, "What we do know ... suggests that probably between 50 and 75 per cent of the poverty group is stable over a two–to–three–year period and probably much longer."

A U.S. study offers more complete information on this question. The results can only be applied with caution, but they are suggestive. The Survey Research Center at the University of Michigan has followed a sample of 5,000 U.S. families from 1968. The sample was carefully designed to be representative of the total U.S. population.[34] That study found that one in 10 of the poor were "persistently" poor, defined as poor for eight or more of the 10 years examined (1969 to 1978). Another four in 10 were "intermittently" poor, defined as poor for from three to seven of the 10 years. On the other hand, 50 per cent were poor for only one or two years. The study also found that a substantial number of people live so close to the official poverty line that their designation as "non–poor" amounts to a cruel joke. The "temporarily" poor — about 90 per cent of the poor who remained in that state for from one to seven years of the 10–year period — have characteristics that are not too different from those of the population as a whole. For the "persistently" poor, however, three characteristics stood out: households tended to be elderly or black or headed by a female. In fact, 65 per cent of the "persistently" poor households were headed by women.

The Canadian studies also show that a large proportion of poor people suffer fairly long episodes of poverty. The high rates of poverty among female single parent families, and the evidence of a persistence of poverty over time, suggest that many childhood poverty episodes are of considerable duration. Since the average durations of single parenthood for Canadian women are quite long, the evidence points to a lengthy period of chronic poverty for a large number of poor Canadian children during their younger and more formative years.

The relationships between poverty and family breakdown are intimate and complex. Frequently, family breakdown precipitates a fall into poverty, particularly for single parent mothers and their children. Men are often able to escape court–ordered obligations to their former wives and children. One Status of Women study reported that the national average of men who default on maintenance payments ranges between 50 and 85 per cent across the country.[35] For some of the few men who obtain custody of the children, the loss of the second income can lead to a period of family poverty, although the duration is typically about one–half of that faced by women in similar circumstances. On the other hand, economic stress and difficulty can help precipitate a family's disintegration, leading inevitably to a worse economic situation, again especially for women and children. For example, during the recession of the late 1970s and the early 1980s, some areas of Ontario's golden horseshoe suffered elevated levels of unemployment (up to 20 per cent in Windsor, for example). Social service agencies there reported an increase in family problem caseloads of from 25 to 377 per cent as families began to fall apart under the economic stress. Increased unemployment led to a rash of mortgage defaults, rates of alcohol and drug problems spiralled, child and wife abuse became epidemic, and separation and divorce rates marched upward.[36] In other words, while family breakdown often leads to poverty, unexpected unemployment and episodes of poverty sometimes lead to family breakups.

The economic consequences of family breakdown can be extreme. For example, a study probed the backgrounds of 142 young homeless in Montreal aged 18 to 30 years. Most came from broken families and lived on the very precipice of daily survival. They tended to have serious mental health disorders, exacerbated by the routine abuse of drugs and alcohol.[37] Another Montreal study tried to obtain a more complete characterization of the poor. It was found that in 1981 23 per cent of all Montrealers were officially poor, but one–half of these were "very poor." One in three of these "very poor" were found to be aged 18 or less, and half of them lived in single parent families, amounting to nearly 44,000 children.[38] There are also the new emerging episodically homeless, often single parent mothers with small children, who have been described as the "peripatetic poor," living on inadequate welfare payments and moving from temporary home to temporary home.

Furthermore, the problems of economic stress often result in serious family disruption as a prelude to family breakdown. Children of unemployed parents can suffer enormous mental stress that is psychologically worse than that of the parent losing the job. Such children quickly lose any sense of expansive optimism about the future, tend to see the world as a disordered place in which they are unneeded and unwanted burdens, and tend to suffer elevated risks of clinical depression. They also more frequently experience physical abuse.[39]

On the more positive side, a stable and secure family is vital in establishing a child's sense of self–esteem and in fostering a sense of personal control over one's world.[40] Not surprisingly, it has been found that well–adjusted adolescents tend to come from families with higher levels of socioeconomic status. They have experienced no physical abuse. They can count on a more comprehensive system of social supports. Their parents tend to be more loving and caring. Their lives contained fewer stressful events, such as family breakdown. And, in general, they tend to have very positive concepts of themselves.[41]

Obviously, the increased levels of economic insecurity for many children resulting from the crisis of the family cannot be separated easily or clearly from the attendant increase in emotional and physical insecurity.

5 / The Emotional Insecurity of Children

Opinion on the emotional impact of family breakdown on children is divided.[1] One sociologist can talk confidently about "the *lack* of a clear–cut impact of divorce on children," insisting "it is unclear exactly *what effect* divorce has on children."[2] Others assert, "few children are untouched by divorce, but ... over 50 per cent are indistinguishable from others five years later,"[3] which suggests a considerable, prolonged negative impact. Psychiatrists and psychologists are much less divided: they flatly insist that divorce and/or separation have enormous negative emotional consequences for children. Why this divided opinion?

Part of the explanation can be found in the sad limitations of social science. Divorce or separation is the end of an often long and stressful process. And, of course, it continues to plague the separated spouses and their children. Further, the economic consequences are often disastrous. Therefore, separating cause and effect is virtually impossible. Are the problems of the children of divorce the result of the years of conflict and unhappiness that led up to divorce? Or of the divorce itself? Or of a precipitous fall into poverty? There is no way of knowing with precision.

When we talk about the emotional consequences of marriage breakdown for children, we are not just talking about the singular event of divorce or of the final signing of a legal separation document. We are clearly talking about a process that involves a variety of surrendered hopes, shattered dreams, violated expectations, economic strains, and unfulfilled cravings, often over many years. And how people work these through, or collapse under the stress, will be as unique and varied as their personalities and circumstances.

Sociologists quickly reject the evidence of individual cases because they do not allow us to make general statements about the consequences for children of parent loss. Indeed, one sociologist has argued that sociological findings on the emotional consequences of divorce for children tend to be much less negative and pessimistic than psychiatric findings. It is alleged that psychiatric findings will be more negative because psychiatrists will obviously be approached by those seeking help, not by those adjusting nicely. On the other hand, sociologists tend to try to base their conclusions on samples of all those affected by divorce or separation, scientifically drawn to assure some approximation of representativeness. But this argument tends to ignore the fact that many psychiatric studies do impose rigorous scientific controls and engage in careful comparisons between affected and unaffected groups.

Besides these scientific problems, there are ideological reasons why opinions on the emotional consequences of divorce or separation for children remain at variance.[4] Attitudes to divorce and separation have changed dramatically in less than a generation. Prior to the 1968 divorce reform, if an average person entered into an unhappy marriage, then by and large he or she was expected to put up with it. The breakup of the family was considered to be an overwhelming evil, especially for the children. Remember all those James Cagney gangster movies? Invariably the gangster had suffered the early trauma of parental divorce, separation or desertion. Children of divorce were on the slippery slope that led to the reformatory or the penitentiary. Divorcing parents were seen to be criminally self–indulgent, emotionally truncated, monumentally insensitive, or socially irresponsible, perhaps all four. The sub-message was clear: you may have made a bitterly unhappy marriage, but think of the children ... And again, the message was particularly aimed at women: do everything, accept everything, sacrifice everything, but, above all, keep the family together.

The new feminism contributed to a decline in such attitudes, attitudes that oppressed women with domestic slavery, subordination to the needs of husbands and children, and large doses of guilt. One of the early responses to the burgeoning women's movement was the amendment of the divorce law. Subsequently, in the 1970s and early 1980s there was, Richardson notes, "a tendency to romanticize divorce as a creative, rehabilitative, and liberating process."[5] And so it obviously was for those in unhappy marriages. Whenever the issue of the emotional consequences of divorce for children was raised, it was repeatedly confirmed that it is infinitely worse for all members of the family to remain in conflictful, unloving, and unhappy family situations. But to concede that does not therefore justify ignoring the negative emotional consequences of divorce for children. Children in unhappy families suffer the most; next come children of divorce who suffer a great deal.

Divorce or separation may be necessary and even good, but it is emotionally costly. Just as the new right tends to blame feminism and the women's liberation movement for the decline of the traditional family, so they assign similar blame for the emotional difficulties generated by family breakdown. It would not be surprising, therefore, to expect supporters of the rights of women to minimize or overlook the negative consequences of marriage breakdown. A far better response is to admit that great social changes often involve emotional suffering. Let us, therefore, assess the emotional consequences, bad and good, of divorce and separation and address them through policies and programs. After all, more than one in two children will spend part of their lives in a single parent family.[6] Richardson estimates that as many as 100,000 children each year are affected by divorce and separation.[7] Therefore in the more than 20 years since the changes in the divorce law it can be conservatively argued that between one and two million Canadian children have been touched by some form of marriage breakdown.

Experts have noted a dramatic increase in recent decades of children with emotional problems serious enough to require professional intervention. According to one child psychiatrist, in the 1960s about one child in 10 suffered from an emotional or mental illness serious enough to require professional help. In the 1970s, that figure grew to about one child in 6.5.[8] In 1983 the Ontario Health Survey studied a sample of 3,000 children aged four to 16 and found the prevalence of psychiatric disorder to average over one in five.[9] Between the 1950s and the 1980s teen–age suicide and suicide–attempt rates have risen by 300 per cent in Canada,[10] and the director of the Suicide Research Unit of the U.S. National Institute for Mental Health reported a 66 per cent increase in suicide among the young between the 1970s and 1980s.

Since social support systems are crucial to emotional well–being, the collapse of such systems is typically implicated in the onset of psychiatric disorders.[11] As a result, psychiatrists have not hesitated in pointing the finger at family breakdown as a major reason for the rising rates of emotional distress among children. One child psychiatrist said, "the nuclear family is disintegrating and children have fewer support mechanisms to help them through difficult times,"[12] and another drew a larger portrait of the choice before us:

> Prostitution, child abuse, alcoholism, vandalism, suicide and depression are symptomatic of social malaise. Escalating divorce rates, increased mobility, changing social conventions, the erosion of institutional supports of church and school, all contribute to a sense of rootlessness and anomie.[13]

One study reported that from 15 to 25 per cent of the children touched by divorce require psychiatric treatment. Though most divorced spouses with children remarry within three to five years, 20 per cent experience another separation, compounding the earlier emotional problems. From 50 to 80 per cent of the patients treated by Canadian mental health clinics are from separated families.[14] And the negative emotional effects of parental loss through divorce or separation or death do not end with the end of childhood. Rather, it has been found that parental loss was the "single most powerful predictor of adult psychopathology."[15] And if parents divorce, the chances are much greater that the child will.[16] A study of families of almost 8,000 U.S. women aged 15 to 44 found that women who spent part of their childhood in a single parent family, when compared to those from two parent families, are more likely to marry and have children at a younger age, more likely to have children before marrying, and more likely to experience the breakdown of their own marriages. The authors concluded, "Parental role models and parental supervision are the major factors in determining an offspring's future family–formation orientation."[17]

Emotional Impacts

Though sociological studies are sometimes hesitant to draw firm conclusions about the specific emotional impacts of divorce, none deny they *are* serious. Very large scale studies show clear negative patterns among children from broken homes. One study of 18,000 U.S. children showed that children from broken homes exhibited significantly greater tendencies to demonstrate delinquent behaviour, to leave school before completion, to suffer from various illnesses, and to attempt or commit suicide. Another researcher reported that children of divorce are more isolated and withdrawn; act out more often; exhibit more absent–mindedness, moodiness, and inattentiveness; and present with more physical symptoms of illness.[18] A study of over 2,000 suicide–attempting children aged six–and–a–half to 17 found that the rate of such incidents went up by almost four times from 1977 to 1982 and that the "pathogenic family influences" included family conflict and separation or divorce.[19] As well, it has been long–noted in North America that separation and divorce are the single most striking characteristics associated with attempted adolescent suicide.[20] Such persisting patterns of emotional distress among children affected by family breakdown have been repeatedly confirmed, and they stand as monumental evidence of the emotional burden imposed on children as a result of the transition from traditional to new family forms.

Additionally, clinical studies are beginning to give more details about specific impacts. One study of 100 adolescents consecutively discharged from a provincial psychiatric hospital found that at the time of admission 84 per cent either lived apart from their parents or with only one parent.[21] Seventy–four per cent were diagnosed as having a conduct disorder associated with an emotional disturbance, usually further complicated by an overlying depression. Another study of 51 families referred to various agencies for assessment in custody and access disputes assessed the adjustments of the children involved.[22] Older children demonstrated more disturbance than younger children, perhaps because older children had faced an average four years of parental loss, while younger children had faced an average of two years. More optimistically, the study suggested that only one in 10 of the affected children studied manifested maladjustment serious enough to warrant clinical intervention.

Probably the best clinical studies have been done by E.M. Hetherington and her associates.[23] The researchers reported evidence of extreme stress during the first year following breakup. Children of divorce were found to exhibit more negative behaviour, to express more dependency, to be less affectionate and obedient, and generally to whine and nag more. One year after divorce, both boys and girls were still highly dependent, made excessive demands for help, acted out a great deal, and were resistant to parental authority. Boys seemed to manifest more problems than girls. In a six–year follow–up of 60 children of divorce, Hetherington confirmed the negative behaviour scenario, but she found that the problems were more persistent for boys and actually increased in boys after remarriage, but other studies have failed to find such a clear difference between the behaviour reactions of boys and girls.[24]

Furthermore, it has been shown that the responses of children affected by divorce differs by age.[25] Pre–school and kindergarten kids, aged two to five, tend to regress at first, expressing fear of being deserted ultimately by both parents. They also express guilt feelings, believing somehow that they were responsible for the divorce. They also complain of nightmares and sleeplessness and are often afraid to sleep alone. They frequently complain of headaches and stomachaches. Early school age children still suffer from some of these complaints, but they also tend to begin to deny the separation and to claim that they are experiencing no problems. But further clinical probing uncovers a sense of profound and lingering loss. Among older school age children, those aged five to eight, clinicians report great sadness and explicit grieving. As well, about one–half of the children in this age group exhibit learning problems. By the pre–adolescent age of nine to 12 children tend to express a more thoughtful response to the divorce, yet they feel it necessary to assign blame to one parent and to view the other as the victim. Children in this age group still report some somatic symptoms — like headaches and stomach upsets — but of a more mild sort. When such children do express negative symptoms they are usually indirect, such as acting out, rebellion, running away, and stealing.

Adolescents, those aged 13 to 18, suffer the most. They express greater worries about sex, future marriage, degrees of intimacy, and the nature and extent of emotional commitment.[26] They reveal a profound sense of anger and loss and are torn by conflicting loyalties. All this leads to a greater risk of serious delays in their normal psychosocial development and maturation.[27] These adolescents also present more problems on parental remarriage, including more open grieving about the lost parent and anger that the divorce is now irrevocable.

These negative effects of divorce tend to persist into young adulthood. Studies have suggested that young adults with divorced parents tend to be explicitly anxious about their marital futures, less likely to want to have and raise children, and more prone to postpone marriage. Young women tend to find parental divorce more stressful than young men, manifesting a longer delay in adjustment to the breakup. Furthermore, young women are more split in their post–divorce relationships with parents, tending to side with their mothers while experiencing an erosion in their relationships with their fathers. About two in three such young men and women express anger directed at one or both parents and worry about their parents' future adjustment and happiness, especially about the mother's ability to cope.

There is, therefore, actually very little disagreement about the negative consequences of divorce for children. In general, most children suffer varying magnitudes of serious sadness, grieving, anxiety, and depression during at least the first year after divorce. About two in three of such children return to a reasonably satisfactory normal adjustment, but a third continues to exhibit significant problems. One five–year follow–up study found that these children were still quite distressed and unhappy. But to reiterate another constant theme throughout the literature:

Living with parents who have lost feelings for each other is infinitely worse.

One team of psychiatrists put it this way:

If we accept that there is good evidence of the deleterious effects of divorce, how might we attempt to mitigate these effects? One answer would be to make divorce much more difficult to obtain. This certainly would change the statistics, but it is unlikely that it would improve the lot of the individuals affected. Indeed, at least for the child, the effects might be even more negative than being involved in the divorce; Hetherington's work indicates that children in intact high–tension families are worse off than those whose parents have gone the route of separation and divorce.[28]

Children are, then, among the more serious emotional casualties of the collapse of the traditional family and the transition to new family forms. Men and women usually divorce for a variety of good and sensible reasons. Some women seek divorces because of a spouse's verbal and/or physical abuse or excessive consumption of alcohol. Some women seek divorce because their husbands refuse to support them in breaking out of the confinement of traditional roles. Some working women divorce because their husbands resist taking on a fair share of the domestic work and emotional burdens of home and family. As women become more and more economically independent, the former economic constraints tying them to an unhappy marriage are loosened. It is not surprising that among those most at risk of divorce are married couples where both spouses have independent incomes. Among those at a much lower risk are very high income couples, dependent primarily on the husband's salary. Some men divorce because they wish to recapture the roaming freedom of their youth. Some because they cannot accept being replaced by a baby as the main focus of their wives' emotional attention. Some because they can't accept their wives' assertion of independence, others because they can't accept their wives' tendency to cling to traditional, dependent roles. Some men and women divorce because they fall out of love, but more usually because they fall into a new, more satisfying love. Usually men and women divorce reluctantly after many efforts to salvage a relationship. The typical divorce happens after about nine years of marriage, a lengthy emotional investment by any standard. Therefore, when a decision to divorce is made it is not impulsive: it is a considered, deliberate, and painful act.

Children cannot fully understand or accept this. For them, the divorce shatters the centres of their lives. Studies cited by Richardson are instructive.[29] Children of divorce are confused, shocked, and disbelieving. Even when there had been spousal violence and quarrelling, such children felt "their family life was basically happy" and that their parents' conflicts did not justify divorce. For them almost anything is preferable. And we should not expect children, even older children, to accept the ebbs and flows of emotional events in adult love relationships. A man or a woman wants love and fulfillment, sexual and otherwise, emotional meaning, and happiness out of a marriage relationship. From their parents children want love, protection, serenity, and security ... above all that the world as they have known it should go on in the future as it has in the past. To trade that for a search for personal happiness seems out of proportion for children. After all, it is a father or a mother being lost, not just a husband, wife and lover. Husbands, wives and lovers can, with some pain and difficulty certainly, ultimately be satisfactorily, perhaps even more happily, replaced. "Real" mothers and "real" fathers can never be replaced, and such a loss remains a lingering blot on many children's experience even into adulthood.

These psychological and emotional costs must be entered into the ledger recording historical change. And in the section of the ledger that records the costs of the transition of the family, there are many pages to be filled with those borne by our children. But there are even more to be recorded. The transition to new family forms also threatens the physical security of many of our children. These are the permanent, forever irretrievable casualties.

6 / The Physical Insecurity of Children

When we read reports that 40,000 of the world's children die of starvation and/or disease each day, we can perhaps be forgiven for being thankful that a wealthy nation like Canada remains immune to tragedies of such magnitudes.[1] The Canadian family still retains the institutional responsibility for the primary care, protection, and socialization of children. And the care we lavish on our children makes them among the world's most fortunate. But there is also a darker side. The Kid's Help toll–free phone line, recently established in Toronto, receives over 700 calls from distressed children each day. The callers range in age from three to 19, and counsellors estimate that 20 per cent of calls come from physically and/or sexually abused children and that 20 per cent are from children contemplating suicide. Experts estimate that one in eight Canadian children suffer emotional or physical abuse — over 900,000 children.[2] For many children the family promises only terror, cruelty, and suffering, and it is estimated that between 60,000 and 100,000 Canadian children aged 10 to 16 run away from home each year. Studies have shown that such children are fleeing from homes in which 73 per cent suffered physical beatings and 73 per cent of girls and 38 per cent of boys suffered sexual abuse.[3] A growing proportion of Canadian children are thus physically at risk. Like all linkages between social causes and effects, the one between the physical insecurity of children and the problems involved in the transition to new family forms is difficult to prove. Sometimes the evidence is abundant, clear, and irrefutable. Other times, it is indirect, suggestive, and tangential, but convincing because of its preponderance.

We have already considered the relationship between child poverty and the family's transition. Clearly many of the negative consequences of poverty for children are the direct result of poverty *per se*, yet when poverty is itself a consequence of family breakdown or family change, the causal chain is more complex. We know that poverty for many women and children follows from family breakdown. Therefore, when we say that child abuse, for example, is caused by neglectful and emotionally uncontrolled parents, ought we not to ask what circumstances generate such parents? Or when we say that a child commits suicide because he or she feels bereft of hope and support, ought we not to ask how the child came to such a stark conclusion?

In what follows we will be examining the growing physical insecurity of children — health and mortality, suicide rates, child abuse, child and adolescent homicide, and the proportion of our children in formal state agencies of care. Only a small minority of our children face such appalling situations, but it is a much larger minority than people generally believe. If many children are suffering avoidable injury and death, then clearly the family is somehow tragically failing them.

The facts can be clearly stated. More of our children are being injured, many fatally, as a result of avoidable accidents.[4] More are committing suicide. More are apparently suffering physical and/or sexual abuse. More are the victims of homicide. And more are being taken into forms of state care. This growing physical insecurity of our children can only be understood in the context of the transition from traditional to new family forms and must be seen as part of the costs of this social change.

Child and Adolescent Mortality

In the early 1970s so-called "social injuries" passed illness as the leading cause of child death in Canada.[5] "Social injuries" result from situational circumstances and might have been prevented had there been greater care or more attention paid to the child's environment. Typically in these fatal injuries no individual blame is assigned. In the 1970s Canada had one of the worst records among industrialized nations for child deaths as the result of accidents. Among boys aged one to 14, Canada was third from the bottom, and among girls of the same age, second from the bottom, in a group of 24 industrialized nations. A survey of 17,000 injured children who annually went through Toronto's Hospital for Sick Children from 1974 to 1978 found that the injuries resulted from 5,000 falls and 3,000 "bumps and blows," while the others were the result of violence, burns, poisoning, either self–inflicted or inflicted by others. It is estimated that about one in 10 pediatric injuries result from deliberate abuse, while another one in 10 result from neglect. A B.C. study in 1978 found that violence was the leading reason for hospital admission among the province's children.[6] Another study reported that children under five years of age are more likely to be run down and killed in parking lots or by parents backing out of a driveway than they are in street traffic. Those over five are more likely to be killed by running unexpectedly out into oncoming traffic. [7]

Who is responsible for such "social injuries"? Clearly, more adequate care and closer supervision by adults would dramatically reduce them. Why is such care not available to many of our children? Is single parenthood a factor? Are two working parents a factor? Are kids being left unattended more often?

The pattern is quite general, and more disturbing because of its generality. In 1961, the five leading causes of death among boys aged 15 to 19 years were, in order of frequency: 1) traffic accidents; 2) cancer; 3) diseases of the circulatory system; 4) suicide (tied with #3); and 5) congenital abnormalities. Of these, traffic accidents and suicide can be considered as "social injuries." In the same year, the five leading causes of death among girls the same age were: 1) traffic accidents; 2) cancer; 3) diseases of the circulatory system; 4) congenital abnormalities; and 5) influenza, bronchitis and pneumonia. Of these, only traffic accidents are "social injuries."

Twenty years later, in 1981, the situation was disturbingly different. Among boys the five leading causes of death were; 1) traffic accidents; 2) suicide; 3) cancer; 4) homicide; and 5) diseases of the circulatory system. Among girls they were: 1) traffic accidents; 2) cancer; 3) suicide; 4) congenital abnormalities; and

5) homicide.[8] Therefore, three of the five leading causes of death among our adolescents are now in the "social injury" category.

How do we explain this? At one level, such statistics are a commentary on our medical successes in defeating disease and illness among children and adolescents. But now we face the daunting fact that most child and adolescent deaths are caused by "social injuries." Why has not society committed the kind of public resources to combat these social causes of child death that have for generations been committed to combatting illness and disease? How can traffic deaths be related to the crisis of the family? If children had better supervision, many such accidents would not occur. For adolescents what one might view as the sad price of greater independence — the unsupervised use of automobiles — is somewhat tempered by the contention by some child psychiatrists that many adolescent traffic fatalities are really cases of disguised suicide. At least part of the explanation of these changing patterns of mortality must be sought in the changing nature of the family.

A much less dramatic spotlight on the relationship between children's health risks and changing family forms was provided by a U.S. study of children in the eighth grade in Los Angeles and San Diego, which found that "latchkey" children, regardless of their parents' wealth or marital status, were more likely to smoke, to drink alcohol, and to experiment with marijuana.[9] Clearly the risk of greater rates of more serious misadventurous behaviour is also higher among such children in what is euphemistically called "self–care."

Parents find it harder and harder to provide appropriate levels of care for their children, and the question, "Who's minding the children?" takes on greater and greater urgency.

Child and Adolescent Suicide

Suicide is the ultimate act of despair and hopelessness. Rates of child and adolescent suicide have escalated since 1961, going up by a factor of four times between 1960 and 1986 among the 15 to 19 year age group (from 5.3/100,000 to 20.2/100,000 population).[10] The overall suicide rate in 1986 (14.6) was double the rate

from the 1920s to the early 1960s (7.5) and has even far out-
stripped the rate during the dark decade of the Great Depression
(10). But the most dramatic age specific rate increase has occurred
among adolescents. And it is estimated that there are from 30 to
40 suicide attempts for every one that is successful.[11]

Child suicide, suicides among those under 15, is still rare but
increasing.[12] In 1966, there were 19 suicides among children and
68 suicides among adolescents representing, respectively, 1 per
cent and 4 per cent of all officially recorded suicides. In 1986 there
were 25 child suicides and 241 adolescent suicides representing,
respectively, 1 per cent and 7 per cent of all suicides. It is not
unusual to find at least one case each year of a child between five
and nine years of age taking his or her own life.[13]

The fact that child suicides have remained constant must not
be cause for too much comfort. The trend in absolute numbers of
suicides each year among children has been upwards, because the
total number of children in the age groups in question has declined
steeply. Furthermore, all experts agree that official suicide rates
are far below the actual, since many apparently accidental deaths,
or deaths by misadventure, are in reality hidden suicide. Suicides
are often covered up by families, aided by sympathetic physicians
and officials, particularly in the case of child suicide, which devas-
tates a family beyond imagining. Although the favoured suicide
technique among children is hanging, many ingest lethal over-
doses of drugs. In the absence of clear evidence to the contrary,
either event can be easily construed as accidental death.

In the case of adolescent suicide the evidence requires very
little supplementary explanation. Despite probable underreporting, despite the declining number of adolescents as a whole,
despite the rising overall suicide rate, adolescent suicide has sky-
rocketed in absolute numbers, as a proportion of all suicides, and
as rates per 100,000 population.

Again, it is possible that in the 1960s there was a greater
tendency to cover–up adolescent suicides. However, the increase
has been so great that a decline in the willingness to cover–up
suicides is simply an insufficient explanation of the steep rise.
While data will never finally become available, adolescent suicides are much less easy to cover–up because of the typical means

used and of the ages of the victims. Adolescents are more likely to use guns or motor vehicle exhaust fumes, which are more difficult to interpret as accidents. Hanging and drugs are also more difficult to interpret as misadventures in this age group.

The facts, then, are harrowing. More and more of our children and adolescents prefer suicide to continued existence. Why? In *Growing Up Dead: A Hard Look at Why Adolescents Commit Suicide*, Brenda Rabkin surveyed a variety of troubled backgrounds and individual coping responses. Her final judgement says it well:

> Young people commit suicide because of unbearable pain and a conviction that life is without hope, that new tomorrows are just miserable repeats of old yesterdays; so to continue living is pointless ... Each act of suicide is as idiosyncratic as the individual committing it. To view suicide solely in terms of theories and statistics is to ignore the human agony that prompts the act.[14]

Although it is difficult to disagree, if there are larger social patterns in child and adolescent suicide, they ought to be sought. Some studies have discerned significant patterns in child and adolescent suicide, particularly the psychosocial risk factors.[15] Among them are a number that are not particularly surprising — higher risk groups include those who had previously sought psychiatric or psychological help; those who had experienced the suicide of a member of the family or a friend; those with parents requiring psychiatric help; those who had attempted or threatened suicide in the past; those who had experienced a recent break–up with a boyfriend or girlfriend; those who abused alcohol or drugs; those who had lost a parent or parents through separation, divorce, or death; and those who had been physically and/or sexually abused by a parent or parents. Other risk factors include problems with the police, academic difficulties in school, and unemployment. Many of these factors are intertwined and many child and adolescent suicides are characterized by multiple risk factors. As Thompson says, after studying all completed child and adolescent suicides in Manitoba between 1971 and 1982 (190 cases):

The most common risk factors for the population as a whole were alcohol abuse, a recent breakup with a boyfriend or girlfriend and a recent marital or family dispute … Alcohol abuse is related to a recent breakup in a relationship and to a recent death among family or friends. Previous attempts were associated with psychiatric contact and suicidal ideation. Unemployment was associated with a history of drug abuse and school problems. A suicide note was found statistically more often when there was a history of parental separation and divorce.

And there are a series of significant overall relationships among the identified risk factors:

Alcohol is the leading risk factor overall, agreeing with previous studies … The association of this drinking with a recent breakup or death of a loved one suggests that these teenagers turn to alcohol in times of emotional stress … The association between previous attempts, psychiatric contact and suicidal ideation probably stems from attempts leading to psychiatric contact. When a suicide is completed the psychiatrist is contacted and ideation reported. Many previous studies agree with our finding that this cluster occurs more often in females. That it occurs in both genders in the 18–20 year range likely indicates increasing duration of pathology with increasing age.

Finding a suicide note after a parental separation or divorce is more common in the 15–17 year range, as are school problems. One wonders if the notes left behind, which often apologized for what they were about to do, are not apologizing for a sense of responsibility for the breakup of the parents' marriage.[16]

The extent to which the intertwining of these risk factors dovetails with the emotional consequences of divorce or separation for affected children is remarkable. Indeed, the pattern of the relationship between family breakdown, the negative emotional consequences for affected children, and the emergence of risk factors for suicide among children and adolescents has been confirmed and reconfirmed. A related risk factor is ongoing family conflict, which may or may not lead to ultimate divorce, and it is again hard to separate the emotional consequences of an unhappy family experience over some years and the final breakup.

Indeed, family dysfunction or family breakdown remains among the most common risk factors in the background of children and adolescents who commit suicide. Psychological consequences of family problems and family breakdown, like low self–esteem, depression, anger, social isolation, school problems, acting out behaviour, and excessive moodiness and absent–mindedness, parallel quite closely the psychological profiles of suicidal children and adolescents. Epidemiologically, suicide rates among children and adolescents affected by family breakdown range all the way from two times the rate among children with only one parent present in the home to four times the rate in homes where both parents are absent.

Epidemiological patterns do not *prove* a direct causal link; rather they are merely strongly suggestive that a causal connection between two associated phenomena is more probable. Reproduced below are two graphs, one charting the divorce rate in Canada between 1951 and 1986, the other charting the rate of suicide among adolescent males (the pattern for females is similar, but the rate is much lower).

Figure 1: Divorce Rate, 1951–1986

Source: Owen Adams, "Divorce Rates in Canada," Statistics Canada, *Canadian Social Trends* (Winter 1988): 19.

Figure 2: Suicide Rate for Boys Aged 15-19, 1960-1986

Source: Renée Benoteau, "Trends in Suicide," Statistics Canada, *Canadian Social Trends* (Winter 1988): 23

What does this suggest? We can fairly safely say that the crisis of the family, as manifested in divorce and separation, is strongly associated with the rise in rates of suicide among adolescents.

Let us be crystal clear about what is and what is not being said. Divorce does not *cause* suicide in children. Indeed, many children from particularly unhappy families might have been more likely to attempt or commit suicide had the divorce not intervened. For many children, divorce leads to a happier future. Nor is every child in an intact family immune from suicide. What is being said emphatically is that separation and divorce, and the whole complex of subsequent emotional consequences of the family's breakup, place the affected children and adolescents *more at risk* of suicide.

Child Abuse

The case that most galvanized public opinion and spotlighted the problem of child abuse in Canada was that of 19–month–old Kim Ann Popen, who was brutally beaten to death in 1976. The immediate cause of death was fatal injuries to the head, but the autopsy revealed a litany of sexual and physical torture: bruised and cut genitals; a torn hymen; broken ribs; and an anus three times the normal size. Baby Kim had been subjected to repeated beatings and was under the care and protection of the Sarnia Lambton Children's Aid Society when the fatal decision was made to return her to her home. As a result, County Court Judge H. Ward Allen conducted an inquiry into the death and concluded that the following persons and agencies had failed to protect Baby Kim: the Social Services Ministry; the police; the Crown Attorney; the Lambton Health Unit; individual social workers; and all those family members and friends who knew of her plight. But the judge most strongly condemned the Children's Aid Society, insisting that the child would not have perished had the agency lived up to its responsibility to protect her.[17]

Hardly a week goes by without another gruesome tale of starvation, crushed skulls, biting and beating infants to death, ruptured stomachs, broken bones at different stages of healing, or blindings, or burnings. And often it is reported that the authorities knew of the abuse. No purpose will be served here by an endless repetition of such horror stories — the social scientific and medical literature are full of them. Much more important are the questions: just how extensive is child abuse in Canada and what appear to be the factors that precipitate such abuse? Just what leads a parent or another adult to physically or sexually abuse his or her charge? Since the early to mid 1970s, when national attention focussed on the problem, there have been many studies and inquiries documenting this distressing phenomenon.[18]

Estimates vary on how extensive the child abuse is. Partly, that is a matter of definition. When we speak of abuse, are we talking about physical and sexual abuse, psychological and emotional abuse, or abuse resulting from deliberate neglect and deprivation? A recent Decima poll found that one in three Canadian parents admit to slapping or spanking, and parents of young children under six are twice as likely to use physical punishment as parents of older children.[19] Is this abuse? The law says "no," since the Criminal Code permits adults in charge of children to use "reasonable force ... by way of correction" of children. But experts worry about where the line is drawn. The 1980 Senate Report, *Child at Risk*, estimated that there are between 5,000 and 9,000 Canadian children suffering potentially damaging or fatal abuse. The Badgley Report estimated that one in three males and one in two females in Canada have been victims of unwanted sexual acts

— with about 80 per cent of these acts occurring during childhood or adolescence.

Perhaps a firmer estimate is provided by a 1988 Gallup poll which found that one in seven Canadians (14 per cent) say that they have "*personal* awareness of a *serious* instance of physical abuse of children by a parent," a much higher estimate than even the most impassioned anti–abuse activist has ever dared suggest.[20] Even more worrisome is that 37 per cent took no action whatsoever to intervene. Further, when compared to a Gallup poll on the same question taken in 1982, the 1988 results suggest a significantly increased awareness of serious child abuse. In 1982 Gallup found that only 11 per cent of their sample admitted personal awareness of a serious case of child abuse.

The doctrine in the literature is that there is no reason to believe that child abuse is any more prevalent now than it ever was. Indeed, it is often argued, the apparent increase is merely an artifact of increased reporting of actions that in former times were hidden and even tolerated. But two arguments qualify an uncritical acceptance of this view. First, it is remarkable that child abuse has persisted and apparently increased at a time when it is almost universally condemned and when serious interventions, including legal sanctions, are for the first time being more or less systematically applied. This persistence is much more remarkable than the fact that hidden and more or less tolerated abuse of children went on systematically in the past. Even more significant, however, is the emerging evidence of the stressors that seem to be associated with child abuse. Clearly if they can be related to the current crisis of the family, then we can argue not only that child abuse might be increasing, but also that its causes are shifting and becoming more and more rooted in the problems associated with the transition to new family forms.

Throughout the literature on child abuse, especially feminist literature, there is a centrally recurring theme that child abuse, as well as other forms of family violence, must be viewed in the context of male domination and the patriarchal family. Males are socialized to be more prepared to use violence to defend and assert their power, authority, and position. Males are socialized to have a limited emotional repertory, and they are therefore more quick to see violence as an effective means of resolving conflicts. There-fore, when children intrude on men's spaces, resist their authority, or behave vexatiously, males are more likely to use physical punishment. Furthermore, we live in a society that celebrates violence and the macho male, in sports, in politics, in war. As well, in our political culture those with power and authority routinely defend themselves from challenges through legitimate violence.

A 1987 Montreal case is a horrifying example of the implica-tion of traditional patriarchal attitudes in instances of child abuse. The story was movingly told by Janet Bagnall in the 21 October 1989 edition of the Montreal *Gazette*.

It was December 28, 1987, three days after Christmas. In a small, fourth–storey apartment in north Montreal, an 8 year–old boy broke a household object. His social worker won't say what he broke, but she said it was neither valuable nor important.

In the child's mind, though, that wasn't the point. The point was that he would get another beating from his father. But this time, he panicked. He just couldn't face his father's belt across his back one more time.

He opened the door which led to the apartment's balcony, climbed up on the railing and jumped, intending to die.

Fortunately, the child lived, suffering only a badly sprained ankle thanks to a heavy groundcover of snow. In the aftermath the child was taken into protection and placed in a foster home where he is reported to be doing well. The boy was repeatedly beaten, and burned with lit cigarettes, by his father. Social workers ap-proached the father to see if he would co–operate in dealing with the problem and cease his abuse. As the boy's social worker said, "Over the next few months I tried and tried and tried with the father, but it was no good. As far as he is concerned the child is his property and he can do what he wants with him. It is not safe for the child to return home."

Patriarchy is therefore a crucial factor in child abuse. Indeed, the overwhelming majority of child abusers are male, upwards of 85 to 95 per cent. But, if we accept this general argument, then we ought to be able to argue further that today such a causal pattern might lead to more child abuse, or at least to changing patterns of such abuse. Today the dominant male patriarch is threatened on all sides — women are more assertive, attitudes more disapproving of the traditional male role are more widely shared, even children are more assertive. A traditional husband and father, who 20 years ago was able to rule the home with benign authoritarianism, backed up always by the ultimate threat of force, might now lash out emotionally and physically more often to defend his position.

What does the literature tell us about the stressors commonly associated with child abuse? Is the threatened patriarchal male the major perpetrator? Or is it a more pathetic figure? Does the crisis of the family provoke child abuse in other ways? The literature fails to confirm clearly that child abuse can be largely explained as the result of the desperate efforts by threatened patriarchs to salvage their prerogatives and privileges. The child abusing male is a much less a looming and tragic historical figure. Child abuse is much more complex.

Poverty, unemployment and economic stress have been frequently associated with child abuse. Despite its repeated confirmation, some experts simply reject its meaningfulness and argue that child abuse cuts across all classes and income groups. An Ontario nurse, who deals with child abuse in her work, testified before an all–party committee of the province's Legislature examining child abuse that the poor are more prone to physical child abuse because they suffer more stress and have fewer supports and resources to cope with problems and crises. Wealthier parents who abuse their children are more likely to engage in forms of emotional abuse and neglect, she alleged.[21] Both a Tory and an NDP member of the Committee attacked this notion. The Tory argued "Child abuse crosses all economic stratas [*sic*]. You just can't say that upper classes are more negligent and lower classes use physical abuse." The New Democrat argued that lower class abuse tends to get reported, while upper class abuse tends to be underreported saying, "I think we have some stereotypic views of the working class family where the father rules the family with an iron fist and that everything is calm and smooth in the upper–class family."

The resistance to admitting poverty as a major stressor in precipitating child abuse seems to come from two sources. Some feminist writers dislike any argument that deflects central attention away from the patriarchal family, and male supremacy in the family hierarchy, as the major background factor in child abuse. Poverty, unemployment and economic stress as factors do just that. Others feel that an association between lower economic status and child abuse unfairly attacks working class and poor men and women, heaping emotional insult on economic injury. It is easy to understand the concerns. We ought not to lose sight of the power relationships in the traditional patriarchal family, as a context conducive to child abuse, nor should we overlook the fact that wealthier people tend to be more immune from intervention by authorities and less likely therefore to be reported as abusers, particularly in cases where the evidence is marginal. But, and it is an important "but," again and again the association between poverty, unemployment, economic stress, and economic failure, on the one hand, and child abuse, on the other, has been found.

Marital conflict is also strongly associated with the incidence of child abuse. For example, it tends to be more frequent in families with young parents, families headed by single parent mothers, families affected by strife and conflict, and families on the threshold of parental separation and/or divorce. Furthermore, husbands who abuse their wives also tend to abuse their children. And abused women often, in turn, abuse their own children.[22] Children in families which are socially isolated from family and friends are also more at risk of suffering abuse. Studies in Britain have found that battering mothers tend to be young, poorly educated and victims of abuse themselves, while battering fathers tend to be poorly educated and former victims of child abuse. The typical abusing couple, for child abuse is often a form of *folie à deux* particularly in the collusion to cover–up the crime, tended to have married young in defiance of their parents, to have few or no friends, to live a great distance from their families in increasing economic misery, and to have children who were frequently unplanned and premature.

Just these two — poverty and marital discord and breakdown — are repeatedly associated with child abuse, and they are closely related to the problems provoked by the family's transition. Typically there is a cluster of multiple stressors afflicting families at greater risk of child abuse: family instability and breakdown; poverty and/or unemployment; and other forms of social and economic stress. As well, there are a series of characteristics of the child which tend to put him or her at greater risk of abuse. Premature infants, for example, are more at risk of abuse. Experts speculate that because such infants spend weeks and sometimes months in hospital emotional bonding fails to occur with the parents. Furthermore, they frequently continue to present the family with medical difficulties. Other children who are handicapped, or who present the family with ongoing medical and behavioural problems, are also more at risk of abuse. The "problem" or "difficult" child, medically or emotionally, is in general more at risk, because of the added stresses on the parents.

Such stressors do not, of course, alone explain child abuse. There are some crucial parental psychological characteristics that alone, or in combination with serious stress, set the stage for child abuse. The most commonly associated factor in child abuse is that child abusers suffered abuse themselves when they were children. They themselves grew up in situations of emotional deprivation, physical abuse, parental rejection, and family conflict. Child abusers tend to be young and unprepared for parenthood and with unrealistic expectations about appropriate behaviour in children. Typically female abusers have exaggerated dependency needs, while male abusers often possess sociopathic and/or psychopathic personality characteristics and have criminal backgrounds. Further, child abusers often have a high level of dependence on alcohol or other drugs. Abusers are frequently described as inadequate personalities with low self–esteem and high levels of psychological insecurity.

Child Homicide

The end result of child abuse is sometimes murder. Researchers at Johns Hopkins University recently reported that murder is the leading cause of death by injury among U.S. infants under one year of age.[23] One in three of these infants died of child abuse or as a battered child. Others died of suffocation, strangulation, deliberate drowning, stabbing and gunshot wounds. Another large category died of "neglect–abandonment" — defined as deliberate neglect "with intent to injure or kill."

Child murder is nevertheless quite rare, though it is more commonplace than in the 1960s. In 1966 there were 48 murders of children up to the age of 14 and 13 murders of adolescents aged 15 to 19. In 1986 the figures were 58 and 35, respectively. Murders of babies up to the age of four remained fairly static — 34 in 1966 and 32 in 1986 — but we must recall the sharp decline in the total population of infants between 1966 and 1986. The most disturbing increase is that of adolescent homicide, which has grown incredibly in absolute numbers despite the decline in the total adolescent population. Again, we have no idea how accurate these official figures are, but if they err, they err on the side of underreporting.

The murder of a newborn is typically done by the parents, most often the mother. One psychiatric study reports that such mothers are usually young, single and immature. Yet they are not clinically mentally disturbed; rather they tend to be passive and unable to cope.[24] Such acts are clearly acts of desperation on the part of a young, frightened, unwilling mother. A recent Canadian case history confirms the pattern, reporting the attempted murder of her newly born infant by a 16–year–old high school student. She had hidden the pregnancy from her mother and had the baby alone in the bathtub.[25]

A recent Statistics Canada survey of solved homicides shows no dramatic upward trend in domestic homicides.[26] But the figures remain deeply disturbing nevertheless. Of those surveyed, 11 per cent were cases of fathers and 9 per cent were cases of mothers killing their children. In the single year of 1986, 55 of 191 domestic homicide cases were children killed by their parents.[27] Parents who murder their children tend to be young. About one–half of mothers who killed their children were under 25 years of age, and one in five were teenage mothers. Similarly, about one–half of fathers who murdered their children were under the age of 30.[28]

Clearly, for the domestic victims of child homicide the family was neither sanctuary, nor haven, nor a place of love and happiness. And for those many victims of child homicide whose deaths were the final episode of repeated abuse and neglect, the thought of the months, weeks and days preceding death is too devastating for words to express.

State Care

The family systematically fails about one in every 100 Canadian children who, for a time, lives in forms of state care.[29] Of these children, 60 per cent live in foster homes, 20 per cent in group homes, and another 20 per cent in juvenile institutions and treatment centres. About two in three come from officially poor families. Similarly, about two in three are taken into care as a result of "parental neglect or incapacity."[30] Up to date national figures are hard to come by, since the area is one of provincial jurisdiction, and provinces use different criteria and categories for "care." But experts in the area suggest that one in 100 remains an adequate estimate,[31] and there is some indication that the figures may be rising.

But such figures do not begin to reveal the total number of children placed in forms of emergency or exceptional care. Many families in distress rely upon networks of relatives and friends to take over the care of threatened children, turning to official agencies only when authorities intervene. Furthermore, many child care workers are constrained by government policy to take children into care only in the most extreme of circumstances, and workers are encouraged to reunite children in care with their natural families often without much regard to the risk to the child. Additionally, many child care workers are reluctant to take children who are at risk into care simply because the official state child care system is so bad.

The appalling situations in many of our state–sponsored or supported foster homes, group homes, and institutions have regularly made headlines. The allegations have included numerous serious assaults and other forms of abuse and maltreatment,[32] including the use of behaviour modification and aversive therapy techniques on children incarcerated.[33] Treatment meted out in some foster homes is often not much better. The recent exposure of the case of Dereck O'Brien's treatment in a foster home in Mount Pearl, Newfoundland, in the 1960s shocked most. O'Brien alleges that his state–approved foster parents forced him and his brothers "to scrounge through garbage for food, to drink water off a basement floor, to use a dump as a bathroom."[34] I can recall a television documentary exposing the child–rearing practices of foster parents who adhered to fundamentalist Christian doctrine that instructed them that systematic beatings of children were necessary for a good Christian upbringing. In 1986, David Tickell, then the Saskatchewan Ombudsman, released a report indicting the province's child care system for permitting, frequently knowingly, the widespread physical and sexual abuse of children under the care of the system, sometimes in foster homes, sometimes by failing to act quickly enough in a known case of abuse or neglect, other times by returning the child to the original home prematurely.[35]

The nation was reminded again in 1989 of the serious deficiencies in the state–sponsored child care system by the revelations of repeated physical and sexual abuse of children at the Mount Cashel Orphanage in St. John's, Newfoundland, and allegations of physical abuse at the Bosco Homes in Saskatchewan.

Recently Quebec's Commission de Protection des Droits de la Jeunesse reported that even those young people (aged 12 to 17) who expressed positive feelings about the benefits of stays at provincial rehabilitation centres face a "bleak, barren future." Camille Messier described the kinds of children in such centres:

> More than a third had broken with their parents, close to a third were the victims of an abusive home life; 19 per cent were 16 and 17 year old boys who were facing criminal charges under the Young Offenders Act and whose parents consequently had washed their hands of them; and a last group — about 15 per cent of the total — were the children whom the youth–protection system had failed.[36]

These children, who reach legal adulthood at 18 and therefore must leave the state's care system, unrealistically dreamed about returning to their family homes or of setting up housekeeping on their own. Instead, they typically face isolation, unemployment, and poverty, with no network of support. These children are the most prominent victims of our failing family system — the "official" and reluctantly recognized victims. Yet too often the system designed to rescue and protect them fails.

Although there is clearly significant overlap among the categories, evidence shows that over one million Canadian children flounder in poverty; upwards of 900,000 suffer from forms of physical and sexual abuse, and for many thousands such abuse is life–threatening; another perhaps 1.4 million experience some form of emotional or psychiatric disorder; many thousands are injured or killed each year by forms of "social injury"; hundreds commit suicide, while more dozens are murdered each year; and finally tens of thousands languish in forms of state care. This situation reflects not only a tragic failure on the part of our whole society, but, more specifically, a growing incapacity of our changing family forms to fulfill the family's primary institutional obligation to provide care, comfort, love, security and protection. Children are among the front–line victims bearing the costs and consequences of the family's social transition.

They are the first casualties. Their innocence and helpless vulnerability make their plight particularly horrifying, but their parents are also victims bearing the costs of these changes in the family's massive transformation. We must recognize that the parents too must cope with and adapt to social forces beyond their personal control. It may be true that Canadian men and women are not completely innocent of the plight of many of their children. Yet neither are they completely guilty.

PART III

Victims of the Crisis: Women

"Equal with men? Yes, the law says we must be.

And we also have to be equal with horses to get the strength."

Tatyana Geoshvili,
working Soviet wife and mother,
Globe and Mail, 8 March 1989.

Introduction:
The Oppression of Women

The oppression of women in Canada remains a fact of daily life, apparently remarkably resistant to all our efforts to the contrary. Oppression — defined eloquently and simply by the *Shorter Oxford English Dictionary* as "the imposition of unjust burdens" — afflicts women in virtually every social, emotional, political and economic aspect of their lives. Whether they are CNR crew dispatchers subjected to "sexual touching, bum patting and ... sexual molestation;"[1] or rape victims whose complaints are dismissed as "unfounded;"[2] or a vocational school student stripped of her office as student president when she became pregnant out of wedlock;[3] they are constantly reminded that they are sexual objects. Patriarchy may not be entirely well after the last 25 years of assault by the new feminism, but it remains unmistakably alive and frequently even robust.

On paper and in theory, laws, regulations, and official promulgations make gains for women look and sound impressive. But the practical reality is something else. Laws are only good if they are systematically enforced. Declarations and promulgations are not worth the paper they are written on if no serious action is taken to realize even the most eloquently stated goals. The two young women at CN, for example, were obliged to go through a degrading arbitration process before being vindicated. In 1974 the RCMP began hiring women officers, about 800 by 1986, but these women officers exhibited five times the resignation rate as a result of "sexual harassment and rampant sexism."[4] Canadian women won another victory in 1980 when 52 women were finally admitted to Canada's military colleges, but five years later a confidential Department of National Defence report obtained by the *Globe and Mail* justified the exclusion of women from combat and near-combat jobs on the grounds that women lacked the necessary endurance and strength and that the presence of women would lead to sexual and romantic hanky–panky.[5]

There has been a grand deception going on and the gap between our rhetoric and our actions regarding the situation of women in Canada has never been greater. And women have been required to fight for modest real gains through a sort of trench warfare, almost on a case by case basis, fighting to gain ground inch by reluctant inch. Victories are frequently won at great cost, financial and emotional. And they are often Pyrrhic victories — victories that too often have all the taste of defeat. What women can win in public is often stolen in private as they are subjected to sexual harassment, perhaps less overt career discrimination, and personal hostility. In a sense then, women, as they escape old oppressions, confront new ones.

This is particularly true when the impact of the crisis of the family on women is examined. While the traditional family relied on the largely silent oppression of women in the home, the new family forms frequently impose even greater unjust burdens. Women are still assumed to be primarily responsible for child care and for keeping the family unit running smoothly, even as they take on equal burdens in the work world. Women therefore carry the major burden of the current family crisis— whether it's earning that all–important second income while continuing to meet most of the old domestic expectations, or picking up the pieces and putting them back together with the children after separation or divorce, or managing the many tensions of a reconstituted family, or putting up tolerantly with male angst in response to rapidly changing sex roles.

One of the best documented aspects of women's new oppression is the price exacted from working women if they wish to establish a family and have children.[6] Inevitably they put less time and energy into education, career training, and advancement. Even those who make it into high–paying professional or business jobs find it necessary severely to scale down career aspirations if they wish to marry and to have children. Therefore while women have fought to gain equality in the world of work with men, they have found many of the fruits of such gains snatched from their grasp because of their continuing child–bearing and –rearing tasks.

This is not a new insight. In 1976 Dorothy Dinnerstein argued forcefully that the new feminism can never achieve full equality for women as long as women continue to be primarily responsible for child care.[7] A decade later, Sylvia Hewlett went further, arguing that the U.S. feminist movement had made a strategic error by fighting for strict equality with men while ignoring the costs to women of bearing and raising children.[8] By pursuing an abiological notion of equality with men, such as is embodied in the Equal Rights Amendment, the U.S. women's movement failed to fight for and secure a system of family supports. Meanwhile, the European feminist movement struggled for equal rights in tandem with demands for programs to help working women deal with family obligations. Consequently, women in Europe have not only succeeded in more significantly narrowing the pay gap with men, but also in winning generous full–pay maternity leave benefits and high levels of state aid to day care.

In Canada the situation is similar. Precious little action has been taken on issues like maternity leave, day care, and other kinds of family support programs. As a result, the women's movement in North America is moving increasingly from ideological issues to very practical ones. Increasingly, men are asked more practical questions — do you support state aid to day care? do you support effective affirmative action programs for women? do you support equal pay for work of equal value? do you support programs of full–pay maternity leave? do you support women's right to choice on reproductive matters? Increasingly, the focus of the women's movement has moved to the concrete issues of pay equity, child care support, reproductive choice and the fair sharing of domestic work.

That such a practical focus has become pre–eminent is understandable. A 1985 world survey of the situation of women concluded that the changes in the status of women in the world since World War II have been "modest."[9] The survey concluded that there is no place on earth where women enjoy wage parity with men. Furthermore, as a result of un– and underemployment, low pay, job ghettoes, and residual responsibility for the children after family breakdown, women are facing an accelerating process of the feminization of poverty.[10] A group of Commonwealth experts reported in 1989 that "the recession of the early 1980s and subsequent budget cuts by governments around the world have been particularly damaging to women and issues that concern them." The report goes so far as to assert that recent government policies "have halted and even reversed the progress ... which women enjoyed in the preceding three decades."[11]

A 1989 Gallup poll revealed just how far Canadians believe women have come.[12] Asked if they believed that women in Canada "get as good a break as men," 45 percent answered yes, while 54 per cent said no. In 1971, the figures were 64 per cent and 36 per cent, respectively. In other words, Canadians believe that the situation has worsened. Revealing the public's level of cynicism, 57 per cent agreed that "men are willing to let women get ahead but only if women still do all the housework at home." Another 46 per cent agreed that "a woman who takes years out of her career for child care can never make up for it on the job." Interwoven with these attitudes and perceptions — some of which perhaps conceal a degree of hostility to women's aspirations — lies women's albatross: the primary responsibility for raising the children. Fully 56 per cent of Canadians still believe that married women with families impose a "harmful effect on family life" if they work outside the home.

Such attitudes and opinions are sustained by and reflect the structural reality of patriarchy and the continuing oppression of women. They are the result of a continuing sexist socialization, on the one hand, and a neglectful miseducation of the young, on the other. Sociology and social psychology have long known that in the socialization process children absorb norms, values, behaviours, and attitudes much more from what they observe than from direct instruction. Therefore, if our children still have sexist attitudes, it is because we still live our daily lives in a sexist and stereotypical manner.

Sexual stereotypes still bombard us in the media. We know that children from the age of two to 11 watch an average of about 19 hours of television each week and are relentlessly bombarded by many hundreds of commercial messages as well as the stereotypical content of most shows. The media — especially television — play a big role in the socialization process, impacting on aspirations, future hopes, and basic achievement orientation and thereby helping shape styles of life, educational choices, and occupational selection as well as marital and sex role behaviour. The Canadian Radio, Television and Telecommunications Commission (CRTC) has exerted pressures for self–regulation, but progress has been very slow.

The reading materials in our schools, after more than two decades of study and critical assessment, are still blatantly sexist and biased against women. A 1987 study commissioned by the Ontario Federation of Women Teachers' Associations, a follow–up of a 1975 study, concluded that the reading material used in grades four through six still present children with "a male–dominated world in which women's place is limited and specific."[13] Male characters — men and boys — were "vastly over–represented," and women's occupations were frequently family–based. The tasks performed by men and boys differed greatly from those performed by women and girls. In one reader, "boys handled equipment, played piano, danced, argued, collected stickers and protected mussels," while "girls became afflicted with 'the vanity of city girls,' abandoned a ballet recital, went on a diet, dreamed sad dreams and cried."

The results of such miseducation and missocialization has shown up in studies done on the aspirations and expectations of adolescent girls.[14] Research in the 1950s and 1960s suggested that adolescent girls saw their wage work as only temporary, while boys contemplated vocations and careers. But despite the great changes throughout the 1960s and 1970s, studies in the 1970s reported "that adolescent girls still plan to stay home with their children until the last child is in school, even though they also expect to have paid employment." As well, studies in the 1970s and even up to the turn of the decade "indicated that adolescent girls still see their lives in very traditional and romanticized terms."[15] Furthermore, girls often begin to scale back their career aspirations to meet the sexist expectations and limited opportunities they confront:

> While male students concentrate on putting more effort into getting into university or establishing themselves in a trade, female

students are dreaming of marriage. The heavy emphasis on appearance and relationships channels girls' energies away from career planning at the very time it is most important.[16]

In the 1980s, Baker studied adolescent girls and adolescent boys across Canada, and the results were deeply disturbing. Most girls expected to attend university, and those who mentioned specific jobs anticipated professional or managerial posts. About three in four expected to get married and almost the same number expected to have children, but few expected divorce, or if they saw divorce as a possibility, thought that it would not have much of an impact on their lives. Most saw marriage in highly romantic terms: relaxed evenings with their husbands while untroublesome children slept contentedly.

One of the most distressing findings has to do with sexuality and unplanned pregnancy. Only 9 of the 122 girls said such a pregnancy would not happen because they would use birth control or would not indulge in sexual intercourse. Among the others, 34 would seek an abortion, 5 would put the baby up for adoption, while 14 didn't know what they would do. Almost half, 60 girls, said they would keep the baby, either alone or in a marriage or common–law relationship. They were quite oblivious to the stark implications of such a decision. There were 6 teenage mothers in the study and their lives were bleak and hopeless compared to those of the other adolescent girls.

> The unmarried mothers ... who usually had about Grade 10 education and generally came from lower SES [socioeconomic status] families, spent much of their time watching television or reading romantic novels when they were not caring for their child. Their child–rearing took so much of their time and energy that most had little desire or opportunity to look for work outside the home or to improve their educational qualifications ... However, they seemed uncertain how to improve their lives. They saw their lives improving when their child grew older and they could get out more often.[17]

Perhaps this lack of realism, this romanticization of sex and relationships, and an almost fatalistic approach to the future on the part of adolescent girls explains the continuing growth of teenage pregnancy. Trends indicate that the pregnancy rate is dropping among every other age group of fertile women.[18] Adolescent girls who keep their children add over 17,000 single parent families to the rolls in Canada each year. A 1983 Ontario study reported that such mothers often live in deep and abject poverty, have little education and no job skills, and suffer from "quashed hopes" and deep discouragement.[19] One study found that adolescent mothers were less happy with the pregnancy, had a weaker network of social support to assist them through problems, and far less support from the father.[20] This phenomenon of children having children is another dimension of the crisis of Canadian families.

Clearly the women's movement faces the difficult problem of reconquering the psychological terrain among each new generation of women in a milieu that continues to foster traditional attitudes in both boys and girls. While the structural oppression of women is relatively easy to document, this internalized oppression — "like a garrison in a conquered city" after Freud[21] — is more difficult to overcome. Externally imposed unjust burdens may anger, but self–imposed burdens merely eliminate options. Susan Brownmiller says, "Femininity, in essence, is a romantic sentiment ... of imposed limitations ... but while the extremes of masculinity can harm others (rape, wife beating, street crime, warfare and a related inability to concede or admit defeat), the extremes of femininity are harmful only — only! — to women themselves in the form of a self–imposed masochism (restraint, inhibition, self–denial, wasteful use of thought and time)."[22] One thinks immediately of the adolescent girl who cannot separate spontaneous romantic love and sex and therefore fails to plan birth control. Or of the girl swept away in the romantic vision of traditional marriage and children. Only later will they come to realize the full consequences of the burdens they have embraced with naive enthusiasm.

The crisis of the family cannot be separated from the oppression of women. Just as women bore the major economic, physical, and emotional burdens of maintaining the traditional family, today they bear the major burden — with the children — of the transition to new family forms. The more closely the situation is examined, the more clear it becomes that women will *never* achieve full liberation until the family's crisis has been resolved. And it will not be resolved until women's fullest liberation has been realized. In the meantime a heavy toll is being exacted.

7 / The Double Burden

Women's work in the home has typically been endless, invisible, unrecognized, and taken for granted.[1] No wages are paid and there's no discernible product that goes on the market. And because such work carries no recognition in the larger society, full–time housewives receive little prestige or attention from social scientists who study work. As the Armstrongs note, in *The Double Ghetto*, "conventional social science has treated women's work in the home as merely another aspect of her feminine role, not as a job."[2] But in the last two decades feminist social scientists have documented the nature of housework and the time women traditionally have had to devote to it. The Armstrongs usefully categorize women's domestic labour into four task areas: housework; reproduction and child care; tension management; and sexual relations. The last two will be more appropriately considered in the chapter on emotional oppression. For now, the focus will be on housework and child bearing and rearing.

All the research on domestic labour suggests it was (and is) clearly the work of women. When sharing occurred, men tended to take on the more interesting tasks — entertaining the kids with games or a book — while women cooked, cleaned, ironed and so on. Men often argued that they did the regular "men's work" around the home — home repairs, painting, etc. — *and* brought home the bacon, so it was only a fair and reasonable division of labour that women should take the major responsibility for housework and child care. Most traditional wives in the past probably agreed. Indeed, men would often point to the fact that women significantly outlived men, presumably because they lived sheltered lives, free of the stress and competition out there in the market jungle.

All this changed as more women moved into the paid labour force and as the women's movement began its sustained critique of women's oppression both inside and outside the home. The palpable reality of working women — who are also wives and mothers — has confronted many men with the formerly "invisible" work of the housewife. And women who have remained full–time housewives at least now enjoy more recognition for the work they do, if not much more prestige. Research has told us that in Britain and France full–time housewives with children put in around 75 hours of domestic work each week. In 1989 the Canadian Advisory Council on the Status of Women asserted that women's unpaid domestic work accounts for 37 per cent of the total working hours of all Canadians and that full–time housewives put in 50–hour weeks.

Increasingly the real economic value of housework and child rearing is recognized, though it remains unpaid. A Statistics Canada study, using 1981 data, estimated the annual value of such work at between $121 billion and $139 billion, representing, respectively, about 36 per cent and 41 per cent of the GNP.[3] The lower figure was based on the estimated costs of hiring people to do the work, the higher on an estimate of foregone labour market earnings of people doing unpaid domestic labour. Further, as families have become increasingly dependent on two earners, the costs of services to replace a wife have astonished many men. Whether it's the escalating costs of day care, or the investment in the "new necessities" like freezers, microwave ovens and dish-washers,[4] or the 30 cents of each food budget dollar that families of full–time working women spend on eating out,[5] it is impossible for Canadians not to recognize the economic value of domestic labour. Indeed, "pay for housework," a proposal that enjoyed some brief prominence in the feminist movement over a decade ago, only to be largely rejected because it did not solve the alienation, isolation, and psychological oppression of housework, now is being picked up by the anti–feminist lobby. Chantal Devine, the wife of Saskatchewan's premier, proposed that perhaps women might have to be paid to stay home with the children in order to defeat "the anti–family agenda led by radical feminists."[6]

According to the Economic Council of Canada, the contribution of husbands to average family income between 1973 and 1986 *dropped* by 5 per cent, while the contribution of other family members, largely working wives and mothers, *rose* by 46 per cent, mainly beause there has been no real growth in earnings since the mid–1970s.[7] How has this massive change affected the sharing of housework and child care between working husbands and working wives?

A fair distribution over time of domestic and child care work is still exceptional. Studies in the late 1970s and early 1980s generally found that husbands resisted sharing domestic work, and studies in the mid–1980s suggest there has been only a marginal improvement.[8] In 1985 a Toronto Family Services Association survey found that when both spouses work full–time outside the home, the men contribute less than one–half the time to housework that the women do and one–third the time to child care.[9] When women moved from part–time to full–time work, their husbands contributed an average of nine minutes more a day to housework, while actually contributing one minute less per day to child care. Men also enjoyed much more "passive leisure time" — reading or watching TV — than women. In 1988, a Dalhousie University survey found that working married women did three–and–one–half hours of housework each day compared to one–and–one–half hours for their husbands.[10]

In 1989 Hochschild and Machung reported on their eight–year study of dual–earner families and the sharing of domestic work in the U.S.[11] They found that about 20 per cent of men shared "the second shift" equally, about 70 per cent did more than one–third of the domestic work but less than one–half, and there was a 10 per cent group of hard–core hold–outs who did less than one–third. Further, Hochschild and Machung found that even in those marriages which came closest to equal sharing, the women got the less satisfying tasks while the men got the more interesting ones. In other words, men with working wives are just doing a bit more of the same kind of domestic chores as they did for non–working wives.

The stress of the double burden for women, and the resentment provoked among them by the unwillingness of men to share the second shift, have increased dramatically as the dual–earner family has become a permanent fact of life for a majority of husband/wife families. Furthermore, the situation becomes worse with the arrival of children. While the working wife of a childless couple might accept a husband's failure to share domestic work fairly, when children arrive the problems redouble because children require "compulsory and full–time" care.[12]

A study of the transition from childlessness to parenthood among dual–earner couples reports that women experience much more pressure than men and that sometimes the stress is "extreme." Yet, interestingly, new parents in single–earner families experience a steeper fall in "life satisfaction" than new parents in dual–earner families.[13] A study of 680 husbands and wives by Ross and Mirowsky found that the impact of a wife working on the psychological well–being of a family depends on four factors: the presence of children; the type of child care used; the presence of difficulties relating to child care; and a husband's participation in child care.[14] The results represent yet another setback for advocates of the traditional family. For wives with jobs outside the home, levels of well–being were not affected by the presence of children but by whether there were difficulties relating to arranging child care and by whether the husbands shared child care responsibilities. Wives whose husbands did not participate in child care experienced higher levels of depression and lower levels of psychological well–being than those whose husbands helped. Indeed, working mothers and wives who had problems arranging child care and who had the *sole* responsibility for child care manifested "extremely high depression levels." Yet, in general, it was found that wives who did not work also experienced high depression levels when children were present.

As a result of this primary responsibility for child care and domestic labour women at work suffer great stress. A U.S. study of 30,000 employees at 30 corporations found that 40 per cent of working women with babies and toddlers claim that worries about child care make them less productive at work, 50 per cent turned down transfers and 30 per cent turned down promotions because of child care difficulties, and more than 50 per cent felt stress both at work and at home because of the conflicts between work and family obligations.[15] A recent Conference Board of Canada survey found that most firms estimated that at least 25 per cent of employee absenteeism resulted from work/family conflicts,[16] and a larger, 1988 study found that two in three employees experienced difficulty reconciling work and family obligations, and 80 per cent of these said they experienced stress and anxiety because of such conflicts.[17] A report prepared for the Canadian Advisory Council on the Status of Women asserted that the stress resulting from balancing domestic and job obligations is also a hazard to women's physical health since stress is implicated in as much as 80 per cent of all illnesses.[18] A University of Michigan study found that, on average, working women sleep 25 minutes less a day than working men because of their primary responsibility for domestic work.[19] So far there is no evidence that such increased levels of stress have begun to close the age of death gap between men and women, as many traditionalists warned; long–term paid employment does not appear to increase women's average risk of mortality, even among those struggling under the double burden.[20] At least, not yet.

In *The Second Shift* Hochschild and Machung note that working women have developed three basic stratagems for dealing with the double burden. Some try to excel at both job and home, pursuing the superwoman or "supermom" course. Some cut back their commitment to work, thereby relinquishing some of their career aspirations. And some cut corners at home, scaling down the high expectations they previously had about what they could do as a wife and mother. And many have surrendered and discontinued putting pressure on men in an effort to ease domestic tension. Overall, Hochschild and Machung found that there is a novel secret to marital happiness in this era of the changing family. And it has nothing to do with candlelight and wine. Women are now increasingly claiming that the most important component of marital bliss is rooted in a husband's willingness to share domestic and child care work fairly. Not very romantic. It may be hard for men to realize that the secure way to a woman's heart is through the mop pail, the laundry room and the kitchen sink. But there it is.

While Hochschild and Machung's work suggests that many working women swallow their resentment in the interests of marital harmony, there are contrary indications that it is coming more and more to the surface. The U.S. National Center for Health Statistics recently reported that about 62 per cent of divorces in the U.S. are initiated by women, 33 per cent are initiated by men, and the rest are mutually initiated.[21] The figures are similar in Canada. But the U.S. report also tells us that when children are present, 66 per cent of divorces are initiated by women, while when no children are present, only 57 per cent are. These figures suggest, at least in part, that the double burden becomes truly onerous for women with the arrival of children.

Perhaps we should let some women experiencing the double burden speak for themselves in order to get a full sense of their feelings of injustice and resentment.[22] One cook and the mother of two says,

> A mother that works and raises a family has to be pretty strong, very strong. I really feel sorry for the mother with the little kids — have to bundle them up in the morning and take them to the daycare centre and pick them up again at night. I wouldn't go through that again that way. It's too hard.

Another comments on the problems of reconciling traditional sex role socialization to the new family reality:

> It's still very different for men and women. You can divide up all the tasks in the world, but the feeling of responsibility of every working mother I know is vastly different [from that of] her working husband. I mean, I don't know any man who would call home to see what's doing with the babysitter. You know, the men walk out the door and that's the end. But for the mothers, there's a sense of responsibility and there are different levels of guilt.

Or take the case of a woman lawyer who said she was reaching her "breaking point" in her marriage. Involved in a difficult case, she had called her husband at work and asked him to pick up the children at the day care "just this once." "He absolutely refused, said it was impossible. He had an important meeting, and I had to do it."

Finally, a working mother of two explains why divorce and the absence of a husband brought a measure of relief:

> Remove the male and it's easier to organize. It is true. When I was a single parent I found that there is yourself. And it's easy to deal with yourself by yourself. You know that you have to do these things. No one else is going to be there to do them. You make your decisions whether they're right, wrong, whatever ... It's much easier. You can come home and throw on a hot dog.

The double burden borne by women is a central dimension of the family crisis provoked by our rapid move to new family forms. As the Canadian husband/wife family has come to rely on two earners, women have been forced to assume two jobs. The resulting stress and resentment have in no small part contributed to the rising rate of marriage failure. Men's general failure to accept a fair sharing of domestic and child care tasks has presented many women with a hard choice: either accept the double burden in order to sustain the family or opt for divorce and a period of single parenthood. More and more women are making the second choice.

As we examine the three central areas of women's continuing oppression — economic, emotional, and physical/sexual — the reality of the double burden, and the fundamental sexist assumptions and structures it is based upon, permeates all the other costs women are bearing, willingly and unwillingly, as a result of the transformation of the family.

8 / Women's Economic Oppression

The General Pattern of Economic Oppression

Women do not get paid as much as men for the work they do. In 1900, full–time working women earned about 60 per cent of what full–time working men earned.[1] Such comparative income data on the sexes only began to be regularly collected by Statistics Canada in 1967 when it was found that full–time working women earned just over 58 per cent of the pay earned by full–time working men.[2] In 1977, the figure was an unimpressive 62 per cent.[3] By 1985 the figure had climbed slowly to just under 65 per cent. Two years later it had inched up to 66 per cent.[4] Thus the twenty years characterized by a Royal Commission on the Status of Women, an inundation of studies and inquiries, a blizzard of laws forbidding sexual discrimination, and countless specific programs to improve the economic position of women resulted in only a very modest upward shift. Indeed, this slight improvement may have had little to do with such symbolic acts and more to do with women's improved labour market qualifications as they flocked to universities in the last two decades in record numbers, now taking up over 50 per cent of undergraduate and 37 per cent of graduate places, compared to just over 25 per cent and 15 per cent, respectively, in 1961.[5] And in the 1970s and 1980s more and more women have entered university specialties formerly the near–exclusive preserve of men.

The picture that emerges is one of chronic and change–resistant economic injustice.[6] Full–time working women aged 45 to 54 earn 61 per cent of their male colleagues, while those aged 15 to 19 earn 87 per cent. Women with grade 8 or less earn 59 per cent of equivalent men, while those with some university training earn 70 per cent. Married women earn 61 per cent of married men, while single, never–married women earn 94 per cent of single men. Women in male–dominated professions earn 71 per cent of what men in those professions earn. A survey of 201 occupations based on 1980–81 data found that in the top 10 occupations by annual earnings, women ranged from a low of 46 per cent of men's earnings to a high of 66 per cent, while in the bottom 10 occupations by annual earnings, women ranged from a low of 47 per cent of men's earnings to a high of 84 per cent. Perhaps an illustration from Statistics Canada's statistical report, *Women in Canada*, published in 1985, makes the point most dramatically regarding the systematic pay inequities women face. In 1982, a woman with a university degree earned just $1,602 *more* than a man with some high school education. Meanwhile, a man with less than grade 9 earned $2,466 *more* than a women with a post–secondary degree of diploma (other than a university degree). Comparing those with university degrees, a man with a degree earned about $12,000 *more* than a woman with such a degree.

Typically the pay gap between the sexes is explained in terms of the ghettoization or segregation of women in the labour force. In the early 1900s two in three working women were employed in the following occupational categories: (1) professional (mainly nursing and teaching); (2) clerical; (3) commercial and financial; and (4) service. In 1980, four in five Canadian women in the labour force were employed in those categories.[7] Armstrong and Armstrong refined this further by identifying the ten leading female occupations in Canada in 1971 and 1981, occupations in which women made up over 72 per cent of the occupation and which in 1981 accounted for the employment of about 40 per cent of all working women.[8]

With the exception of graduate nursing and teaching, such jobs are largely unskilled, labour intensive, and characterized by low levels of productivity and low levels of unionization. As a result, the pay is low, and it is not surprising that global female earnings lag well behind those of men. As long as women as a group remain in such jobs, they will not succeed in closing the overall pay gap. Indeed, the segregation of women in the labour force appears to

Table 3: The ten leading female occupations, 1981

	Females as a % of occupation	% of all females working
Clerical	99	10
Sales	56	6
Personal service	93	2
Teachers	64	4
Selected manufacturing (largely textiles)	81	3
Graduate nurses	95	4
Waiters and bartenders	82	5
Nursing assistants, aides, and orderlies	83	2
Telephone operators	95	1
Cleaners	41	2
Totals	**72**	**40**

Source: Adapted from Armstrong and Armstrong, *The Double Ghetto* (Toronto: McClelland and Stewart, 1984), pp. 36–37. All percentages are rounded.

be worsening. Statistics Canada has reported that 63 per cent all jobs gained in the first half of 1988 were in the clerical and sales sectors where women predominate.[9] In fact, as of 1988, 73 per cent of *all* working women were employed in either clerical, sales and service positions, or in teaching or health services, mostly nursing.

The occupational segregation argument by no means explains the pay gap completely. In fact, men in the leading female occupations still earn significantly more than women, ranging from a low of women earning just 55 per cent of men's wages in sales occupations to a high of 96 per cent of men's wages in nursing.[10] Male nurses often move up to supervisory roles. Male teachers tend to be principals and vice–principals in primary schools or to be high school teachers. Male waiters often quickly achieve petty management roles. So, in fact, women face a double segregation: not only do they tend to be concentrated in low–paying occupational categories, but they also tend to be at the lower paying end of those categories.

But this still cannot fully account for the enormous wage gap between the sexes. Thus another argument is added on to the

segregation argument. Owing to their socialization, women tend
to have less training and experience than men. This contributes to
the wage gap since they do not move upward in a chosen career
path, either because of lower motivation or of interruptions in their
labour force participation. This perspective is frequently posed in
sexist terms. In the House of Commons, Alberta Tory MP Doug
Fee recently claimed that women themselves are to blame for their
failure to achieve job and pay equity because they put their
personal lives ahead of their careers.[11] Nova Scotia Tory MP Bill
Casey echoed similar sentiments when he claimed that women
think differently than men and as a result they are less competitive. Despite the fact that Prime Minister Mulroney rebuked these
two members the next day for their "offensive" comments, such
attitudes are widely held.[12] Usually they are expressed with a little
more restraint, but they are held by many influential men.

As Phillips and Phillips point out, as with the occupational
segregation argument, there is some small truth in this.

> Studies both in Canada and elsewhere that try to standardize for
> training and work experience suggest that about half the difference
> in earnings at the level of the broad occupational categories is
> accounted for by the above two factors. That is, if women had the
> same training and work experience as men, women's earnings as
> a percentage of men's would rise from around 60 per cent to
> approximately 80 per cent.[13]

Such model building cannot control or account for the effects of
sexist attitudes and discrimination. Such discrimination is so
widespread that an Economic Council of Canada study expressed
a shocking conclusion:

> In short, full–time native born paid employees who are women
> earn less than men because they do not benefit from their income
> relevant characteristics (education, training and experience) in the
> same manner as men.[14]

The fact is that as of 1980 only women with a university education between the ages of 45 and 54 earned more in wages than the average male worker in the labour force.[15]

Nowhere in this made more starkly clear then when we leave the low–paid segregated occupations of "women's work" and examine what happens to the women who join men in the more highly paid and privileged occupations. A study of 800 executives in the U.S., reported in the *Harvard Business Review*, carried out a survey of women executives and their experiences, comparing 1965 and 1985.[16] Although there were 150 per cent more female executives in 1985, the study still found that women had to be exceptional to succeed and that even then they failed to win dollar recognition equivalent to men — 48 per cent of male executives, compared to just 10 per cent of female executives, were earning $100,000 a year or more.

Professional Advancement

In Canada, women have made remarkable progress in breaking into male–dominated professional occupations.[17] (A professional occupation is defined by Statistics Canada as one where 45 per cent or more of the incumbents in 1981 had at least a bachelor's degree. A male–dominated profession is one where 65 per cent or more of the incumbents in 1971 were male). In a Statistics Canada survey of 46 professional occupations, including 34 male–dominated professions, between 1981 and 1986, women accounted for 69 per cent of the growth in all professions and over 52 per cent of the growth in the male–dominated professions. Between 1971 and 1986, women's participation in the male–dominated professions grew from 11 per cent to 23 per cent. Indeed, female growth in some of the male–dominated professions has been so marked that a number of them no longer fit Statistics Canada's definition of a male–dominated profession. But women in these male–dominated professions in 1986 earned only 71 per cent of their male colleagues, while women in other professions earned 83 per cent of their male colleagues. Even though one could argue that some of this difference has to do with the fact that the recent female arrivals are younger and less experienced and therefore, as a group, will tend to earn less than men, the fact remained that when women and men aged 25 to 34 were compared the earnings gap did not disappear — women earned 81 per cent of their male colleagues. Evidently a professional women of that age loses 19 cents of every salary dollar for no other apparent reason than she is a woman.

In the legal profession the situation is similar, but worse. Between 1966–67 and 1982–83, female full–time enrolment in Canada's law schools went up from 281 (just over 5 per cent of law school places) to 4,153 (just over 40 per cent of places) — an increase of 1378 per cent![18] But in 1980 female lawyers earned just 58 per cent of what male lawyers earned, and by 1985 that limped up to 60 per cent. This was partly because women lawyers were more likely to be salaried or to work part–time than their male peers. And job segregation is also at work since women lawyers in Canada tend to be in the lower paid legal jobs and the smaller practices, including family law, legal aid, and government jobs, while men dominate the high profile, much more highly paid positions.[19]

Women have also made great gains in medicine. In 1987 women made up 43 per cent of all medical students in Canada, including close to 60 per cent in Quebec, and comprised over one in five of all practising physicians.[20] Over 40 per cent of medical school graduates in 1987 were women. And an examination of medical students training for specialties in 1987 indicated that women outnumbered men in general practice (53 per cent), and have come close to matching them in pediatrics, obstetrics, and gynecology (about 47 per cent). But job segregation afflicts women in medicine as well, since they have failed to break significantly into the glamorous specialties like cardiovascular surgery (8 per cent) and neurosurgery (9 per cent). And the pay gap remains; women physicians earn about 60 per cent of their male counterparts. Furthermore, ironically women's emerging pre–eminence in certain medical areas is occurring just when a process of relative proletarianization is taking hold, as incomes for non–specialist physicians and family specialists fall relative to other incomes in general and particularly relative to the incomes of the male–dominated medical specialties, and as governments move to put caps on billings, to control access to billing numbers, and to continue to underfund medicare. By the time women come to dominate the lower ends of the medical profession in Canada, as they must in the next decade if present trends continue, they may find themselves no better off than their sisters in the Soviet Union where women dominate the profession but cannot expect to earn much more than a technician.

One final example. Women have also made great strides as teachers at Canada's universities.[21] In 1960 there were fewer than 750 female university teachers in all of Canada. In 1985 there were almost 6,000 — an increase of 713 per cent. Though the number of women university teachers has grown more rapidly than that of men, the gap has not greatly narrowed. In 1960 11 per cent of full–time faculty were women; in 1985 the percentage was 17. Job segregation also characterizes women's participation in university teaching, both by discipline and rank. Women faculty tend to be concentrated in the areas of education, social sciences, humanities, and health sciences. And female university teachers tend to be concentrated in the lower academic ranks and tend to advance much more slowly than men. Therefore, overall, women teachers at Canadian universities are paid less than men — in 1985, 81 per cent of the median salary paid to men. Furthermore, women in the same academic rank and with the same qualifications as men earned significantly less than their male colleagues in 1985.

All this is not to diminish the significance of women's tremendous advances in acquiring post–secondary education and in breaking increasingly into the professions. But many women have experienced dismay and even anger at the continuing barriers. A 1980 Statistics Canada study comparing almost 30,000 men and women university graduates found that men generally obtained significantly higher paying jobs and that in many areas of work men earn more than women for the same job and with comparable qualifications and experience. A later Statistics Canada study of the employment outcomes for degree holders in the humanities and sciences, based on the 1986 census, confirmed the problem.[22] As expected, a university degree improved women's employment prospects and salary levels, but not as much as for men. Not only do women graduates in the humanities and sciences have lower levels of employment than men, but they earn less. Women aged 25 to 34 with degrees in the humanities earned 87 per cent of their male colleagues, while in the sciences they earned 84 per cent. And things do not seem to improve with age — women aged 45 to 54 with humanities degrees earned 81 per cent, and with degrees in the sciences 68 per cent, of their equivalent male co–workers. Though the sex wage gap remains for female university graduates, it is not as large as the average gap faced by all working women as a group. All full–time working women from age 25 to 34 earned 74 per cent of what all full–time working men of that age earned, while from age 45 to 54 the gap widens considerably. Such women earned only 60 per cent of men of the same age.

Another aspect of the sexual segregation of women in the labour force is that such segregation also tends to limit women's opportunities for advancement at any level. The 1980 study of university graduates found that many women stay in traditional female jobs even when they get an education in a typically male area — for example, a male graduate of a business school tends to get on the career track to a management job, while a female graduate often gets side–tracked into the career dead–end of a clerk.[23]

This lack of opportunity has persisted throughout the 1980s. Among Canada's 120 diplomatic missions, only 10 are headed by women.[24] Among 4,538 managers in the federal public service, only 481 are women. Among 22,702 scientific and professional personnel in the federal public service, only 5,563 are women. Among Canada's 366 full colonels, there are 5 women, and among our 87 brigadier–generals you can only find 1 lonely woman. Among the higher reaches of Quebec's 1987 public service there were 2,319 men and 179 women — and this excluded the public service stratosphere of deputy ministers, associate deputy ministers, and directors of government commissions and agencies.[25] Among the army of women who work in six Canadian banks — the Canadian Imperial Bank of Commerce, the Toronto–Dominion, the Royal Bank, the Bank of Nova Scotia, the Bank of Montreal and the National Bank of Canada — who outnumber men by a ratio of 70 to 1, there are almost no women in upper management.[26]

Thus, even access to the formerly male–dominated professions does not narrow the pay gap to anywhere near equity because doors to advancement within such professions remain closed once women have overcome the hefty entry barriers. The former head of the Canadian Bar Association's Committee on Women's Issues noted that a central reason why women lawyers tend to concentrate in the lower paid areas is that women lawyers reach a sort of "glass ceiling" beyond which it is very difficult to advance,[27] a barrier their male colleagues don't see.

Women in Canadian universities also hit a glass ceiling within the system. This inequitable situation has been documented and redocumented. The frustrations resulting from lack of gains led two scholars to conclude that blatant sexism is the only possible explanation of women's lack of opportunities to gain *access* to university faculty jobs and the lack of opportunities for *advancement* for those few women who have gained access.[28] In 1986 the University of Western Ontario won a prize for its voluntary affirmative action plan to advance women. Three years later Western actually had to admit that the percentage of female professors was in fact *lower* than it had been in the 1930s and 1940s.[29] As Michele Landsberg noted, "All parties to the debate seem to agree that this grotesque imbalance is the result of widespread, covert and entrenched discrimination against women in university hiring."[30]

As a result of Ottawa's 1986 Employment Equity Act a clearer picture of the global situation is emerging. The legislation requires that federally regulated businesses file reports regarding the situation of women, and in 1988 371 such reports were filed. *Globe and Mail* analysts reviewed reports filed by 27 organizations employing around 400,000 people.[31] The reports reveal that women continue to occupy the "lower work rungs" and receive lower salaries compared to men. Women tend to be concentrated in jobs paying less than $25,000 annually, while men tend to be concentrated in jobs paying more than $35,000 a year. Air Canada reported they have 18,800 full–time male employees and that 1,373 of these earn more than $70,000 per year. Meanwhile Air Canada had 6,300 full–time female employees, only four of whom earned more than $70,000. According to Canada Post, most male and female employees earned between $25,000 and $30,000. But the corporation also has 5,400 women earning less than $20,000 and 7,600 men earning between $30,000 and $70,000. The survey concluded that "in almost every enterprise, employers favour men when hiring or promoting middle managers, skilled tradesmen, and semi–skilled and manual workers." Women benefit in only one category of hiring and promotion: clerical.

This helps explain the results of a Statistics Canada study on the changing wage distribution of jobs.[32] The study uncovered a worrisome trend that began in the 1970s and accelerated dramatically between the 1981 and 1986 Census years. It seems that the lowest paying jobs in the Canadian economy are the fastest growing category of jobs, and most of these are taken up by younger workers. As a result, the wages enjoyed by younger workers are declining in relative and real terms, while the wages of middle–aged and older workers are climbing. However, if men and women as groups are compared, the wages of women workers as a group fell while those of men rose. Women therefore experience an additional disadvantage to add to job ghettoization and barriers to opportunity. As relatively recent arrivals in the labour force, many women have hit the job market at a time when low–waged jobs are more and more the only ones available and at a time of declining real wages for young workers.

Given the situation of women in terms of pay and opportunity, it is not surprising that there is an increasing "feminization of poverty" in Canada. The fact is "women face a greater risk of poverty than men in almost every category" and "make up a larger percentage of the poor ... in most categories."[33] The ratios of female to male poverty rates in the different categories show a consistent pattern of women's greater risk: all persons, 1.24; persons in families, 1.18; all family heads, 4.30; aged family heads, 1.9; non–aged family heads, 4.62; unattached individuals, 1.32. The only poverty categories in which men face ever so slightly higher poverty rates than women are "children" and "aged persons in families." And in these categories the rates are about equal, 0.99 and 0.93 respectively.

Economic Oppression and the Crisis of the Family

This general economic oppression of women is intimately linked with the crisis of the family and the unjust burdens that it imposes on women. The "revolution in women's labour market participation" in the 1960s, 1970s, and 1980s most importantly included a massive movement of "married women between the ages of twenty–four and fifty–five" into paid work.[34] And in the early 1980s, this movement most dramatically included married women with young children. Clearly this revolution is the result of a complex web of causation, and no doubt the growing instability of marriage has contributed to women's determination to decrease their economic dependence. Yet a major push has to do with the economic needs of the family. In 1989 Statistics Canada reported that the traditional two–parent, one–earner family experienced a slight *decline* in real family income between 1980 and 1988 — from $37,449 in 1980 to $37,351 in 1988.[35] Meanwhile average family income ($46,185) had experienced "little real growth in the 1980s" and will remain "flat for the foreseeable future." The only families that experienced growth in real terms during the 1980s were those with two earners ($51,780 in 1988). In fact, in November 1989 the Economic Council of Canada reported that rises in real family income during the last decade and a half have been the primary result of married women entering the labour force.

Women pushed into the labour force by family income pressures are clearly at a disadvantage. They will take any job available, and most will end up in traditional female job ghettos. Part–time jobs tend to be lower paid and carry few benefits.[36] In 1988, 72 per cent of Canada's approximately two million part–time workers were women, and one in four of these worked part–time because that was the only job they could find.[37] But the unwilling acceptance of part–time work is but part of a larger problem that plagues the careers of many women in the labour force. Studies in occupational mobility have confirmed the importance of the "occupation of entry" for future occupational attainment.[38] Take the earlier case of a young man and a young woman, both graduates of a business school. The young man succeeds in obtaining a place in a management trainee intake program — he is on the career track toward promotions and higher pay. The young woman, on the other hand, because of family income pressures, takes the first job she can get — a clerk in an accounting firm. Their work futures will be heavily influenced by these occupations of entry.

Taking any job available is only one of many labour market sacrifices women routinely make. Much of the economic inequity women experience occurs long before they enter the labour market. Socialized to see themselves realizing a central aspect of their identities as wives and mothers, women are often not encouraged to take their role in the world of work seriously. Therefore, they tend not to be as well prepared as men when they launch their careers. That is why, in a study over the decade of 1976 to 1985,[39] it was found that men obtained twice the rate of trade certificates as women; that women, though earning more undergraduate degrees than men, were far less likely to pursue graduate work; that, despite female predominance as university undergraduates, women still only occupy a tiny percentage of places in the more employment–oriented university courses like mathematics, sciences, and engineering; and that women were far more likely than men to pursue university education on a part–time basis.

If women choose to marry and to have children, they make major labour market sacrifices. They drop out of school. They attend part–time. They leave their jobs to have kids. Then they look for jobs compatible with raising kids. They enter, exit, and re–enter and then enter, exit, and re–enter again to suit the ebb and flow of family demands. They search for part–time work to reconcile the need for income, the desire to work, and the demands of children and husbands. They look for work that fits the day care they can find, when it becomes impossible to find day care to suit the work they want to do. Even highly motivated and well–educated women, having embarked on the first steps of a rewarding career, find such career compromises inescapable.

Women who work, and then opt to have children, or women who have children and then realize that they must find some paid work, learn very quickly that often only the inferior jobs can be easily reconciled with being wives and mothers. For the overwhelming plurality of women these are jobs in the traditional female ghettos. For female teachers, it involves the "choice" not to pursue further education for a high school job or an administrative post — or perhaps to do "just a few years" of "subbing." For female nurses, it involves the "choice" to work only two or three days a week. For the female doctor, it involves giving up post–graduate training, "at least for now" and perhaps practising part–time. For the female lawyer, it involves a part–time job at a legal aid clinic. For the aspiring female university teacher, it involves putting off the Ph.D. and "teaching the odd course" until the kids are in school. The variations on the theme are endless.

The modern family's success therefore rests importantly on the abandoned aspirations of many women: foregone training, postponed education, rejected promotions, transfers dismissed out of hand, jobs unapplied for. This point is made considerably more drily by the Canadian Mobility Study:

> Additional sex differences in the occupational attainment process among married men and women occur with child–bearing and child–rearing. Number of children depresses the occupational attainment of women under age 45 but it has no influence on the attainment of married men.[40]

And while it is true that many of these working mothers, perhaps most, make significant career sacrifices willingly, the fact remains they have no real choice. Unlike men, women cannot easily "have it all."

Indeed, the one group of women in Canada who have come closest to closing the sex pay gap are "single, never married" women, who in 1987 averaged 94 per cent of the pay gained by single men.[41] And the women who have succeeded in breaking into the male–dominated professions are more likely, compared to women working in other areas, *not* to be married, and to have *fewer* children, or *none* at all. They are also most likely to have *never* married. As Katherine Marshall says, in her study of women's success in male–dominated professions, "it is still far easier for men to maintain both a professional career and a family. For many women, unlike men, the decision to pursue such a career may mean limiting marital and parental options."[42] A study of women lawyers who did advance to reach near equality with their male colleagues found that such women did so at "great personal sacrifice." The fact is that "most successful male lawyers are married and have children, most successful female lawyers are not."[43]

A decade ago a U.S. executive search company surveyed 485 women executives in the 1,500 largest U.S. corporations. The study found that the highest paid women executives tend to work longer hours and to be divorced when compared to less well-paid women executives. Over one in three was divorced. Fewer than half had children, and those under 40 were less likely to have children than those over 40.[44] Almost a decade later Edith Gilson's study of 250 U.S. women executives, appropriately entitled *Unnecessary Choices: The Hidden Life of the Executive Women*, found that things had not improved, indeed they appear to have deteriorated in some ways.[45] Success for women in the U.S. executive suite can be emotionally expensive for some women: loneliness, unhappiness, unsuccessful marriages, childlessness. And even success brings lower pay than men, fewer promotions, less recognition, and pressure to deny and suppress their femaleness as they learn to model themselves on successful men in order to get ahead.

And, of course, at work such successful women, despite their sacrifices, still face forms of discrimination that inhibit their advancement. As a result of differences in behaviour and personality, women are often judged differently from men.[46] Professor Ron Burke reports that compared to men, women executives tend to be friendlier, more willing to help associates and subordinates, better listeners, and more prone to try to persuade others to their point of view rather than using confrontation. Hence such women may speak up less at conferences and meetings and therefore might be viewed as "timid" or "reticent" and hence less valuable. Nina Colwill found similar sex differences in behaviour in corporate boardrooms: women allow themselves to be interrupted more often than men, are more polite in their business interactions, and tend to make "softer" requests and suggestions. In other words, the behaviour that earns maximum rewards in the executive suite still tends to be that expected of stereotypical males. Further, even women who have made it into management and have decided either to postpone children or to ensure children do not disrupt their careers face prejudicial attitudes. Dr. Alice Nakamura found that whether or not a woman quit upon bearing a child was predicted more successfully by the woman's past work record than by the fact of having a child. A woman who worked 48 weeks in the previous year and bore a child was almost as likely to continue to work after the child's birth as a woman who bore no child.[47] It appears, then, that even those women who are determined not to allow children to disrupt their careers suffer from the assumption on the part of their employers that children will interfere with their continuing commitment to the job.

New Patterns

As a result, some astute women are seeking success first and postponing having children until their careers are well–established. This strategy is not without its costs, costs that men do not have to bear. One cost is the act of deferring children until a later age, thus postponing the emotional fulfillment ten or twenty years. Another is the increased risks of bearing children at a later age.

This trend also includes senior women executives leaving work to have a baby and to spend a few years at home. Corporations that have committed themselves to the advancement of women up the ladder are now concerned about how flexible they should be with talented and successful woman asking for time off to have a baby. More and more are responding with extended leaves, flex–time, temporary contract work, and extended part–time work. Yet such attitudes are rare. And the number of women willing to, or able to, postpone children until they reach managerial success are few. There is just not that much room at the top. As Judge Rosalie Abella found in her Royal Commission on equal employment opportunities, prejudice and discrimination against working women of all classes are so widespread and tolerated that only harsh interventionist measures will succeed in achieving equity in the world of work for women.[48]

One of the choices women can make to avoid trying to balance work and family is simple. They can stay single and childless. More and more women are doing just that — in 1986 Statistics Canada estimated that 14 per cent of Canadian women would never marry, up from about 10 per cent in 1971.[49] But the choice most women make involves work, spouse, and children. A woman making that choice faces clear consequences. Her career takes second place to that of her husband and to the needs of her children. She will always earn much less than her male colleagues, even those with the same qualifications and experience doing the same work. She will routinely lose out on promotions, partly as a result of her family obligations and partly as a result of discrimination. Her husband will give her little help with child care and housework. She will find little support and sympathy, and almost no career concessions, from her employer and her colleagues when she decides to have children. Family crises and problems that disrupt, or *appear* to disrupt, her work commitment and job performance will most definitely be held against her. Indeed, the fact that such disruptions *might* occur will be held against her almost as much as actual disruptions. She will work 12 to 16 hour days once the kids arrive and until they grow up and leave home. She will work almost as hard on weekends and holidays as on regular work days. The other option is to remain single and childless, at least until she has fulfilled her career aspirations. She will have to work harder than her male colleagues, and routinely outperform them, in order to receive the same treatment. Or nearly the same, since she will still receive less pay on the average. Promotions will be harder to come by than for men, but easier than for her married sisters, especially those with children. She can come and go as she pleases at home, weekends and holidays will be hers, and her psychological space after work will not be cluttered with the insistent demands of husband and children.

Life's choices are rarely posed with such clarity. Indeed, we have often made life choices without realizing it until much later. But faced with such a set of choices, I have no doubt which option most men would chose without a moment's hesitation. The fact that the overwhelming majority of women choose the messy and

difficult choice involving work, husband, and children is a confirmation of their abiding commitment to making the family work.

And at no time is that commitment more clearly revealed —
nor is the reality of women's economic oppression more unmistakably confirmed — then when the family breaks down. The
economic consequences of family breakdown for women — and
for their children, as we've seen — is catastrophic. Families headed
by working women not only lose the man's income, but now rely
on the women's income, which is much less from a job with fewer
prospects. Further, single parent mothers have a greater difficulty
maintaining their commitment to the labour force. In 1988, only
42 per cent of female single parents with pre–school age children,
and 63 per cent of those with kids aged six to 15, were in the
labour force. (This compares with 57 per cent and 70 per cent,
respectively, for married women with children of those ages.[50]) It
is not surprising therefore that female single parents and their
children are among the major beneficiaries of social programs like
welfare, unemployment insurance, and family allowance.

Furthermore, despite improvements in laws affecting the sharing of family assets after marriage failure, women still do not
experience economic justice upon family breakdown. Judges now
more frequently insist that a divorced woman, even those who
remained at home, should eventually become self–sufficient.
Thus, ongoing support awards, as distinct from the one–time split
in all family assets, are tending to be smaller in amount and shorter
in duration. As one Montreal family lawyer put it,

> Divorce judgements used to reflect the fact that the husband
> definitely had to look after her. Now women are being told to fend
> for themselves. You change the rules in the middle of the game
> and it creates very grave handicaps.[51]

Further, such awards are rarely realistic. The same lawyer alleged that support orders — including child support payments —
are often less than half the cost of raising a child and often go no
higher than 20 per cent of the husband's net income. As a Manitoba
study argued, courts are increasingly operating on the mistaken
assumption that Canadian men and women have managed to

achieve something approaching economic and social equality, "but the reality is that Canadian women ... have fewer resources, lower status and less flexibility."[52]

But even court–awarded maintenance and child support payments, however inadequate, often do not find their way into the hands of divorced single parent mothers. In 1985 a Canadian Advisory Council on the Status of Women study reported that 50 to 85 per cent of divorced husbands and fathers default on such payments,[53] and the situation has not improved much.[54] Only about 26 per cent of Ontario's 62,000 court–ordered support payments in 1989 were complied with — up from 15 per cent in 1987. These results were achieved through the Ontario Attorney–General's department spending about $14 million a year on enforcement. The success rate in Alberta is about 33 per cent, and in Quebec it is about 50 per cent. These modest success rates have been achieved as a result of Ottawa's, and most provinces', recent "get tough" policies with delinquent ex–husbands and fathers. Contrary to popular belief, such court–ordered payments are largely for the support of children. For example, 97 per cent of Ontario's cases are orders for men to pay; of these, 73 per cent are orders for the support of children, 16 per cent are for an ex–spouse and children, and only 11 per cent are orders for the support of the ex–spouse alone.

Clearly the major cause of the trend toward the feminization of poverty has to do with the economic consequences of marriage breakdown. In Quebec an estimated 10,000 women and their children have been forced to go on welfare as a result of defaulted maintenance payments. From 1987 to 1989, over 16,000 Ontario ex–spouses, overwhelmingly women, and their children received welfare because of support payment defaults. In Ontario about 70 per cent of families on social assistance are headed by single mothers, and two in three of these mothers were previously married. Throughout the 1980s, the percentage of female single parent families below the official poverty line has been shocking: 1981, 53 per cent; 1982, 57 per cent; 1983, 59 per cent; 1984, 60 per cent; 1985, 60 per cent; 1986, 56 per cent.[55]

Women's economic oppression cannot be separated from their roles as wives and mothers. In the traditional family the economic sacrifices women were expected to make were clear. They were expected to devote themselves to domestic careers. Thus, they became economically dependent and vulnerable. That domestic legacy affected the fate of women as they moved into the labour force and sought to reconcile domestic obligations and paid work. Whether it was in the form of "women's work," or of lower pay, or of the assumption that women's commitment to the paid labour force was temporary, women were (and are) expected to make economic sacrifices because their primary tasks remained domestic. When women's commitment to the labour force became clearly permanent and irreversible and families increasingly needed two earners to survive and flourish, that domestic legacy continued to demand economic sacrifices of women. Most of the economic crises of the changing family are imposed primarily on the shoulders of women.

9 / Women's Emotional Oppression

The emotional oppression of women is not simply a consequence of the difficulties imposed by the double burden and economic injustice. Indeed, the double burden and the new forms of economic oppression are themselves merely the more recent historical expressions of women's general oppression. Women have always been economically, emotionally and physically oppressed in the interests of the family. Certainly that oppression is taking novel forms as the family changes and as women's resistance increases, but in many ways it's the same old oppression.

The emotional sacrifices women have made, and continue to make, for the family have been thoroughly documented. As the traditional guardians of hearth and heart, women were assigned the "expressive functions" in the family, according to functionalist Talcott Persons, while men were assigned the "instrumental functions."[1] For men, women are expected to provide emotional support and reaffirmation. For children, women are expected to provide "warmth, security and unconditional love." Different authors have selected different words, but the reality is the same: women are viewed as the primary emotional guardians and sustainers of husbands and children. And in order to do so women have been expected to give emotional priority to the needs of husbands and children. Indeed, women's personal aspirations, their access to an enjoyment of privacy, their emotional needs, and even their health are expected to be forever offered up on the family altar.[2] For example, one classic study in the U.S. found that women in "adequate" or "normal" families were "overwhelmed with responsibility," "obese," "psychosomatically ill," and "sexually dissatisfied," while the men were "functioning well" and felt no sexual dissatis-faction.[3] As Luepnitz argues,

> Thus, according to the authors, an adequate family consists of a husband and children who are functioning adequately and a wife who is not ... There is no greater devaluation of female leadership ... nor a more profound training in sex roles than in a family in which a mother's needs are sacrificed for the good of the whole.[4]

In the orthodox psychological literature, characteristics tradi-tionally associated with the male — assertiveness, independence, autonomy — are usually posited as those which come closest to characterizing an emotionally mature and mentally healthy adult, while the traditional female characteristics — dependence, sub-missiveness, responsiveness, subordination — are typically as-sociated with an emotionally immature and less than psychologically healthy adult.[5] A report for the Canadian Mental Health Association argues that since women in the family are "devalued" and "oppressed," they have "poor self–esteem" and "lowered aspirations."[6] As the role of housewife is viewed as less important in the "real" world, women who occupy that role re-ceive less attention and concern and less recognition of their desires and problems.[7] Indeed, there is a new pathogenic category increasingly recognized in psychiatry: "the belittled wife."[8]

The belittling process goes beyond merely a devaluation of women and their role in the family. Women are also frequently blamed for the emotional problems of others. In the clinical lit-erature mothers are routinely blamed for 72 different categories of psychopathology.[9] They are blamed for their own problems as well as the problems of other family members: they "provoke" their husbands' physical abuse, they contribute to their husbands' alcoholism, or they neglect their psychologically maladjusted chil-dren. Even for psychological disturbances among young women in which fathers play a significant role — depression, anorexia, agoraphobia — the mothers are often still blamed.[10] As a result, women often accept the blame and consider themselves inade-quate. The tendency to engage in "mother blaming and father coddling" is so widespread that one therapist concluded that the family in "modern culture is irrefutably father–absent ... and patriarchal."[11]

Marriage and Mental Illness

The overwhelming preponderance of evidence tells us not only that women benefit less from marriage than men, but also that marriage appears to increase the risk for women of falling victim to forms of psychopathology.[12] For women, marriage brings with it an increased risk of social and psychiatric problems, often of marked severity. Married women who remain at home, and therefore dependent on men, experience a greater risk, compared to single women, of anxiety, phobias, and depression. In fact, married women experience a greater risk of depression than single women, and married women with three or more children have a higher risk of depression. Between 60 and 80 per cent of mothers experience emotional problems after the birth of a child, and one in five such mothers experiences serious depression for many months after birth. For unemployed wives the arrival of children increased levels of depression; but for employed wives, depression was not affected by children, but by the ease or difficulty of child care arrangements and whether husbands helped out.

Overall, rates of mental illness among women are higher than those among men. Married women experience higher rates of anxiety than single women and men in general. Girls, for example, suffer three times the rate of clinical depression of boys, largely as a result, one suspects, of their preparation for future roles where they will be expected to define themselves and their priorities as based on sustaining others in relationships. In fact, the higher rates of anxiety and depression among women suggest that these psychopathologies are quite sex specific: anxiety and depression result frequently when one feels worthless and useless as a result of a fear of failure or failures in fulfilling responsibilities and obligations to others. Anorexia nervosa and bulimia nervosa, which are clearly women's psychopathologies, have mushroomed in recent years, and clinical descriptions of young women most at risk sound very much like a characterization of the psychological and emotional problems and contradictions women typically face.

Girls and women who are particularly vulnerable appear to be those who have a premorbid sense of helplessness and powerlessness about their lives ... their sense of self–efficacy is impaired ... most of these women identify problems with appropriate identification of internal feeling states, perfectionistic attitudes, trouble with expression of direct and appropriate anger, difficulty with assertiveness and decision–making, and trouble with appropriate separation and autonomy from the family of origin.[13]

Of course, a global comparison of psychopathological rates between men and women is deceptive. Married women are more at risk of mental illness than married men. But unmarried men have a greater risk than unmarried women. Hence the conclusion is rather stark: marriage is psychologically bad for women and good for men; singleness is psychologically good for women but bad for men.

As a consequence of the increased risk of psychopathological disturbance women face, other facts make sense. Women and girls receive anywhere from 66 to 72 per cent of tranquillizer prescriptions.[14] Indeed, they are increasingly the treatment of choice among many doctors for middle–class housewives. One study at the University of Ottawa found that women aged 45 to 65 receive most new prescriptions for tranquillizers, suffer more frequently from emotional crises and seek psychiatric help more often. Another clinical study at Queen's University found that women were 30 per cent more likely to be prescribed tranquillizers than men for the following categories of presenting problems: tension headaches, anxiety, alcohol abuse, marital and sexual problems.

A common explanation of the mental health differences between men and women is that women are more willing than men to seek help for their problems.[15] Some feminists have also alleged that male physicians and psychiatrists tend to see women as emotionally weak and therefore too readily diagnose psychological problems. Others argue that women in fact appear to suffer more than men. Vancouver psychiatrist Susan Penfold believes that indeed many male psychiatrists have a sexist bias and embrace traditional views of women. They tend to see unhappy women as needing help to cope with their family life situation but rarely suggest that their family situation could be part of the problem and could be changed. Also, she concedes that male psychiatrists might be quicker to label women's problems as emotional rather than situational. But the evidence also shows that women do suffer more. Furthermore, as Montreal psychiatrist Suzanne Lamarre argues, women suffer more anxiety because of a "sense of powerlessness." Women are simply not allowed to refuse demands placed upon them by husbands, children, or employers. In the context of low control in a situation containing high and ever–escalating demands, the resulting stress makes women more vulnerable.

Other Data

Other data tell us, however, that traditional marriage and dependency is also very much implicated in women's greater vulnerability. As women become less dependent economically and psychologically, their risk of psychopathology decreases dramatically. Married women who work outside the home are not only less vulnerable, but positively psychologically healthier than women who do not. As women become less dependent, they attain a greater sense of self–determination and mastery. Furthermore, since work extends the self into the larger community and establishes a wider network not only of support but also of social confirmation as a person independent of husband and children, women have stronger identities and more coping resources. Despite the great stress for working wives and mothers of juggling the double burden, they are psychologically healthier than those locked up in traditional roles in traditional families.

Let us leave for the moment the area of greater psychopathological risk and focus on the "normal" situation. Besides the emotional sacrifices all women are expected to make for husbands and children, what are some of the other specific emotional frustrations women in general bear? Two U.S. studies, one at the University of Michigan and the other at the University of Washington, provide some insight.[16] Neglect, condescension, unfaithfulness, physical or verbal abuse, sexual aggressivity, and inconsideration were all listed as male characteristics that make women unhappy.

By far the biggest concern had to do with the way men dealt with their own and their partners' emotions. Women complain that men are too emotionally constricted, too unwilling to work through emotional matters. Men typically seek action solutions— "You're unhappy, well what can we do about it?" — whereas women are frequently looking for an open discussion of the situation. Furthermore, men and women appear to have opposing views on the relationship between sexual intercourse and emotional intimacy. For women, physical love–making is part of the expression of love and intimacy. For men, women complain, sex is too often the necessary prerequisite for a time of emotional intimacy. Women also want to hear actual expressions of love and respect, which men too often take for granted.

That men and women largely live in two emotional solitudes — responsive, emotionally sensitive women and unresponsive, emotionally controlled men — is all part of the traditional package of sexually stereotyped behaviour. Some progress has been made, and many men today are much more emotionally open and responsive than their fathers and grandfathers were, but it is slow. A 1989 Gallup poll confirmed that men are more likely than women to see their spouses as romantic.[17] Women are more likely than men to see themselves as romantic. Men are more likely to forget birthdays and anniversaries and less likely to give gifts at times other than special occasions. Women are almost three times as likely as men to feel they do not receive enough attention from their mates. Women are less likely than men to see sex as important in their relationships and more likely to feel that the excitement has gone out of the relationship. Over twice as many women as men would not marry the same person again (11 in 100).

Single women may be statistically psychologically healthier than married women, but they are not necessarily more emotionally satisfied. Women marry, usually, for love, a desire to have children, and to construct a meaningful and fulfilling family life. But if the emotional consequences of marriage are difficult for women, those of marriage breakdown and divorce are even more so. For many women, divorce is not only an economic but also an emotional catastrophe.

Certainly divorce is no where near as psychologically devastating for men and women as it is for children. But neither is it painless.[18] Rates of mental illness among divorced or separated adults are up to twenty times higher than among the married. Divorce and separation have been causally implicated in depression, suicide, homicide, alcoholism and increasing risks of various serious physical illnesses. Studies have found that both estranged partners, one year after separation, "feel anxious, depressed, rejected and alternate between anger and despair." Women suffer from these reactions more deeply and for a longer time. Divorced couples are afflicted by very ambivalent feelings about each other, but "the anger and resentment are sustained far longer in women than in men." The only significant psychological advantage women experience after divorce is that they tend to have a stronger network of support and that ultimately they tend to become more happy than men "with their post–divorce lives and suffer lower rates of mental illness than divorced men as a result."[19]

Single mothers and poor women experience the greatest risk of mental illness. And when a woman is both poor and a single parent, as is usually the case, the risks are that much greater. One study of 83 female single parent families found that the psychological trauma of divorce, combined with the resulting economic hardship, seriously disrupted the women's ability to cope, dramatically lowered their self–esteem, and undermined their sources of social support.[20] Other studies report that the dire economic problems associated with female single parent families seriously impair the mothers' relationships with the children. Further, such women often have problems just coping with routine domestic work and lead highly constricted social lives.

Upon remarriage — which happens to three of four divorced women — women's emotional problems do not end.[21] Balancing the new family is difficult, and women see such emotional relationships complicated by orchestrating their new husbands' relationships with his children from the previous marriage, her children from the previous marriage, and the joint children of the new marriage. The memory of the previous failures is inescapable. The children are suspicious, resentful, and resistant; both partners are uneasy and uncertain. Family boundaries are unclear because of the continuing obligations, both tangible and emotional. Economic problems are complex and full of conflict. Through all this the woman feels enormous stress to keep it all together. So do men. But men are more prone to "let things work themselves out." By their socialization and emotional training women are expected, and expect themselves, to work diligently to ensure success. And failure — which occurs very often in remarriage families — still tends to be blamed on the woman.

What is most striking about the emotional oppression of women in the context of the crisis of the family and the emergence of new family forms is that it has not lessened. Indeed, in some ways it has worsened. Whether it's earning that needed second income, or taking on the double burden, or trying to cajole a recalcitrant and perhaps bruised male to new insights and new behaviours, or repairing as far as possible a fractured family as a single parent, or walking an emotional tightrope as a remarriage wife and mother, women today bear an infinitely more complex emotional burden than their mothers and grandmothers. It is true that the emotional burdens of the traditional family always weighed heavily on women. Today that burden is composed of contradictory expectations, aspirations, and dreams. Before, a woman, a domestic and emotional slave in the home, knew what she had to do. Today that clarity and certainty are gone: she is to be her own person yet also the person of others; she is to slug it out in the job market yet also maintain a home and raise children; she is to be free yet encircled with marital and maternal obligations; she is to be equal and autonomous yet also be there whenever she is needed.

There is, however, one crucial difference. Today a woman has a choice, at least much more so than formerly. An unhappy marriage need no longer be endured endlessly. Lost dreams, surrendered hopes, and forever postponed happiness need no longer be embraced as endless "reality." But often, as women try to exercise this newly won choice, they face the final line of defence of a threatened patriarchy — physical and sexual oppression. Options and choices can only be exercised fully in the absence of a fear of consequences. Today many women fear the consequences of freely exercising their freedom to make choices. Many also suffer the consequences they feared. And often the consequences are fatal.

10 / The Physical and Sexual Oppression of Women

Violence against Women

The phenomenon of violence against women has dominated our front pages for almost two decades now. Apparently rising rates of wife abuse, of sexual assault, and of sexual harassment have provoked both widespread debate and deepening concern. Is it just that violence against women has come out of the family closet? Is it that women victims of non–family violence are laying more public complaints? Is it, in the context of the rise of feminism and women's assertiveness, that male patriarchy, threatened, defied, and frustrated, is lashing out more often? We will never know for certain. As John Boswell notes in his fine study of child abandonment in the premodern period, "Conjugal relations, reproduction, and the interior life of the family are, in fact, among the most reclusive and private aspects of human existence, jealously guarded from public view in most cultures, and less likely than almost any other interpersonal activity to leave written records."[1] And it is probably even more true that the darker aspects of "the interior life of the family" were among the least likely to find their way into the public record. Similarly the true extent of non–family violence against women did not find its way into the public record because of the response of the community: disbelief; woman blaming (she asked for it); and if the case were proved, often rejection ("damaged goods"). Today women are more willing to come forward to lay complaints. Public agencies of order are more likely to take the charges seriously. And the attitudes of the community have changed considerably.

However, the underreporting of violent events against women persists. In 1985 a report prepared for the Solicitor General found that 750,000 Canadian couples experienced one or more episodes of conjugal violence a year and that "domestic dispute" calls were the largest category of requests to police for help. Yet only 10 per cent of such events were recorded, and there were only two prosecutions for every 10,000 incidents. Forty to 70 per cent of all violent crimes in North America occur between people who are married or living as married.[2] A Secretary of State study by Linda MacLeod estimated that one in four women in Canada can anticipate being sexually assaulted at some time in her life, one–half before the age of 17,[3] and U.S. estimates are similar. An Alberta study found that one in nine women in a marriage or common–law liaison is subjected to abuse,[4] and the national estimate is that one in 10 married or common–law women can expect to be abused.[5] The 1981 Canadian Urban Victimization Survey, carried out by Statistics Canada, found that four in every 1,000 Canadian women, aged 16 years and over, were subjected to physical and/or sexual assault by a spouse or a former spouse, and only 44 per cent of these events were reported to the police.[6] In 1980 rape was the fastest growing crime of violence in Canada.[7] Eight years later the Women's Legal Education and Action Fund claimed that sexual violence against women had reached the status of a "national crisis,"[8] and in 1988 Gallup found that fully 23 per cent of Canadian adults claimed personal awareness of the physical abuse of wives by husbands.[9] Clearly, if all such events were acted upon through our formal agencies of justice, Canada's criminal justice system would be inundated by a tidal wave of cases having to do with family and non–family violence against women. But this has not happened. As the Metro Toronto Action Commission on Violence against Women and Children declaimed,

> We see sexual violence tolerated by our institutions, celebrated by our media, excused by our criminal justice system and ignored by many in our governments.[10]

The fact is that violence against women is still not taken seriously by many. If found guilty of beating his spouse a man rarely faces jail or a fine, usually receiving a suspended sentence or an absolute or conditional discharge. Among the 56 per cent of women reporting abuse in the Urban Victimization Survey, and who did not report the event to police, most did not do so either because they believed the police would do nothing or because they feared future retribution. This was a realistic fear, since court orders restraining assaulting husbands from contact with their victims are "routinely violated without penalty."[11] As for sexual assault, federal statistics in the early 1980s revealed that the police were more prone to refuse to take seriously a complaint of sexual assault than any other kind of allegation of criminal wrongdoing.[12]

Reforms and changing government policies have slowly improved the situation, especially regarding wife assault. In the early 1980s only 10 to 20 per cent of reported wife batterers were charged in Ontario. By 1987 47 per cent were charged. In Metro Toronto the figure reached 61 per cent. But punishment is still lenient. For example — two in three cases resulted in probation and one in five cases resulted in a jail sentence, usually of one day.

Similarly, there have been efforts to improve the effectiveness of the system in dealing with cases of sexual assault. In 1983 Canada's old rape laws were replaced by new sexual assault laws, designed to make prosecutions easier by being more lenient regarding rules of evidence and by being less harsh on the victim. Victims no longer as often find their sexual histories on trial, nor need the prosecution fulfill the formerly excessively strict evidentiary rules regarding corroboration. This did not, as many expected, lead to a massive movement of victims coming forward and appears to have resulted primarily in shorter sentences for offenders. There have been more convictions, but these have typically been for the less serious forms of sexual assault.[13]

One of the major problems is that many judges harbour traditional attitudes. Some seem to believe that rape by a man known to the woman is a less serious matter than rape by a stranger. A Dauphin, Manitoba, man received a six–month jail sentence and probation for a year when convicted of the extremely violent rape of his wife. An Ontario Supreme Court judge in one case remarked that a raped erotic dancer "was in a profession that promoted lust." A Sault Ste. Marie, Ontario, man convicted of a sexual assault, involving beating and raping a woman behind an arena, received a ninety–day sentence to be served on weekends, despite the prosecution's request for a penitentiary term.[14] The judge felt that the man came from a good family, and had learned his lesson. As for the woman, a divorced single parent who had been followed by her rapist from her 27th birthday party in a hotel, the judge remarked that though the assault had been traumatic, it was of short duration.

Women frequently do not fare much better in cases involving family violence. The Alberta Crime Compensation Board found that a 24–year–old woman was 25 per cent responsible for the beating she received from her former boyfriend because she went to his house to collect a debt despite her knowledge that he tended to be violent.[15] And in the family violence trial that probably received the most media attention in Canada's history, Kirby Inwood received thirty days in jail after his conviction for assaulting both his Russian wife, Tatyana Sidorova, and their year–old baby.[16] The judge felt that Inwood should not be made the scapegoat for Canada's family violence problems. Such selective illustrations suggest that the old pattern of woman–blaming and man–coddling continues even when dealing with events of serious violence.

Troublesome attitudes about violence against women remain deeply held. In 1985 a survey of 245 women and 194 men at Washington State University found that 5 per cent of the women and 19 per cent of the men did not believe that forced sexual intercourse on a date is definitely rape or that the man's behaviour in such a situation is "definitely unacceptable."[17] It is not therefore surprising that a survey of women students at Cornell University found that almost one in five "had intercourse against their will ... through coercion, threats, force or violence." A 1987 survey of 1,700 Rhode Island students in grades six to nine seemed to suggest the situation may even be worsening. One in four boys, and one in six girls, said it was "acceptable for a man to force a woman to have sexual relations if he has spent money on her."[18] The researcher commented, "Basically, the kids were very much into blaming the victim of sexual assault." Among the survey's findings: one–half of the students believed that "a woman who walks alone at night and dresses seductively is asking to be raped; ... 65 per cent of the boys and 57 per cent of the girls in grades seven through nine said it is acceptable for a man to force a woman to have sexual intercourse if they have been dating for more than six months; 87 per cent of the boys and 79 per cent of the girls said rape is acceptable if a couple is married." The prevalence of such attitudes helps us understand why a Queen's University student council's anti–rape campaign around the slogan "No Means No" was responded to by some men at the university with slogans like, "No Means More Beer," "No Means Harder," "No Means Kick Her in the Teeth," and "No Means She's a Dyke."

Sexual Harassment

A related, but considerably less serious, manifestation of the physical and sexual oppression of women is sexual harassment, particularly in the workplace and other public places. A 1983 survey by the Canadian Human Rights Commission reported that 1.2 million women faced forms of sexual harassment at their places of work.[19] Sexual harassment does not just include unwanted sexual attention and overtures, though that is its most common form. It also includes "any unwelcome [sexual] action, whether verbal or physical, that humiliates, insults or degrades."[20] It happens to women in the lowest service jobs and in the highest–paid professions. It can be expressed crudely or in highly subtle ways. But it all adds up, in the words of the Canadian Bar Association's Committee on Women's Issues, to the same thing: "some men apparently continue to have problems separating the image of women as romantic possibilities from the reality of women as professionals." It can involve betting on how a female co–worker will react to having her breast pinched.[21] Or leaving doors off toilet stalls. Or sexist jokes. Or touching, bum patting, and sexual molestation. A most extreme form occurred in the New York jail system where some female corrections officers were not only subjected to the typical forms of sexual harassment by their supervisors — dirty phone calls and offers of promotion for sexual favours — but were told, when they became pregnant, to get abortions or resign their jobs. Again, like the more extreme forms of women's oppression, sexual harassment in the workplace is coming more into public view as a result of changes in human rights laws and important precedent–making arbitration and human rights commission decisions, which have encouraged women to come forward with complaints. And both union and management frequently have moved to establish policies and procedures to protect victims who complain and to ensure such complaints are taken seriously and acted upon fairly.

Sexual harassment in other public places continues, affected only by public disapproval. Sexual harassment can be worse for women on the streets and in the shopping malls. Sexual ogling and comments by passers–by, suggestive body language, and facial gestures are all constant backdrops for women when they are out in public. Only rarely can a woman take meaningful action — such as in the University of Toronto case of the professor who wore flippers and goggles in order to ogle women in the university swimming pool. As one woman journalist put it,

> Women know what it's like to have to walk past a crowd of teen–agers after dark and try to ignore their jeers and threats.
> Women know what it's like to have total strangers comment on their physical appearance or stare at their breasts before bothering to meet their eyes — if they bother at all.
> Women know what it's like to face this day after day ... the small, daily indignities that degrade us — and degrade all men who perpetuate them.[22]

It is important to reflect upon the typical role of violence and harassment in the history of human affairs. They are used to control the behaviour of others through fear, retribution, and example. Violence punishes those who break or resist the established rules of power and privilege and alerts them to the consequences of continued resistance. Public violence against members of an oppressed group has a demonstration effect, warning through graphic example what can be expected. We find this easy to understand, if not accept, when dealing with violence between racial, economic, national, or religious groups, or with the application of legitimate violence by the state. Both critics and defenders of such violence understand why it occurs.

When feminist and other social theorists make similar arguments about the nature of violence against women, many are uneasy, regarding it as outrageous to see male violence against women as a systematic effort of a patriarchal society to defend male privilege and to keep women contained and controlled. Where are the meetings where men as a power group make such policy decisions? Where are the documents to validate such claims? Of course, there are none. And most men are deeply offended by violence against women and are hurt by suggestions that violence against women is a male campaign to suppress them. Perhaps we would all like to believe that these violent acts are perpetrated by deranged individuals. Yet experts tell us again and again that rape, and other sexual assaults, are more acts of violence and domination than sexual acts. The same is true for family violence. We determinedly seek individual pathological explanations, all of which are certainly pertinent, while overlooking the larger structural issues, the persistent patterns that refuse to go away.

One lawyer has argued that sexual harassment in the workplace is part of the social oppression of women. As one of the ways in which women are kept in their subordinate place, the lawyer drew an analogy to racial harassment.[23] Most white people deplore it when white supremacists attack black or native people. But the attacks occur and take their toll, not only among the particular victims, but among all blacks and natives as they experience fear and hesitation in living and working at ease in the world.

Clear Evidence

Certainly there is clear evidence that violence against women has engendered fear among many, perhaps most women. A 1982 Victimization Survey of 61,000 residents 16 years of age and older in seven major Canadian cities, carried out for the Solicitor General's office, found that Canadian men are almost twice as likely as women to face violent crimes, yet women are much more fearful of violence.[24] This fear results from the nature of the violent crimes women face — sexual assault and personal theft. In *The City for Women: No Safe Place* Linda MacLeod reports that 56 per cent of women do not feel safe and secure when walking alone after sunset in their own neighbourhoods.[25] Women experience fears serious enough to lead to self–imposed restrictions on their and their childrens' lives. Women who experience repeated battering by their husbands often claim that it was the fear of their husbands and the potential public shame that kept them silent victims in abusive relationships.[26] Rape victims are often fearful, depressed, and unable to work as effectively; they feel vulnerability, humiliation, and a profound loss of control.[27] Even some wife batterers concede the purpose of violence against women: "We've [men] been raised in a society that teaches us we're expected to have power and authority and be served by women. When those expectations are either denied or frustrated, we will use violence to regain control."[28] Therefore it is safe to conclude that one of the consequences of violence against women is that women are more likely to be fearful, controlled, and re-strained in their behaviour.

The whole debate about violence against women — its sources and its consequences — was horribly crystallized on 6 December 1989 by the bloody and tragic events at L'École Polytechnique in Montreal.[29] Shortly after 5 p.m. Marc Lépine, 25, armed with a .223 calibre semi–automatic rifle and two 30–clip magazines of ammunition, entered the engineering school affiliated with the Université de Montréal. Twenty minutes later he had roamed three floors of the building, killing 14 women, most with shots to the head, wounding 13 other men and women, until he ended his massacre by committing suicide near the bodies of his final four victims on the third floor. Lépine's actions were cold and calcu-lated — at the first classroom he entered he separated men from women, ordered the men out of the room, and began methodically shooting the women. Witnesses heard him say, "You are all a bunch of feminists. I hate feminists" ("Vous êtes toutes une bande de féministes. J'haïs les féministes."). When asked what he was doing he replied, "I am fighting feminists" ("Je lutte contre les féministes"). Police found a three–page letter on Lépine's body which characterized his act as a political gesture ("un geste politique") against feminists whom he accused of ruining his life. The letter also contained a list of the names of 19 prominent and successful women in Quebec society.

In the aftermath, considerable effort was made to avoid the sexual politics of the tragedy. Violette Trépanier, Quebec's minister responsible for the status of women, characterized it as "a completely isolated act" ("un geste complètement isolé"); Claude Ryan, minister of education, called it "a tragic event everyone was powerless to prevent" ("un fait tragique contre lequel on ne peut plus rien"). Others suggested it was the act of a deranged individual. Still others insisted it was merely another reflection of the growing general problem of violence in our society. *The Journal*'s Barbara Frum almost pleaded with commentators that the event could not possibly best be seen as a deliberate act of political violence against non–traditional women and a violent gesture against feminism.

Many such reactions were understandable, and some were even accurate. It was thankfully, an isolated event. By any reasonable standard, Lépine was deranged, at least temporarily. And yes, violence is escalating in our society. But Lépine did not just shoot people at random, nor did he just shoot women at random. He deliberately chose to shoot women engineering students. It was an act of deliberate mass murder of non–traditional women for the sole reason that they were non–traditional and symbolized feminism, which Lépine felt was his scourge and nemesis.

Although sketchy, some of the details of Lépine's life are disturbingly suggestive: an emotionally scarred product of a broken home where family violence led to family breakdown; a failure in his relationships with women; a difficulty in forming close friendships with men; a familiarity with firearms and a recognized expertise as a marksman; a chronic failure in most things he tried; unrealistic aspirations. We will probably never know the full details of his psychosocial chemistry, but we do know that before his suicide he was determined to make "un geste politique … contre les féministes."

Those who still believe that this was just the isolated act of a madman should reflect on the subsequent comments of Tyler Benson, a prominent anti–choice and anti–feminist activist in Regina.

> Violence against women is dramatically increasing in direct proportion to the success of the feminist movement in destroying the traditional family unit and values generated within that unit. If we are to eliminate such violence, we have to acknowledge the frustration, anger and hate generated by the things feminists do ...
>
> Feminists are advocating a lawless society ... the safety of women depends on how successful we are at destroying the feminist movement ...
>
> The Quebec incident was just the beginning of the backlash against feminism. Very few, I am sure, will resort to such violent methods, but there will, from time to time, be someone unable to express the agony and hate they experience in any other way.
>
> Many innocent people will get hurt in the process, but there is a war going on.[30]

There it is. Feminists are destroying the family and engendering "frustration, anger and hate." They advocate lawlessness. They must be destroyed. "There is a war going on." Extreme misogynysts who perhaps secretly applaud Lépine's rage against feminists, if not his actions, can find further inspiration in the public utterances of people like Tyler Benson.

Violence and the Changing Family

This present work cannot deal extensively and completely with the wider problem of violence against women in contemporary society, but we must turn our attention to family violence as it affects women and how part of the price women are paying for changing family forms is the increased risk of being abused, beaten, and murdered *within* the family. We do know that the tendency to seek violent solutions to problems is typically first confronted and learned in violent families. Most concede that wife beating was a fairly common event in the past, but I suspect that the factors that shape the risk of women being beaten have changed considerably. Perhaps women who were beaten in the past were put at greater risk when they defied patriarchal authority, when their husbands came home angry and stressed and perhaps drunk, or when they didn't serve their husbands with the alacrity expected. Such themes recur in old movies, novels, and plays. However, we now know more about the extent of family violence against women and the factors that put certain women more at risk and that make certain men more prone to use violence against their spouses.[31]

First, the extent. Both of Linda MacLeod's studies on wife battering (1980 and 1987) estimate that about one in 10 women in Canada who is married, or lives as married, is battered each year. Based on a survey of various studies, she claims this is a very conservative estimate.[32] A 1986 Alberta study put the figure at one in nine, and the 1982 Canadian Urban Victimization Survey (CUVS), carried out by Statistics Canada and the Solicitor General's office, found that four in every 1,000 women aged 16 and over suffered physical or sexual assault by a spouse or former spouse.[33] The discrepancy is probably the result of MacLeod's wide definition of wife battering as involving physical and sexual, as well as psychological and verbal, abuse. The CUVS study included only actual assaults and excluded all those assaults carried out by male friends or partners the victim did not describe as a spouse or ex–spouse. On the other hand, a 1986 survey of Canadian men aged 18 and over, carried out to assure anonymity, found that 12 in 100 men admitted to using physical violence against their spouses or girlfriends.

Overall, 12% of men reported that they had pushed, grabbed, or shoved their mates at least once during the previous year, and in two–thirds of these cases, the incidents had occurred more than once. Another 9% reported they had thrown an object at a mate.

Rates of more serious types of violence were lower: 6% reported kicking, biting, or hitting with a fist, 5% reported slapping, and 5% said they had hit with an object or had attempted to do so. Fewer than 3% reported beating their mates, while less than 1%

claimed to have either threatened to use or actually used a knife or gun.[34]

Less the small percentages deceive the reader, it should be noted that in 1986 there were over 9.1 million men in Canada aged 18 years and older. This means that almost 1.1 million men used forms of physical violence against their romantic partners in 1986, including 80 to 90,000 who threatened to use, or actually used, a knife or gun. This suggests that MacLeod's one million battered wives figure may be an underestimate since she includes psychological abuse. The male violence survey included only physical abuse. The survey also found that 18 per cent of married men — or over 1.1. million men — engaged in at least one in a list of eight violent acts. Further, 10 per cent of married men — or about 630,000 — committed at least one of the five most serious violent acts which carry "a high risk of serious injury." Suffice it to say, then, that wife battering is very widespread. When Canada had 71 transition homes for battered women in 1979, they were almost always full and had to turn women away. In 1987, when Canada had 264 such shelters, again they were virtually always full, and it is estimated that one woman was turned away for every one that gained entry. There is no reason not to believe that the need will more than fill any foreseeable expansion of emergency shelter and support programs.

The nature of wife battering runs the whole gamut of violent, degrading, and abusive actions and words. Beatings with fists, feet, and weapons; bitings; scaldings and burnings; rape and sexual degradation of unspeakable kinds are all part of the pattern. Psychological abuse, belittling, and terrorization that frightens, controls, and degrades are also common. Indeed, frequently episodes of physical and sexual abuse and psychological terrorism alternate, increasing the victim's fear and uncertainty. An important point is that wife battering and abuse is ongoing, repetitive, and persistent. MacLeod attempts an encompassing definition:

> Wife battering is the loss of dignity, control, and safety as well as the feeling of powerlessness and entrapment experienced by women who are the direct victims of *ongoing or repeated* physical,

psychological, economic, sexual and/or verbal violence or who are subjected to *persistent* threats or the witnessing of such violence against their children, other relatives, friends, pets and/or cherished possessions, by their boyfriends, husbands, live–in lovers, ex–husbands or ex–lovers.[35]

Its long–term psychological effects can be destructive of a woman's self–esteem, fostering feelings of self–hatred, leading to an increasing withdrawal from contacts outside the home, and often resulting in the overuse of drugs and alcohol. The batterer seeks to control through an insidious process involving the systematic dismantling of the victim's autonomous personality.

The short–term physical effects can be serious as well: bruises; cuts; concussions; burns; wounds; and broken bones. In the CUVS study cited above, 75 per cent of incidents of wife abuse were acts of physical violence: one in three caused injury serious enough to require medical attention. Wife battering can also lead to death. About 40 per cent of homicides in Canada involve victims and suspects in a domestic relationship. The most common type of domestic murder is that of men killing their legal or common–law wives.[36] York University researchers studying murders in Canada from 1974 to 1983 found that three times as many husbands kill wives as wives kill husbands,[37] and Statistics Canada reports that 79 per cent of spousal homicide victims are women. Often, the husband kills the wife and the children of the union at the same time.

Wife battering can also lead to another kind of murder, the murder by the victim of her assailant, of her spouse. In 1987, the number of men killed by wives (33) was the highest since Statistics Canada began collecting homicide statistics in 1961.[38] Just as in the case of physical assaults against husbands, women who murder their husbands typically do so in desperation after years of sustained, life–threatening battering. Two widely publicized cases of the murder of the husband helped spotlight the horrors of wife battering, increased public awareness, and set important legal precedents that for the first time help to protect victims of battering from first–degree murder convictions.

On 9 March 1977 in Dansville, Michigan, Francine Hughes, 30, poured gasoline around the bed containing her sleeping husband, Mickey Hughes, set it on fire, loaded her three children into the car and drove to the Ingram County Sheriff Department.[39] She was charged with first–degree murder and felony murder. Had the death occurred just a few years earlier Francine Hughes would probably have been routinely convicted of murder. On the day of Mickey Hughes' death, he had repeatedly beaten Francine with his fists, terrorized the children, spilled food and garbage all over the floor and forced her to clean it up, smeared food on her face and back and in her hair, torn up her business college school books and forced her to burn them, threatened to smash up her car so she couldn't go to school anymore, ordered her to fix him a meal, and finally forced her to have sexual intercourse with him before falling into a semi–drunken sleep.

At the trial, the jurors and the public were subjected to the sordid details of her 12 years of brutalization at the hands of Mickey Hughes, and her repeated but always unsuccessful efforts to get help from the authorities, police, and prosecutors, even on the day of the death. At the conclusion of the trial, the prosecution claimed that Francine Hughes had deliberately murdered her husband with premeditation. The defence argued that she had suffered a bout of temporary insanity as a result of the years of abuse and further that she acted in self–defence "against an evil force that was threatening her life." After five hours of deliberation, the jury returned a verdict of "not guilty — by reason of temporary insanity."[40]

The Canadian case was similar. In Queen's County, Nova Scotia, late on 11 March, or in the early morning hours of 12 March 1982, Jane Stafford, 33, killed her common law husband Billy Stafford with the discharge of a 12–gauge shotgun.[41] After a day of drinking, Billy Stafford had passed out in his pick–up truck, but only after subjecting Jane to another day in six years of abuse, culminating in threats to kill a good friend of hers and her son by a previous marriage. Jane Stafford was charged with first–degree murder.

After hearing the testimony, and the defence arguments for a manslaughter verdict as well as the prosecution's contention that the murder was planned, deliberate, and without provocation, the jury reached a verdict of "not guilty." The prosecution, the defence lawyer, the whole courtroom was stunned — no one had expected a not guilty verdict. Many were elated, but others were disturbed that it was a mandate for beaten women to take justice into their own hands. (Just weeks after Jane Stafford's acquittal, a woman in New Brunswick shot and killed her battering husband. The jury took just over an hour to find her not guilty.) The Crown successfully appealed, and a new trial was ordered. This time the Crown prosecutor accepted the formerly rejected offer of a guilty plea to a manslaughter charge. After sentencing arguments, the judge sentenced Jane Stafford to six months in jail and two years probation.

Experts claim that these two cases are not all that unusual as serious battering cases go. We know about these cases because of two widely reported, sensational trials that reached unexpected verdicts, verdicts that caused the judicial system and the whole community to take stock.

Because these cases received enormous attention, they, and others like them, contributed to improvements in attitudes and policies affecting cases of battering. But they did more. Together with the fine work of people working in the area, they told us something about the complexity of the phenomenon. Both men engaged in cruel and unspeakable brutalities against their wives and children. They were among the most sadistic of wife and child abusers. Yet their wives loved them, at least at first, and did everything they could to salvage the marriage and the family — including risking their very lives for an extended period of years. Why? What motivates such women? What provokes abuse? What increases the risk of abuse, and of spousal homicide? What motivates the abuser? What kind of men abuse? Why? Are there discernible risk factors?

As with child abuse, there is a widespread reluctance to seek explanations of wife battering in theories of economic stress or social class. However, the evidence from transition homes is clear: battered women tend to come from poor, economically stressed families, and the men who batter them tend to be poorly paid and only irregularly employed. MacLeod's study of battered women in Canadian transition homes in 1985 is revealing.[42] They tended to be poor and young, with an average of two young children. Three in four lived in serious poverty. Only one in five worked outside the home, and those who did tended to be in low–paying jobs. If they left their husbands, a bad economic situation would have become catastrophic. Seven in ten had not finished high school. They often stayed with their batterers because they felt sorry for them, believing that without the relationship the battering men would have nothing left and that the men were somehow psychologically sick. Only 38 per cent of the batterers worked regularly — the others were chronically un– or underemployed. Of those who worked regularly, almost six in ten worked in unskilled, labouring sorts of jobs. Over six in ten had not finished high school.

Back in 1980, faced with similar patterns, MacLeod was adamant: "wife battering is just as common in middle and upper–class homes."[43] But in 1987, having presented even stronger data on class and poverty factors, she was more tentative in her suggestions that battering occurs equally among all class and poverty groups. Her data is derived from battered women who sought the help of transition homes. Other than impressions on the part of transition home workers that many of the anonymous calls for advice come from middle and upper class women, there just aren't hard data to tell us clearly the extent of battering in less economically distressed families.

There are, however, other studies based on samples drawn from the population at large that provide us with some data on the risk factors associated with wife battering. The 1986 University of Alberta study was able to establish some clear risk factors.[44] It found that one in nine married or common–law wives suffered from abuse at the hands of their husbands. Also suggesting that wife battering is more extensive than expected, the study found that 46 per cent of those surveyed knew of cases of physical or psychological abuse. (This compares to the Gallup figure of 23 per cent for physical abuse.) The highest rate by age, about one in five, occurred among younger women aged 18 to 34 years. Recently separated wives suffered rates of physical violence of about 55 per cent, while recently divorced wives suffered rates of almost 44 per cent. Lower income households, $6,000 to $15,999, reported almost twice the rate (13.8 per cent) reported by upper income households (7.5 per cent). The 1981 Canadian Urban Victimization Survey, which surveyed 61,000 people in seven cities and identified 11,000 incidents of physical and/or sexual assaults of wives, reported a similar set of risk factors.[45] The data reveal that separated women suffer a rate of abuse of almost *28 times* that of married women, while divorced women suffer at a rate *9 times* that of married women. As well, women in low–income families (less than $9,000) suffer a rate of abuse of over *3 times* that suffered by women in higher–income families (more than $20,000). Women in moderate–income families ($9,000 to $20,000) experience only slightly higher rates than those in lower–income families. The male domestic violence survey in 1986 suggests similar risk factors.[46] Divorced or separated men were over one–and–one–half times as likely to use physical violence against their wives as married men. The rate of wife abuse among poorer men (less than $20,000 in annual income) was *twice* that among better–off men ($65,000 and over). Younger men are more likely to use violence against their wives than older men — over one in two males admitting domestic violence was 29 years old or younger. Finally, among men aged 18 to 44, those with less education (incomplete high school) showed much higher rates of wife abuse than those with a graduate or professional degree. Interestingly, among men aged 45 years or older the highest rate was found among those with an unfinished university degree.

The male domestic violence survey also found evidence of a clear relationship between economic stress and wife abuse. The respondents were presented with a list of events that they might have experienced in the previous five years. These included: "unemployment for more than one month; personal bankruptcy; a drop in wage or salary; taking an additional job to make ends meet; child support or alimony payments that he did not have before; a move to less expensive accommodations; taking in a boarder to help make ends meet; one or more demotions; loss of income due to a return to school; some other important career setback; some other significant negative change in economic circumstances." The rate of wife abuse was lowest (eight in 100) among men who claimed to have experienced none, or only one, of the events (the overall rate was 12 in 100). Among men afflicted by two or three of the events, the rate of abuse rose to 18 in 100; for those facing four or five of the events, to 19 in 100; and for those facing six or seven of the events, to 33 in 100 — over four times the lowest rate.

Similar risk factors can be found in patterns of spousal homicide. The study by McMaster University psychologists Martin Daly and Margo Wilson suggested that family homicide emerges in the context of a sexual struggle in which the male attempts to dominate his wife, and the woman tries to minimize or resist that control.[47] The psychologists noted some significant risk factors. Women are most at risk of murder by their husbands when they attempt to end the relationship. They also found that very young wives face a higher risk of murder by their husbands — teenage wives suffer triple the risk of murder of older wives. Statistics Canada figures also confirm some of these patterns.[48] A survey of 1988 homicides notes that separated and divorced people are overrepresented, both as victims and suspects. In 1988 such people made up 4.7 per cent of the population, but 16.3 per cent of the victims, and 12.9 per cent of the suspects, of homicide. Over 57 per cent of all female victims of homicide in 1988 were killed by a husband or lover in a domestic relationship (this contrasts with just over 24 per cent of all male victims). Although there aren't clear class and income indicators, Professor Chimbo's earlier study of 34 spouse murderers suggested they tended to come from "the lower socio–economic stratum."[49]

Murder/Suicide

Two recent family homicide cases exhibit many of these risk elements. On Saturday, 23 December 1989 in Drayton Valley, Alberta, Trevor Samuel, a 33–year–old school caretaker, stabbed to death his wife Cindy, 23, and their two daughters, Brittany, four and Erica, six, before taking his own life.[50] The couple had been married for five years, during which Trevor battered Cindy regularly. A good friend of Cindy's reported that Trevor had a "maniacal obsession with controlling his wife" and had threatened her,

"I'll kill you and the kids if you ever leave me." The friend believes Cindy had finally decided definitely to end the relationship the night before her death and her husband "couldn't handle that."

On Monday, 18 September 1989 in Bridgewater, Nova Scotia, Darrell Lowe, 23, shot and killed his estranged common–law wife, Gail Naugler, 34, on the school bus she drove, and then fatally shot himself.[51] Just the week before the murder/suicide, Lowe had been charged with threatening to shoot Naugler and her children, but was released after a promise to stay away from them and not to possess firearms, and was scheduled to appear in court to answer the charge on 27 September 1989. Apparently the relationship had been stormy and Naugler had left Lowe just a month before her death. Many of the typical risk elements were clearly present in both cases, and in both the actual murder appears to have been provoked by the decision taken by the woman to leave the relationship.

What, then, can we conclude about violence against women *within* the family? Those families with lower incomes are at substantially greater risk. Men in lower–income groups, and/or experiencing greater levels of economic stress, are more likely to engage in wife abuse. Men with less education are more likely to engage in abuse than men with more education. Finally, rates of family violence against women tend to be much higher among those women about to end a relationship or who have recently ended it. Regarding this last factor, of course, we don't know if the move to separation and divorce is a cause or a consequence of violence. But we do know that when abused women do begin to show signs of assertiveness, when they begin to make moves toward independence, or when they threaten to leave, the violence escalates tremendously in intensity and frequency, and sometimes escalates to murder.

Clearly these larger social and economic epidemiological patterns of risk have to be related to particular psychosocial profiles of men who batter. The data from MacLeod's study suggest that the battering husbands of women who sought refuge in transition homes were, on the whole, a rather pathetic group — even their victims believed that their lives would be nothing without their wives and kids, whom they abused. High estimated rates of alcohol and drug abuse, high rates of criminal conviction, low rates of regular work — all suggest that these are largely men with seriously flawed personalities, a poor and underdeveloped capacity to cope with their lives, and a tendency to live multi–problem lives. Further, their proneness to use violence is symptomatic of their general inability to cope effectively with life and even its routine difficulties. Perhaps their sense of failure in the context of traditional patriarchal expectations to succeed makes them more likely to target their wives and children for abuse.

Doug Scott has tried to demonstrate the diversity of men who batter, based on a study of battered women who sought refuge at Regina's Transition House between 1976 and 1982.[52] While recognizing that there was a great deal of overlap among the categories, he found nine themes that seemed to capture different "types" of battering and the "social forces" at work.

> Certainly patriarchy is prominent among the forces which promote male violence in the home. However, the association between patriarchy and battering appears more complicated than is commonly assumed. Only three of the factors could be construed as representing the type of "secure," "rational," or "instrumental" violence characteristic of feminist portrayals of battering. Several of the factors suggested that, although the relationships may have contained elements of patriarchal organization, the violence itself was more directly associated with other aspects of the men's situations, including: depression and alcohol dependency, severe loneliness, or insecurity and paranoia. Moreover, even violence which appeared to express "secure patriarchal dominance" was not all of one type. In this analysis, such violence took the form of "disinterested cruelty," "machismo," and "calculated domination."[53]

Scott also found an association between class and battering. Among middle class batterers, stress, "related to incongruities between ... the men's 'status expectations' ... and their actual 'status experiences'" appeared to be a factor. Among blue collar workers, battering seemed more associated with "a form of 'retaliation' ... for what they perceive to be attacks on their self–worth or 'maleness.' " Overall, Scott's work suggests that although the patriarchal context and the effort by men to control women are central features of violence against women within the family, only certain kinds of deeply flawed men feel it necessary to use violence to confirm their significance in the world.[54]

How has the crisis of the family and the emergence of changing family forms contributed to the risk of violence? Many of the risk factors are clearly related to the family's crisis. The traditional one–earner, male "breadwinner" family is in serious economic trouble. Such men find it difficult to "deliver the goods," and they face increasingly stiff competition from growing numbers of women in the labour force. This can only increase the kinds of stresses that the male domestic violence survey found were related to wife assault. Women are increasingly assertive, making control and domination by traditional patriarchal men more difficult. Women are seeking separation and divorce more often, and there's a clear relationship between the risk of wife assault and efforts by women to end relationships. And women have more choices today.

Whether or not violence against women within the family is today more extensive than in the past is finally really irrelevant. Since in the past it was part of the hidden "interior life of the family," it was not a contentious public issue. Today, the context in which violence against women within the family occurs has clearly changed. The public spotlight on violence against women gives the phenomenon, politically speaking, the same impact it would have had, had it suddenly increased.

The economic, domestic, emotional, and physical burdens women bear for the sake of the family are enormous. For the sake of sustaining the family women make great sacrifices, renounce many hopes and aspirations, and often confront continuing abuse. And, when the family breaks down, women bear the lion's share of that burden as well. But women's fate — and that of children — has always been largely tied to the family. And it was, in retrospect, inevitable that the growing liberation of women would finally have to be resolved in a significant structural transformation of the family. So far we've tried to document the costs and consequences of those structural changes for children and women.

But men pay a price as well. Certainly the changes are less costly and the burdens less onerous than they are for children and women, but neither are they entirely without pain and difficulty. While we might not wish to weep copious amounts of tears as we contemplate the plight of the deposed patriarch, we must nevertheless try to understand his plight. There is a special sad poignancy about an emperor who has not only lost his throne, but whose former subjects, pity having replaced fear and respect, look upon him, not without affection, as an historical curiosity.

PART IV

Victims of the Crisis: Men

"Only ... a few acknowledged that the re-wards of power and privilege hardly compen-sated them for the pressures and obligations of masculinity."

Mira Komarovsky,
Dilemmas of Masculinity
(New York: Norton, 1976), p. 248.

Introduction: Elusive Masculinity and Patriarchy

Men remain the clear beneficiaries of patriarchal social structures. Such structures bestow great powers and privileges on them: social, political, economic, and psychological. The control of economic resources, of instruments of political power and authority, and of women and children allowed men, even the lowliest of men, degrees of autonomy, self–determination, and self–indulgence that went far beyond even the wildest imaginings of women in general. During the last two centuries a slow dismantling of structures of patriarchal privilege has resulted in the growing emancipation of women. Women's gains were not given freely by men, and as each enhanced women's power over themselves, it diminished men's control over them. At each step women met general male resistance, followed by a slow erosion of male unity as they were confronted with their own hypocrisy and contradictions, hurried by rapid social and economic changes that made women's liberation not only feasible but structurally necessary.

It may be true, as Simone de Beauvoir argued in 1949, "the males find in women more complicity than the oppressor usually finds in the oppressed."[1] But it is equally true that few oppressed groups have had the lobbying privilege of sharing the bed and home of the oppressor; of being his obsessional object of love, even when such love was paternalistic; and of raising his children in a union that gave to the oppressor a significant portion of his sense of meaning and purpose in life. The continuing fact of woman's oppression and the slowness that has characterized her transcendence of that oppression cannot be easily separated from a degree of complicity on the part of the oppressed or from the complex links of affection that intimately bound oppressed and oppressor together. The complicity of women and the final willingness of men to begin to yield or, at least, to use de Beauvoir's words, "to resign themselves to the new status of woman"[2] are deeply related. And men paid, and continue to pay, a price for their patriarchal privileges. They paid, and pay, a price to keep them. And they pay a price when they lose some of their privileges, whether they render them up willingly, or with resistance and ill–grace.

Men have deeply ambivalent feelings about women.[3] They love them but want to be free of them. They depend upon them but want to assert their autonomy. They need their approval but cannot ask for it. They want them there when needed, but resist the turnabout. According to Chodorow, Dinnerstein and Easlea, this ambivalence results from mother–dominated and father–absent childcare. Mother becomes all–important and apparently omnipotent in the experience of male infants and children. The absence of the father from the child's immediate experience[4] deprives boys of the opportunity to establish a meaningful identification with a male figure in their formative years. This leads to an early sense of sexual insecurity and uncertainty. Since Mother appears all–powerful, the male child develops great expectations which can never be fully fulfilled. There is never enough love. The world is never perfect enough. Feelings of insecurity and anxiety can never be completely laid to rest. Thus the male child, in addition to a strong love attachment, also feels resentment and anger toward Mother.

As the boy grows and develops a need for autonomy, he commences with a rejection of the authority of Mother. The first most crucial steps in his self–determination, then, are taken *against* women. This is exacerbated because the main male role model in his experience — the father— is rarely implicated in the immediate domestic scene. This encourages the boy's view that to be a man is to be absent from, or "free" of, the woman; to be a man is to be aloof from the domestic scene. All this begins and feeds a psychological need to be dominant over and superior to women. Thus the first tentative steps to masculinity are taken against women, and most importantly against the most significant and powerful adult in the boy's experience, Mother. But since masculinity is initially developed in such an ambivalent context, it remains forever elusive, and it must be forever confirmed to others and to oneself. Furthermore, since the first relationship of a boy with a woman is fraught with ambivalence, all future relationships with women are complicated by such feelings.

The content of masculinity in men is full of this ambivalence about women, the need to be dominant and superior yet dependent, and the need to constantly reaffirm their "maleness" to themselves and to others. To be masculine is to be individualistic, competitive, and tough. A man must control his emotions and not express them too freely. He struggles and competes to succeed, but each triumph merely sets the stage for the next struggle. A man grants affection and intimacy only rarely, and in carefully controlled circumstances. Masculinity means to fear intimacy, indeed to strive for power and control. Masculinity means to seek superiority, *public* superiority, and to continue to confirm it. Real men judge each other's jobs in terms of pay, power, and control over others.

Men do of course seek out women, wanting relationships in which they can become dependent without admitting it. The confident macho male of 20 becomes the dependent husband of 40. The sexually satisfied married man still peers furtively at his neighbour's penis at the urinal, comparing size. Men want to escape the charade and the competitive game — usually through love and commitment with a woman — but can never finally do so with complete ease. Because, finally, masculinity is elusive precisely because it is a myth, a myth that collapses almost completely in the absence of supporting patriarchal structures.

And I am not just talking about the traditional masculinity of our fathers and grandfathers. I am talking about masculinity now. Men still feel a need to define themselves against "the other" — women. One family therapist recently argued that masculinity is still seen by many men as a sort of "ritualistic combat" with other men and that "a man's greatest fear is to be thought to be like a woman."[5] A study of 150 male college students found that male fears resulting from the stress of masculinity cluster in five areas: "physical inadequacy; emotional inexpressiveness; subordination to women; intellectual inferiority; and performance failures in work and sex."[6] Another study investigated the extent to which the masculine role — involving "restricted emotionality, preoccupation

with success, and the inhibition of expressions of affection" —
increased the vulnerability of men, compared to women, to the
negative effects of difficult life situations. The researchers found
elevated levels of distress in men as a consequence of the masculine role.[7] A study of "divorce prone" and "marriage phobic" men
found that both groups exhibited a "wariness" of women and felt
an irresistible need to dominate and control their relationships
with women. Marriage phobic men expressed this by withholding
commitment, while divorce prone men made tentative commitments that were quickly withdrawn.[8] In the early 1980s a California psychologist interviewed 227 fathers of recently born or
about–to–be–born children and uncovered a number of "secret
fears" that privately haunted the men.[9] The biggest fear — affecting about 60 per cent of the men — was one of the most ancient,
"uncertain parentage." In a seven–year study (1980–86) of 1,632
couples by a U.S. psychologist it was found that good job news
— like a promotion or raise in pay — tended to increase a man's
desire for sex, while bad job news — like being demoted or fired
— tended to diminish a man's sexual appetite. (By contrast,
women tended to respond to good job news with a small celebra-
tion with friends.[10]) A study relating a child's sex with the content
of father–child interactions with one–year–olds found that men
tend to enforce, often quite rigidly, traditional sex behavioural
stereotypes much more than women.[11] Contemporary studies like
these indicate that men are still ensnared in the masculine role and
remain afflicted by uncertainties, doubts and anxieties that accom-
pany sustaining that role. Evidently a large part of occupying the
masculine role is a fear of failing to live up to the expectations
embodied in it.

The problems posed for men by the masculine role have in fact
increased markedly. Certainly, as Millett asserted, "patriarchy's
chief institution is the family."[12] And as long as the traditional
patriarchal family remained strong and secure, the "dilemmas of
masculinity" were more or less tolerable. The evident benefits far
outweighed the less tangible costs. There was a synchronization
between masculine and feminine roles. But there were still costs
— or renunciations — exacted from the man: the suppression of
his tender side, a loss of freedom, a feeling of oppression by the

economic burdens and responsibilities imposed by the family, the fear of failure, and the awful consequences of actual failure. So while women pointed to their oppression *in* the family, men pointed to how the obligations of the family oppressed them and complained of their oppression *by* the family. Gains for women, like the vote and full legal citizenship, did not fundamentally change the reality of the position of women in the patriarchal family. According to de Beauvoir, "in their exchanges, woman appeals to the theoretical equality she has been guaranteed, and the man to the concrete inequality that exists. The result is that in every association an endless debate goes on concerning the ambiguous meaning of the words *give* and *take*: she complains of giving her all, he protests that she takes his all."[13]

The "dilemmas of masculinity" for men accelerated as women began to achieve a measure of economic independence, particularly since the 1960s. As long as women remained economically dependent on men, the patriarchal family remained secure and women remained locked up inside of it, even if increasingly restively. As Millett noted, "In general, the position of women in patriarchy is a continuous function of their economic dependence."[14] Twenty years earlier, de Beauvoir had made the same central point:

> It is through gainful employment that woman has traversed most of the distance that separated her from the male; and nothing else can guarantee her liberty in practice. Once she ceases to be a parasite, the system based on her dependence crumbles; between her and the universe there is no longer any need for a masculine mediator ... [She has found] a means of economic and social autonomy.[15]

Today the changing status of women, and the new emerging family forms, are confronting men with not just the wisdom and justice of changing their commitment to the old traditional masculine role, but with the necessity of doing so. Twenty or 25 years ago the women's movement appealed to men to renounce their sexist ways. Today the changing structure of the economy and the family are forcing men to do so whether they want to or not.

11 / Men and
Economic Stress

The economic stress faced by the traditional male carrying the sole burden of supporting the family was central to the price men paid for the privileges bestowed upon them by a patriarchal society. A key component of the traditional masculine mystique, the role of economic provider, was fundamental to a man's identity. The stresses and anxieties generated by these obligations were carried without complaint. A real man got out there on behalf of those who depended on him and competed relentlessly throughout his working life to bring home the bacon, to put bread on the table, and to keep a roof over the family's heads. Even if the man were poor and less than successful, even if the bread were day–old, the bacon a tiny portion, and the roof covered a modest slum, he could still stride manfully into the kitchen confident that, within the limitations imposed on him by his station and circumstances, he had done his duty as a husband and father. Such men were portrayed in novels and movies, and the behaviours and expectations involved in living up to the masculine ideal were drummed into little boys from birth onwards. The image of the ideal male was simple and clear. He was a man of few words, a man of action. He felt deeply but never showed it. He would face challenges to his manhood, and threats to his family, courageously. His life was spent on the endless treadmill, the rat race. Even if he succeeded, he kept on competing and striving. There was always someone with a bigger salary, a better job, a bigger house; there was always more to be got for the family.

Few men really measured up to this stereotype. There can be only so many successes in an hierarchical society, and every success means the failures of many others. Even those who

succeeded felt little comfort and security because competition is
not just getting there, but an endless process of staying there. And
there were cultural images of failure, like Willy Loman in Arthur
Miller's *The Death of a Salesman*. But most men confronted their
failure to measure up less catastrophically than Willy. Achievement goals were scaled down. Acceptable rationalizations were
proferred. Bruised and wounded egos were carried gingerly back
to the privacy of the family for mending and reconstruction, with
the essential ministrations of the wife and children. In many ways,
each family embarked on a secret psychological conspiracy to
convince the man that he was a success in his own way, that he
was the most important man in the world, or at least in their world.
And, of course, he *was* the head of the house. His lack of power
and control outside the family was somewhat compensated for by
his power and control within the family.

But this was not always enough, and the stresses were never
completely expunged. The burden of being the sole provider was
overlaid with playing out a role that denied and suppressed a
whole dimension of a man's life—the emotional, tender side. The
toll on a man was sometimes physical; in other cases it was
exacted from the family, when a bitter man came home drunk and
frustrated and hopeless. Most often the toll was a surrender to a
chronic sense of insecurity, of failure, of dissatisfaction, of disil-
lusionment. Since the essence of the traditional masculine role
was impossible to achieve, men were rarely able to be completely
content, even if they succeeded materially. But there were pay-
offs. Those men who did achieve the outward trappings of manly
success, however modest, could hide their inner anxieties as they
enjoyed the deference of those who depended upon them. Even
for those who failed, a submissive wife and loving and obedient
children could go a long way to compensate for perceived or real
failures.

Traditional men today, faced with the changing status of
women and the new emerging family forms, confront enormous,
even insuperable, problems in sustaining their role as sole
economic provider and head of the family. Harsh economic reality
has confirmed the end of the myth to all but the most willfully
blind of traditional men. A traditional husband is having more

difficulty sustaining the economic viability of the family on his income alone. Such families face over triple the risk of poverty compared with two–earner families (13 per cent versus 4 per cent in 1986)[1] and have experienced virtually no growth in real income since 1973. In fact, traditional–earner families experienced a slight fall in real income between 1980 and 1988.[2] Indeed, being a traditional–earner family, relying solely on the husband's pay-cheque, has become one of the major poverty risk factors in the 1980s. At the other end of the scale, traditional–earner families are increasingly less likely to make it to the top of the income pyramid — in 1986 over 80 per cent of all families in the top fifth of income distribution were dual–earner families.

Moreover, traditional men face increasing job competition from women, and the drive for economic justice for women involving affirmative action and pay equity programs can only make their own career and salary potentials more uncertain. Moreover, they see their colleagues in two–earner families able to provide extras and in general to exude a more manifest sense of economic secu-rity. All the things that were supposed to go to the traditional successful male's family are increasingly beyond his grasp, yet within the grasp of dual–earner families in which men have, at least partly, abandoned the traditional role. Today, a man appears to be economically punished for clinging to the old ways.

For a young man, sustaining a family based on the traditional–earner model is even more impossible. As a result of declining real family incomes and declines in real wages for younger work-ers, families headed by young couples have an enhanced risk of poverty, and those dependent on just the husband's income are among the most vulnerable. As of the 1986 Census, only one in four families where the husband was under the age of 45 was a traditional–earner family, while just over one in two families where the husband was 45 or older was a traditional–earner family. If these trends continue, the traditional family, economi-cally dependent solely on the husband's income, will virtually disappear early in the next century.

The economic circumstances of the traditional male in the context of the growing rate of family breakdown are equally bleak. Families headed by single parent men, though much better off than those headed by single parent women, face almost double the poverty rate of families in general.[3] Divorced men on whom the wife and children were solely dependent face child support and alimony payments considerably higher than those faced by divorced men from dual–earner families. Upon remarriage, if such a traditional man wants to continue to be the sole earner and must meet support payments from a previous marriage, the situation becomes even more difficult. In the past, most such men were able to abandon their former obligations more or less completely with relative impunity. This is more difficult today as governments embark on somewhat tougher enforcement and collection measures. A divorced and remarried man, determined to continue to be the sole provider, even one who earns a high income, cannot hope to fulfill his economic obligations without major stress and sacrifice.

A combination of women's insistence on change and economic reality is thus forcing even traditional men to accept the new reality of the dual–earner family. Yet a reluctant move to the dual–job family poses serious adjustment problems. Studies have found that marriage to an "overeducated" wife is often stressful for men; that non–traditional occupations of wives are associated with either divorce or pressure on the woman to move to a lower ranking job; that a wife's income is negatively associated with difficulties in marital adjustment (the higher the income, the lower the quality of adjustment); that "problem" marriages tend to be those where there are serious discrepancies between the couple's sex role attitudes; that the highest marital satisfaction occurs in egalitarian *or* man–dominated marriages, the lowest in woman–dominated marriages; and that among the poorest marriages in terms of quality are those which bring together a traditional male and an even moderately liberated woman.[4]

Such findings merely reflect the painful process of adjustment that is going on as traditional men adapt to the new family and female realities. In individual cases the adjustment may be successful or unsuccessful, but it *is* occurring as men make the transition and as women learn the best means of helping them to do so. Perhaps the whole process is most analogous to a funeral rite: anger and resentment at the loss, followed by mourning for what has been irretrievably lost as a prelude to accepting the loss and getting on with life. Each of us in his or her own way is thus involved in the ceremonial burial of the traditional patriarchal family.

12 / Men and Emotional Stress

The problems of emotional adjustment differ for different men, but they all face the same stressful context. Komarovsky's study of U.S. male college seniors in the 1970s discovered "a basic contradiction" between "sex equality of opportunity outside the home" and "traditional sex–role segregation within the family." Many experienced severe strains in their relationships with women and felt dubious about their personal adequacy. Many complained of the "shallow and aloof paternal relationship" that had characterized the homes in which they were raised.[1] Raised to see women primarily in sexual terms either as potential objects of sexual consumption or as wives and mothers, men increasingly complain about the uncertainties they face about how to approach and relate to women. Therefore male children suffer from a serious cultural lag between the sexist values they are taught and the feminist reality they must face. Such a lag inevitably produces stress. Samuel Luker put it this way:

> The basic challenge facing contemporary men is to develop role models that are consistent with reality ...
>
> The traditional male played the game. He paid the penalty — he died younger, he was out there alone, sort of leading the charge and getting the arrows through his hat — but it was a man's world. If he played the game right, he got the respect of his wife and the love of his children and that was worth it all.
>
> Now, he does all the right moves and he still doesn't get the guarantee that his wife and family think he's No. 1. And it is not just in the working world that men are finding their childhood images of a real man are not up to real life.

Women that I see in my practice want the man to be strong and a provider and all the things that a traditional male did automatically, but now it's not enough, you've got to be strong, you've got to be tender and you've got to be open about your feelings.

The new woman is demanding a lot more of the same old man.[2]

Herbert Freudenberger, the New York psychologist who came up with the term "burnout," concurs, but he goes further by suggesting that "men are in a much more significant state of transition now than women. They are often uncertain, ambivalent about themselves and sometimes quite confused about the meaning of masculinity and what it means to act and 'be a man.' " The reverse of the fact that women "have more clearly defined ... goals and desires" is that "men have lost their sense of purpose" in life.[3] Freudenberger reported that most of the psychologically distressed men in his practice were between the ages of 25 and 50. Often these men were very successful in their professions and businesses, but felt depressed, uncertain about the future, and trapped in orthodox family relationships. They had difficulty adjusting to the new woman. They complained of having limited intimate relationships and of feeling lonely. They sometimes became narcissistic and compulsive, abused alcohol and/or drugs, or dropped out of their traditional supporting roles and became dependent on a woman. While suggesting that both women and men must change and adapt to cope with the new situation, Freudenberger alleges that "the biggest change needs to be made by the men."

Self–evidently, a man who has accepted the need to redress the economic injustices faced by women will find it easier to accept programs of affirmative action or pay equity which may have a negative impact on his own career prospects and future earning potential. But he will still have to cope with the new competition of women and the consequences of his lost privileges. So too, a man who agrees that his wife should work outside the home, and that he ought to do a bit more to help out around the house, will find it less traumatic to cope with the problems presented by a working wife. And clearly when there is more congruence between the sex role expectations of the man and the woman in the relationship, the coping process will be less stressful and marriage quality will be higher.[4] But if the man retains traditional attitudes, resents competition from women, resists his wife's desire to work, or expects to maintain the family's style of life on just his income, the stresses of coping can be quite horrendous. The results can include not only the possibility of failure at work, but the loss of wife and family. A U.S. survey found a clear positive correlation between the divorce rate and the labour force participation rate of wives, indicating that a wife's full–time work is implicated in the failure of some relationships.[5] California psychotherapist Herb Goldberg was much more blunt about the failures of traditional men in the new context. He claimed to have seen evidence of a "role–reversal" throughout the 1970s in which formerly submissive women have left or threatened to leave their macho husbands, despite the fact that such men were "good providers, hard workers and dedicated family men" on the grounds that the relationship was emotionally unsatisfying.[6]

Men and Marriage

Men have had a different stake in marriage and the family than women have had. Just because the traditional masculine role has been instrumentally oriented to the competitive struggle in the marketplace does not mean marriage and the family were of peripheral significance to men. Men have been at least as emotionally and psychologically dependent on marriage and the family as women, if not more so. The nature of the traditional masculine role makes intimacy difficult, particularly with men with whom they compete at work. When men leave their families of birth they seldom maintain as close an emotional relationship as women do with their families. Again, part of the traditional masculine role is to become independent; as a result, they tend to become emotionally isolated, anchored by few close emotional ties that transcend their worldly, instrumental obligations. This has been typically presented as an outward manifestation of male strength and autonomy and as evidence of men's emotional coldness, aloofness, and irresponsibility. But it can be equally seen as a manifestation of men's emotional vulnerability.

Marriage and the family in fact became central to the emotional life of a traditional male. It was in a relationship with a woman that a traditional male found emotional fulfillment and meaning. He needed her love, understanding, and unqualified support. For it was there, in a relationship based on sexual intimacy and bonds of affectional obligation, that he could let down his guard, open up a bit, and be himself. And when children came, the family became the place where a man sought a more complex and rich emotional life.

Marriage and the family therefore became places of emotional permanence and security for traditional men, pivotal anchors in an otherwise insecure and hostile world. In the mind of the traditional man, his wife and children were the reasons for his daily struggle and were the struggle's ultimate justification. Women were simply expected to give the men what they needed emotionally. A women's economic dependence, and careful socialization, ensured she would do so. She was not to question what he did or what he felt obliged to do. But while it is evident that women were therefore subordinated and oppressed in the family, men certainly needed and depended on marriage and the family for their emotional meaning.

That is why, as we saw in the Chapter 9, marriage has typically delivered more psychological benefits to men than to women, benefits delivered largely at the expense of women.[7] Marriage is psychologically good for men but bad for women; singleness is psychologically bad for men but good for women. This stark pattern should tell us more than anything else just how central marriage and the family have been to the traditional masculine identity. Without marriage — and all the material and psychological benefits it brings — men are more vulnerable, more at risk of psychiatric and emotional disorders. Married men live happier and longer lives than unmarried men.[8] And married men live happier, if not longer, lives than married women.

Consequently, the loss of marriage and the family through separation or divorce is a profound shock for many men. As we've seen, divorced adults generally exhibit higher rates of psychiatric disturbance, but divorced men experience higher rates of mental illness than divorced women. Indeed, just focussing on marital status, divorced men have the highest rates of mental illness of all marital groups. One study of educationally and sociodemographically matched groups of married and separated/divorced men found that the latter suffered significantly elevated feelings of "distress" and "loneliness" and a higher rate of more recent physical illness.[9] Another study found that divorced men face a higher risk of suicide, of admission to psychiatric hospitals, of being victims of violence, and of vulnerability to major and minor physical illness.[10] And yet another found that even extremely self–centred, macho men experience severe distress upon divorce.

> [O]ne group of divorced men seem to feel very little. These men come from marriages that involved little sense of commitment. They are the "easy come, easy go" men with narcissistic character disorders; men who are capable of only shallow relationships and low levels of intimacy. *The loss of context of their lives* seems more important to them than the loss of any specific attachment. They may be very angry or depressed about their own immediate disruption, but they quickly move on to new relationships and leave their children behind with remarkable lack of bereavement. These are the true "disappearing" fathers. In stark contrast psychodymamically are the group of men who experience *a severe narcissistic injury, a sense of intense betrayal and damage.* These are frequently the men for whom the wife's leaving was *a total surprise, who were not aware that the divorce was on its way.*[11]

Clearly, some men are deeply disturbed by divorce in all spheres of their psychological life. There is a loss of self–esteem, of purpose, of emotional meaning. For others, the disturbance is real, but for more clearly selfish reasons: bruised egos, public humiliation, a "loss of context in their lives" rather than the loss of the particular wife and children. Caught up in the preoccupation with self, the divorce leaves them bereft of the justification that was so central to their public "presentation of self."[12] Given the tenuous and insecure nature of traditional masculinity, the blow can be psychologically devastating, and for those who deeply loved their wives and children, the blow can be doubly devastating:

not only is the private and public masculine ego in tatters for all to see, but they grieve for the love lost.

There is a clear relationship between divorce and suicide. Travato's analysis of the relationship between divorce and suicide in Canada between 1950 and 1982 demonstrated a clear positive correlation. As the divorce rate went up, the suicide rate went up.[13] This was true for both sexes, but successful suicide is and has always been much more common among men than women, and divorce is also positively correlated to suicide among children, particularly adolescent boys. Indeed, divorce, as a general phenomenon, is positively related to suicide rates in all groups affected by divorce: men, women, and children. From the early 1960s to the 1980s, the suicide rate doubled for both men and women. But since the late 1970s, the rate for women has fallen, while that for men has continued to grow. The most dramatic growth in male suicide between the 1960s and the 1980s occurred among the 15 to 19 year age group, up about four times, and the 20 to 24 year age group, up almost three times. Overall, the rate for men aged 25 to 44 nearly doubled. Up until the early 1960s suicide was most common among older men over 60, but by the mid–1980s suicide rates for men aged 20 to 44 either equalled or exceeded those of older men. And this rapid rise in suicide rates among men, especially younger men, uncannily and almost perfectly tracks the accelerating divorce rate.[14]

The possible reasons for consistently high rates of suicide among men over 60 are easily understandable: terminal illness or physical infirmity; bereavement; the shock of retirement. But for young men, even those on what should be the optimistic threshold of their adult lives, the high rate of suicide is perplexing and bewildering. And the increase has been so astonishing that an explanation must be sought.

Striking Difference

In studying suicide rates in nineteenth–century Europe, Durkheim found patterns similar to the ones noted above.[15] Examining the relationship between suicide and divorce, he noted that the highest rates of suicide occurred among divorced men and women. But the rate was much higher among the men. Indeed, Durkheim found that the risk of suicide goes up for men and down for women as divorce becomes easier to obtain, which led him to talk about the "immunity of married persons" to suicide and the general "preservative effect of marriage and children." But the striking differences in suicide rates between the sexes led him to point to the "salutary discipline" of the family and children for men and to suggest that the consequences of "conjugal anomy" — divorce or separation — included less "calmness and tranquility" and "more uneasiness" for men than for women. He concluded, therefore, that men benefit from marriage more than women.

> Thus we reach a conclusion quite different from the current idea of marriage and its role. It is supposed to have been originated for the wife, to protect her weakness against masculine caprice. Monogamy, especially, is often represented as a sacrifice made by a man of his polygamous instincts, to raise and improve woman's condition in marriage. Actually, whatever historical causes may have made him accept this restriction, he benefits more by it.[16]

Durkheim was trying to demonstrate that even such an apparently personal act as suicide resulted from larger social causes. Suicide, he argued, occurred more frequently when great social structural changes threatened the serenity of people's daily lives. Rising rates of suicide were therefore reflective of the weakening ties of social integration. As people's social structural maps are disrupted, then personal indices of social disintegration, like suicide or divorce, will go up.

Modern men, particularly men committed to the traditional masculine role, are facing major distress. As a result, many men find their expectations out of step with social reality. In an effort to explain the spiralling rate of suicide among men, especially younger men, psychiatrist and suicide expert Diane Syer–Solursh said,

> The strong, silent macho role society expects of young men is a major reason why they are seven times more likely to kill them-

selves than are younger women ... Boys are supposed to learn how to cope alone, to be a man and not to cry. Asking for help has become extremely difficult ... Young men are reluctant to reveal their troubles, and those who could help them — friends, parents, teachers and doctors — are equally unaccustomed to offering assistance. There are taboos for boys; culturally we allow young women to express much more distress.[17]

Traditional men today face many difficulties in obtaining and retaining Durkheim's "preservative effect of marriage and children." Women are less admiring of traditional masculine behaviour, and men are therefore often forced to change their ways. While this can be a positive step, the stress of balancing the inner self with the new outer self can be significant. Further, within the intimacy of marriage the effort to change is difficult to sustain, particularly when families face troubled times. Some men carry on as men have always done, perhaps agreeing to tolerate a more assertive woman than they would really like. But the stress of that compromise, particularly the economic stress if the wife doesn't work, can be great, and such a compartmentalization can quickly disintegrate. A traditional man may even try to carry on when it becomes clear that he is in an impossible situation and snap, as in the case of Lawrence DeLisle of Wyandotte, Michigan. DeLisle, 30, drove his station wagon containing himself, his wife and four children, aged eight months to eight years, into the Detroit River. During interrogration, he allegedly said that "as the car hurtled toward the river" he was "thinking of no longer having to pay bills." In a 1990 statement proclaiming his innocence after he was found guilty of four counts of first–degree murder and one count of attempted murder, DeLisle said, "A father's job is to protect his children, and I failed ... That is my guilt, not murder."[18]

Most adjust more or less successfully. Many do not, and face separation, divorce, and remarriage, perhaps more than once, as they strive to adapt. Many experience depression, anxiety, lowered self–esteem, and uncertainty. Many also experience anger and resentment, which are often internalized and manifest themselves in psychiatric illness, alcoholism, or suicide. Sometimes this anger and resentment are expressed against women and children, whether through abuse directed at his wife and children in the home, or through sexual harassment and expressions of mysogynist sentiments at work. It may be the anger and resentment of the traditional male who cannot accept or deal with assertiveness and independence on the part of his wife, or from women in general. It may be the anger and resentment of the traditional male who cannot accept the fact that his wife has finally rejected him and seeks a divorce.

The Lépine Syndrome

There is no doubt that a goodly portion of contemporary male violence against women and children can be attributed to the strains and stresses faced by men as they try to cope with the impacts upon them of the general crisis of the family. Perhaps it is true that much of such violence in the past was routinely the result of male frustration and failure successfully to live up to the masculine ideal. But today, added to that historical legacy, is the failure of modern marriage and the family, and the larger social structure, to mesh with many men's traditional notions. And although we will never know for certain, many express the uneasy feeling that such violence has been increasing in recent years. Indeed, we may be on the threshold of the emergence of a "Lépine syndrome" in much of male violence against women. In fact, it may well have already emerged, as the events in Montreal ominously suggest. This is male violence, arising from a man's sense of failure and frustration, both in intimate relationships with women and in occupational attainment and economic achievement, directed increasingly and more or less consciously at women who are seen as the causes of his failures. Whether it is the wife who is blamed for the failure of the marriage because she didn't accept or understand the husband, or had been too assertive and independent, or whether it is women in general in the job market who are depriving him of the success that is his due, such women are targetted as scapegoats and become the repository for all his anger, resentment and bitterness. Many men already suffer from a sort of "Lépine syndrome" without the explicit violence, expressing it in anti–feminist attitudes and petty hostile acts.

Perhaps I have painted an unnecessarily dark picture by focussing on the more extreme ways in which men are victims of the crisis of the family (and in which they, in turn, often victimize others). Typically, men's reactions are rarely the extremes — outwardly directed violence against women or inwardly directed violence against themselves. Yet sometimes the reactions are worrisome, and often times they are ominous. I can't help but remember a television interview with an obviously very prosperous male rancher after a fund–raising rally held by Colin Thatcher's Moose Jaw defence committee. At the time, Thatcher had finally been charged with the murder of his former wife, JoAnn Wilson, after a marriage break–up marked by bitter disputes over matrimonial property and child custody. The rancher said that there would be more and more men driven by economic desperation to murder their estranged wives if the legal principle of the equal division of matrimonial property remained unchanged. The impression was that the man believed Thatcher was possibly guilty, but that Thatcher's actions were at least understandable if not completely justified.

Perhaps less ominous, but nevertheless worrisome were Winston Cole's anti–feminist efforts at Dalhousie Law School in the early 1980s.[19] Cole, a law student, established a group called Men and the Law as a reaction against the law school's Women and the Law group, organized to promote women's concerns regarding sexism in the law and its administration. Comprised of 24 men and only one woman, who served as the group's secretary, the group was, Cole admitted, a "half–serious backlash against the feminism espoused by Women and the Law." Men were confused, he lamented, because they didn't "know whether the female students they sit beside want to be treated as academic colleagues or women."

Even more worrisome is the growing use of the law by men to control women.[20] The efforts of the boyfriends of Dodd and Daigle to use the courts to prevent them from obtaining abortions were only the most recent, highly publicized such efforts. More and more fathers' rights groups, largely composed of divorced and angry men, are being established. Although involving a very small number of men (a 1988 estimate by the *Globe and Mail*'s Ann

Rauhala put the number across the country at "about 80"), they are obtaining some supportive responses from politicians and the courts. The groups, like Toronto's In Search of Justice and Kitchener's Fathers for Justice, are explicitly anti–women and anti–women's equality. They are against any special treatment for women; therefore they oppose affirmative action and pay equity programs, the right of women to have reproductive choice, and the disbursement of government money to activist women's groups. They favour the father's right to have a veto on a woman's abortion decision and better legal protections for men accused of sexual assault. One fathers' rights activist said, "Women's groups say rape is rape. Rape is not rape ... we know the difference between a 90–year–old Sunday school teacher and the woman who's screwed every guy in Toronto. In Search of Truth provides aid to men accused of sexual assault by providing peer support and understanding." But the focus of such groups is "family issues — arrangement for custody, access, child support, parental benefits and alimony." Most importantly, they favour compulsory joint custody and forced mediation upon divorce. In an effort to gain wider support, the groups have begun muffling their more stridently anti–women positions, and many have joined the more moderate coalition, the Canadian Council for Family Rights, which calls for more equal treatment for men and women in the case of divorce, especially divorce involving children. As one father's rights activist said, "It's easier to sell equality than rights for men."

The lobby's efforts have had some success. More and more prominent politicians — like MP Sheila Copps and Ontario MPP James Henderson — have begun to support some of the groups' proposals, like sharing maternity benefits between men and women and forced joint custody. The recriminalization of abortion, if successful, will open the door to a whole series of legal interventions by individual men, fathers' rights groups, and the anti–choice crusade to prevent women from exercising reproductive choice by seeking an abortion.

A series of 1989 court decisions restricting the mobility of female custodial parents suggests that fathers' rights groups are beginning to influence the courts. These were cases where women

who had custody of the children after a marriage breakdown
wanted to relocate to another city. In each case, the father was
able to use the courts to prevent the woman's move on the grounds
that it would restrict his access to the children and thus have a
harmful effect on the children. In an analysis of the issue, the
Globe and Mail's Dorothy Lipovenko asked:

> If the shoe were on the other foot, would the courts compel a
> father who had custody to regulate his romantic interests or career
> ambitions around the needs of his children? Or, would a court tell
> a man who had access but not custody that he could not move
> because the children would be deprived of regular visits?

A law professor believes that indeed "the tables have been
turned: the onus is no longer on the non–custodial parent to prove
that changing living arrangements would harm a child's best interests; rather, it's the custodial parent who must now convince a
court that changing the status quo ... would benefit a child." For
Margrit Eichler, what is happening is crystal clear:

> It's an issue of control. What I find interesting is that fathers,
> via the courts, are having more of a say about their ex–wives than
> they did with their wives.

Regarding the generally increasing use of the law by aggrieved
men, Susan Crean agrees: "This is part of an anti–feminist
backlash. It is a regaining of control, or a way of regaining manhood." So does Michele Landsberg:

> It's one of those ironies of history that women, in fighting for
> rights, have handed the weapons to those who want to take away
> all the rights of women. It's all about control. It's really a comment
> on how angry and frustrated men are over the areas that used to
> be under their control.

On the more positive side, there are more than 5,000 men in
various groups across Canada trying to adjust to the new reality
in ways more supportive of women and the changing family. The

biggest network of such groups was set up by Ken Fisher's New Men, Partners in Change. Ottawa has eight groups, Victoria, 15, Toronto, nine; even Olds, Alberta, has one. And there are many others from coast to coast. The specific concerns of the groups vary, but they are all trying to get troubled men together to help each other change. They discuss questions like the restrictiveness of sexual stereotyping, the oppression of the masculine ideal, the price of masculinity, the nature and practice of sexism, the need to support affirmative action and pay equity programs for women, and the sources and consequences of sexual and physical male violence against women. Some of them engage in lobbying efforts on behalf of reforms of benefit to women. A few of the groups are composed of abusive men trying to change their behaviour.

The problems of adjustment men face clearly vary with the kind of family situation in which they participate. Men in traditional marriages face elevated levels of economic stress and a growing contradiction between their old–fashioned family life and the new reality of the increasing economic liberation of women. If their wives are traditional women, then the home front will not pose enormous difficulties, but outside the home in the market place, where they face competition from less traditional women, they will face elevated stress. Remarriage families and male–headed single parent families also pose unique coping problems for men. And the new norm in husband/wife families, the dual–income or dual–career family, requires tremendous readjustments on the part of men.

In fact, the dual–income, dual–career family is the most significant variation among the new emerging family forms, and the men involved in this family are making the most successful adjustment. Such a family is a decisive break with the traditional patriarchal family because it represents a attempted structural reconciliation of marriage and the family with women's growing economic independence. While all men must somehow adjust to growing female participation in the labour force, it is in the dual–income, dual–career family where that adjustment must occur most intimately. A traditional male can avoid or rationalize the new economic reality, and given the continuing advantages enjoyed by men in the world of work, he can even to some extent insulate himself from increasing female economic competition. But such insulation is more difficult to carry off if such a man's wife works outside the home. Even if the woman earns significantly less than her husband, and therefore her income can be seen as merely secondary or supplementary; even if she agrees to put the husband's career first; even if she continues to carry the full childcare and housekeeping load, the new domestic reality forces even the most traditional of men to make adjustments and concessions.

The new future of marriage and the family is being charted by the dual–income, dual–career family. For it is there, if anywhere, that Komarovsky's call for "a more harmonious society, which would release the creative potential of the female half of its citizens and provide a less constricted range of choices for males"[21] will be initially constructed and tested. It is there, if anywhere, that, following de Beauvoir, "men and women [will be able to] unequivocally affirm their brotherhood."[22] It is there, if anywhere, that Ehrenreich's hope for "some renewal of loyalty and trust between adult men and women"[23] will occur. And it is there, if anywhere, that Millett's

> [S]econd wave of the sexual revolution might at last accomplish its aim of freeing half the race from its immemorial subordination — and in the process bring us all a great deal closer to humanity. It may be that we shall even be able to retire sex from the harsh realities of politics, but not until we have created a world we can bear out of the desert we inhabit.[24]

Historically, women's oppression was inseparable from their economic dependence within the patriarchal family. It follows that women can never achieve liberation until the patriarchal family is dismantled and replaced by a family form that deliberately seeks to reconcile women's economic independence with fairly shared marital and parental obligations.

13 / The Double Burden: Men's Version

Although the double burden is primarily a female affliction, the problems associated with balancing job and family obligations are also confronted by men in two–earner families. Eichler has argued that "sexist [social] science fails to understand men" by tending "to downplay or ignore a potential conflict between work and home for men."[1] Surveying the paucity of research concerning the impact of the double burden on men, Eichler noted that in all work–related decisions — hours of work, overtime decisions, shift decisions, commuting distances, accepting a promotion or a transfer — many men seriously consider family impacts. Indeed, the available evidence is that work/family conflicts are felt by men almost as strongly as by women. Existing studies suggest "that men are aware of family/work conflicts within their own roles and that there are situations in which they are obviously willing to give precedence to the family role." Further, according to Eichler, available evidence indicates that men tend to *believe* in the principle of the equal sharing of domestic labour, but fail actually to live up to that belief. There is also a disagreement between the sexes regarding the perception of such sharing: men often perceive they are doing a larger share than the women perceive the men to be doing.

The reality of the double burden for men in dual–earner families was confirmed by Statistics Canada's 1986 General Social Survey of a sample of about 10,000 households.[2] Working men spend slightly under two hours a day on domestic work and childcare, while working women spend just over three hours. Further, "83 per cent of employed women participated in activities such as housecleaning and meal preparation, compared with just

51 per cent of men." On the other hand, men worked at their jobs over an hour a day longer than working women. As a result, "the total time invested in work outside the home and family care by employed men and women are roughly equal." Of course, these averages tell us little about variation among men. The eight–year study of two career families by Hochschild and Machung, cited in Chapter 7, found enormous variations among men regarding their commitment to sharing "the second shift."[3] While four in five men failed to engage in equal sharing, the other one did so. Only one in 10 men took on less than one–third of the household burden. Thus one must conclude some degree of a double burden conflict for nine out of 10 of the working husbands of working wives. Of course, doing the actual work is only part of the double burden. The other part is organizing and orchestrating the domestic campaign. Indeed, some marriage counsellors report that domestic chore conflicts are really of three kinds: conflicts over the sharing of the actual labour and time involved; complaints from wives about the hopeless incompetence of husbands and their need for constant supervision and encouragement; and complaints from husbands that their wives are too perfectionistic and often refuse to let them do certain tasks, preferring to do the work themselves to make sure it gets done right the first time.[4]

It is clear that equal sharing of domestic work is very rare.[5] In those couples where the husband's job is viewed as most important, even when working women do triple the domestic work of men and willingly reduce their own commitment to their jobs, women largely express the feeling that their husbands are doing a reasonable share. Women often continue to choose work easily reconciled with their primary obligation for the family and often consciously assign domestic chores to the husband that least disrupt his sense of "maleness." Interestingly, a husband's share of domestic work tends to go up when his wife's work has high prestige and high income. Indeed, some researchers have found a clear and direct positive correlation between the size of the wife's pay packet and the amount of domestic work the husband takes on. When the wife earns much less than the husband, he does much less domestic work. As the pay gap closes, his share of domestic work increases.

A major study by Gilbert of men in dual–career families found that the men's sex role attitudes were reflected in their participation in domestic work.[6] She identified three categories of such men. "Traditional" husbands help out, but leave the major responsibility to the working wife. "Participant" husbands take on a major share of domestic and childcare responsibilities, but still do considerably less than the women. "Role–sharing" husbands are more strongly committed to doing a fair share and strive to do so. Gilbert's study suggests that the husbands of working wives are going through a significant process of change and adjustment on the question of the double burden: even traditional husbands of working wives are acutely aware of, and concerned about, the injustices faced by women at work and at home.

Family and Job

Yet men do experience serious problems balancing work and family obligations. A U.S. study found that, while women indeed faced the greatest conflict, men were not all that far behind.[7] Twenty–five per cent of working fathers of babies and toddlers claimed that worries about childcare problems interfered with their productivity (this was true for 40 per cent of working mothers). Thirty–nine per cent claimed to have declined transfers, and 22 per cent claimed to have declined promotions, as a result of childcare problems (the figures for women were 50 per cent and 30 per cent, respectively). The study reported that four in five working parents had had to cope with family problems or crises during working hours, and 50 per cent of both working mothers and working fathers claimed to have felt stress both at work and in the home as a result of conflicts between family and job obligations. Among those experiencing stress, the rate of missed work, reports of difficulty getting up in the morning, perceived failures in job performance, and indications of health problems were all elevated. One should be cautious in interpreting such results. How each sex deals with the conflict they both emotionally feel is probably quite different, and the actual consequences might be very different. The man may *feel* the stress but carry on with his job commitments nonetheless. The woman would be more likely to act on the stress, say by cancelling an appointment or leaving work early. At the same time, however, we should not dismiss such evidence either.

There is one group of family men who cannot avoid the full impact of conflicts posed by the double burden — Canada's over 150,000 single fathers, especially the estimated 60,000 working fathers with sole custody. They face the same problems as single mothers but have two distinct advantages, higher incomes and much shorter durations of singleness. But until they remarry, they must balance job and kids and deal with loneliness and isolation, as well as sexual and emotional frustration. They experience much more uncertainty and doubt about their parenting abilities. The social awkwardness of being a male single parent is much greater than being a female single parent, if only because such families are so unusual and violate so many of our traditional sexist norms. Being a single father also challenges a man psychologically. As one social work professor put it: "The problems faced by the working single father are more than merely the logistical problems shared by all working parents. He has to change the way he feels about himself as a man."[8]

Single parent fatherhood interferes with a working father's career, just as it does a working mother's, but the impact can be more traumatic for the man because of his own self–expectations. Two U.S. studies on working single fathers reported that about 5 per cent were fired from their jobs and another 8 per cent quit because of work/family conflicts. Other negative impacts on the job included a reduction in work–related travel, a higher frequency of absenteeism, and more lateness and early leaving. About eight in ten of the fathers in the study found raising children either "very difficult" or "somewhat difficult." Such men have fewer emotional coping resources since they do not have the kind of female support networks to fall back upon that women often have. Obviously, the fact that single fathers have much shorter durations of single parent episodes has to do with their superior economic situation compared to women and the greater ease men have in explicitly pursuing a new spouse. But it also undoubtedly has to do with their desperation resulting from coping with the double burden and the looming potential economic crisis posed

by career setbacks. Such men discover very quickly that successful careers do not mix easily with the obligations of a primary
parent.

Costs and Trade–offs

Clearly, men in dual–job families are not routinely expected to
make career–related sacrifices for the sake of sustaining the
family. Indeed, the assumption that a man's family life and career
or job are quite independent of each other is so widely held that
there is very little research on the issue. The jobs men do are
organized as if the man's family did not exist. Further, men face
stronger negative reactions when they engage in "cross–sex role
behaviour."[9] Women in traditional male occupations are admired,
if stressed, whereas men in traditional female occupations are
looked at somewhat askance. Additionally, when men begin to
take on family obligations in ways that interfere with the job, they
face stronger negative reactions from colleagues and employers
than women face. If a man leaves meetings, declines promotions,
says no to transfers, or throttles back on his time on the job, he is
breaking the first rule of success — the job comes first. And it's
frequently true that men face a double standard: "Employers may
tolerate the tug of parental obligations in a woman, but they see
it as the mark of a wimp in a man."[10] As one executive trying to
balance job success with more time with his family put it:
"There's a cumulative impact of saying no to your kids, but
there's also a cumulative impact of walking out of meetings. It's
a tough balancing act."[11]

Gilbert studied the "costs or trade–offs" perceived by men in
dual–career families.[12] Among men in such families with children, some noted increased stress as a result of "physical and
emotional overload." Some regretted that they had had fewer
children than they might have had, while others regretted that they
had remained childless as a result of the couple's career commitments. There was decreased time for leisure activities and increased time spent on household tasks. A large group complained
of decreased sexual activity, though many conceded this could
have had as much to do with the presence of small children as

with their wife's job commitment. Others noted that their job mobility and career options had been limited. Although many noted that having a wife with a career usually enhanced their prestige among their colleagues, they did experience some hostility, envy, and jealousy, especially economic envy. This was particularly true of their more traditional colleagues and employers. But these men did not appear to express resentments about these "trade–offs," typically viewing them as having been freely negotiated and freely chosen.

Interestingly, only a handful mentioned the loss of male power, privilege, and prestige as costs associated with a commitment to a dual–career family. This suggests that the old patriarchal axiom — men benefit from women's oppression — is beginning to be eroded, especially among men with working wives. At a general level, men clearly benefit from women's economic oppression. Less pay for women in general means more pay for men in general. Fewer opportunities for women mean more opportunities for men. A promotion granted a woman is a promotion denied a man. A pay equity program for women in a corporation or civil service bureaucracy means less of the salary pie left over to be shared out among the men. But that very real set of general structural privileges is less attractive to men in two–earner families. A lower income for the wife means a smaller contribution to the family income and hence more economic pressure on the husband. Fewer opportunities for women means a cut in his wife's advancement and future salary. A pay equity program that increases his wife's paycheque means more family income. In other words, men implicated in the concrete new family form — the two–earner or dual–job family — benefit less and less from the remnants of male privilege and, in fact, *as individuals*, begin to suffer from the structure of male privilege. Structures of unjust and undeserved privilege are shaken by appeals to justice and equity. They are even more shaken when those on whose oppression the structure of privilege rests become restive and resistant and politically mobilized. They finally collapse utterly when those who benefitted from the structure finally realize that the former benefits have become costs. That process is well–advanced in two–earner families.

By and large the men making the most successful adjustment are therefore those involved in dual–income, dual–job families. The adjustment may be tentative, as in the case of one such man who said, "Sometimes I think, 'My father didn't do it that way, my friends don't do it that way, why should I?' But then I realize that those rules aren't in effect and it turns things from black and white to grey."[13] Or the adjustment may be full of lingering doubt, as expressed by another:

> There is no question that the rewards of sharing career, achievement, and childrearing with one's spouse are great, but the price paid can be high. It is a price, finally, that many of us never imagined we would have to pay, and therein lies much of the trouble ... We might learn to exult in the career attainment of our wives, even if we must sacrifice some of our own professional ambitions. We might find the time as well to be with our children and to be involved as a matter of course in the necessary household chores. We might even learn to give up the anger and resentment that is often engendered by the need to do all these things.[14]

But the adjustment is occurring, if sometimes reluctantly, as men come to realize that the only way they can have a satisfying and happy relationship with the changing woman is in the new family form that provides her with a degree of economic independence while presenting him with the need to change his ways. And social science is beginning to explode some persisting myths. One study, for example, found that men in dual–earner families are not more likely to be sexually unhappy than "real men" in traditional families. In fact, the very opposite was the case. Men married to working women were far less likely to suffer from "desire disorders" and "inhibited sexual excitement difficulties" than single–earner husbands.[15]

Gilbert's study found that men in dual–income, dual–job marriages must be consciously committed to making the relationship work, in marked contrast to traditional marriage, which men tended to take for granted and in which women were required to carry most of the load of sustaining the relationship.[16] Men must be willing to be more "flexible," "co–operative," "tolerant," and "accommodating." In other words, family arrangements become constantly negotiable and require continuing renewal through compromise. When a man becomes involved in such a family arrangement, even if he begins as a traditional male, the situation will require that he begin to change, and as his behaviour changes, his views, his self–concept, and his expectations inevitably begin to change. And as the marriage and family survives, and perhaps even flourishes, the man is awakened to the benefits of the arrangement.

In Gilbert's study even the so–called "traditional" men were acutely aware of the benefits of this new husband/wife family. The men agreed that there were three major clear benefits and a few minor ones. The increased family income enriched family life and provided a greater sense of economic security. The men felt that their spouses enjoyed increased contentment. Furthermore, they found that the establishment of independent identities enriched the lives of both partners. Many of the men, especially the traditional men, also noted that they felt less economic pressure. Finally, the overwhelming majority of the men felt they received "greater rewards from parenting."

Even more heartening for the future of the family are the effects of dual–income, dual–job families on the children raised in such families.[17] Most studies have found only positive effects, especially for adolescent girls, who are "more out–going, independent, active, highly motivated" than girls raised in traditional families. The positive effects are only slightly less for boys, probably because they are encouraged to develop positive attributes in any family situation. Children of dual–career families "are more independent, more resourceful ... more able to draw on a wide repertoire of role models ... they feel more self–directed, score higher on tests of verbal ability, and have a more affective relationship with their fathers ... than do peers raised in relatively traditional households." Such children are more flexible and less rigid in their views about sex–role behaviour. Boys raised in dual–career families, most particularly, manifest "fewer sex–related stereotypes." Interestingly and importantly, fathers in two–job families "place greater emphasis on expressivity and independence for sons *and* daughters and less emphasis on conformity to social norms" than fathers in more traditional marital arrangements. The fathers in Gilbert's study confirm this positive picture, mentioning the following benefits for their children of the dual–career arrangement: "exposure to a broader range of values and experiences," "greater independence and responsibility," "happier parents because of their career involvement," "quality time with parents," "the fathers being more involved with the children" and a wider range of "role–modeling." These positive consequences suggest that when the current generation of children, a majority of whom will have been raised in dual career families of some sort, establish families in the next century we may finally transcend the crisis of the family.

PART V

Conclusion:
Easing the Crisis

With comparative new freedom come new problems for which we, as a society, simply have not yet invented solutions. How does one combine the notion of autonomous individuals with that of long–time commitment? How can we create social structures in which individuals find personal freedom as well as personal security? How can we co–operate as equals when most of us have spent (and continue to spend) most of our time in hierarchical structures? How can there be equality of the sexes within families in a basically sexist society? How can we teach our children what we ourselves have not yet learned?

Margrit Eichler, *Families in Canada Today: Recent Changes and Their Policy Consequences* (Toronto: Gage, 1983), p. 343.

Introduction: Toward a New Family Policy

Neither Ottawa nor the provinces have a comprehensive, effective family policy. And vital areas — like child neglect and abuse — that are not politically glamorous suffer from an indefensible neglect. Alberta establishes an agency to deal with family violence and breakups, hoping to keep families together while dealing with family problems in the privacy of the home. British Columbia announces a $20–million counselling program for troubled families, including efforts to convince pregnant women to seek alternatives to abortion. Ottawa promises $40 million over four years to combat family violence, with half the money committed to establishing 500 new shelters for battered women, then suddenly cuts money for women's programs. Quebec offers cash to women for bearing babies, and in his 1989 re–election bid, Premier Bourassa offers to add the right to 34 weeks unpaid maternity (or paternity) leave to the existing 18 weeks of paid leave — and the fertility bribe is sweetened by promising new parents 60 per cent of salary for a full year after the birth of a third or subsequent child. The Tory–controlled Special House of Commons Committee on Child Care brags in its 1987 report about the $4.7 billion annually spent by Ottawa to help Canadian families with children.[1] Meanwhile 1990 Tory Ottawa hastens to assure us that there will indeed be a new childcare program to replace the one jettisoned after the 1988 election. Beset on the one side by a lobby hysterically defending the near–extinct traditional family, loudly supported by aggrieved fathers' rights and anti–choice groups, and on the other by feminists and others advocating family policies based on reality, many politicians equivocate. Others proclaim their unalterable dedication to dragging the family back into a past that exists only in their sentimental memories.

In other words, Canada does not have a family policy worthy of the name. Perhaps this is understandable, for major structural and policy changes inevitably result in pitched political battles. Incumbent politicians would insist Canada does have a family policy. The prime minister would point to family allowance, the maternity leave benefits under UIC, the child tax credit, the child tax exemption, the day care deduction, and the billions Ottawa transfers to the provinces through the Canada Assistance Plan. He would point to long–overdue reforms in family law affecting divorce, birth control, and abortion. And he would point to the equalization of women's legal status as a result of human rights legislation and the Canadian Charter of Rights. Provincial premiers would cite day care subsidies, improvements in the laws governing the division of matrimonial property upon marriage breakdown, family income supports, human rights laws and commissions, child protection agencies, and shelters for battered women. The problem, of course, is that the basic premise of these policies accumulated over the years is the traditional family. Furthermore, governments have not seen their role as intruding into family affairs, except in the most extreme circumstances. The policies were seen as "add–ons" to help the traditional family. And more recently they have often been seen as defences for that family. Even policies that responded to the new realities were implemented piece by piece, rather than as a comprehensive response to general structural change.

As Eichler points out, our existing complex array of policies is fundamentally flawed.[2] They either fail to recognize new emerging family forms altogether or discriminate against non–traditional families.

> The only case in which so–called family policies actually advantaged people on the basis of their marital status were those of breadwinner families, in which the wife is economically dependent on the husband.[3]

Besides this bias against women, which presumes and therefore reinforces their dependency, many such policies, especially those delivered through the tax system, are biased against the poor, and often the poor and women are the same.

The full extent of the failure of Canada's family policies becomes clear when we assess their lack of effect. Family poverty has not decreased significantly since the 1960s, and the slight gains made in the 1970s were largely erased in the 1980s. Income policies have failed to redistribute income at all since the 1950s — the only difference is that low–income individuals and families are now more dependent on government programs for a greater share of their meagre incomes. The programs have not prevented growing poverty among women, and indeed they have contributed to it by failing to address the economic problems of women with children after marriage failure. They have not rescued our children from poverty; child poverty rates have gone up alarmingly in the 1980s. Eichler provides a summary indictment:

> The major problems with the current system of [family oriented] social policies then, are that the system as a whole is confusing and hard to understand. It does not redistribute wealth from the rich to the poor, it penalizes women for bearing and rearing children, and does not facilitate the integration of fathers into the child rearing process.[4]

Canada desperately needs a new comprehensive mix of family policies that accomplishes a number of related, indeed inseparable, objectives. We need policies that recognize the changing nature of the family and contribute to the healthy emergence of the new family forms, without discriminating against those who remain committed to the traditional family. We need policies to help the victims of the crisis of the family — children, women and men — make the transition and the adjustment more easily. These self–evident policy objectives merely amount to a recognition of reality. But we also need policies that recognize that women's oppression, and the slowness of their climb to full justice, has been, and continues to be, importantly linked to their obligations to sustain the family. Further, since Canadian women bear the major burdens of the family's transition, primarily as a result of their child–bearing and –rearing responsibilities, we need policies that ensure a more equitable sharing of those responsibilities. Finally, since women's continuing economic inequality results importantly, though not completely, from the legacy of their traditional role in the family we need policies designed to accelerate women's achievement of economic equality. In a word, we need policies that recognize that the full emancipation of women can only occur when the family's transition to new, non–patriarchal forms has been completed.

These are not auspicious times to be talking about major new initiatives in social programs. All the talk now is of growing government deficits and the need for draconian cuts in public spending. But the same was true during the Great Depression and World War II. However, many persisted in advocating new policy departures in the interests of relieving human suffering and building a better future. Out of that debate Canada embarked on the elaboration of the social security net that we all enjoy today, and with which politicians, even those with sharp knives and gleaming eyes, tamper at their peril. And those programs were proposed, defended, and finally supported by Canadians because they promised a better life for Canadian families.

Today the family is in serious crisis. The policy proposals that follow represent a tentative effort to come to grips with the family's crisis. They are presented as ideas that logically flow from our considerations of that crisis. They are presented as an effort to provoke debate about what we can do to alleviate the self–evident suffering of so many Canadians.

14 / Program Directions in Family Policy

Day Care

The debate about day care has been particularly heated during the last five or six years. But there are certain agreements. Everyone agrees about the need for more spaces. Everyone agrees that more public money should be targeted at day care. In fact, 49 per cent of Canadians favour "increased tax spending to provide government subsidized day–care centres for pre–school children," including 66 per cent of those aged 18 to 29 years and 58 per cent of those aged 30 to 39 years.[1] Very few now argue that day care is harmful to children, and most agree that good quality day care is psychologically beneficial. There the agreement ends. Should day care be non–profit, or should we allow commercial centres? Or a mixture? How can we regulate the safety of the centres and the quality of care the children receive? How far should we extend licensing requirements? Should there be exceptions? How should the federal government's money for day care be spent? Where should day care centres be established?

Certain features of the debate are clear. Governments prefer payments to parents, leaving the actual establishment of day care spaces up to the co–operative efforts of parents, to the market place, or to institutional decisions at parents' places of work.

Parents and day care advocates are more concerned about *quality* and *accessibility*. A working parent wants to know that her or his child will receive excellent care, involving enriching programs and competent staff. A working parent wants day care that is accessible, both financially and in terms of location. Indirect funding makes quality control difficult. If parents receive a fixed subsidy or tax break, they face serious financial constraints on how much they can pay day care workers. A for–profit day care faces market constraints and the bottom line: quality will be as low as the market will bear. Even when governments are strongly committed to quality control through licensing and inspection, corners are cut if for no other reason than the chronic shortage of spaces. Even Ontario, with what is recognized as the best day care licensing and enforcement system in Canada, has an abysmal record on quality. In 1989, the *Globe and Mail* obtained 1,600 Ontario day care inspection reports and found that 40 per cent fell "short of the province's regulations on safety, cleanliness or quality … [W]hat emerged after a review of the reports was a picture of a child–care network whose quality and safety would shock parents."[2] The desire of governments to stay out of direct involvement in day care and parents' desire for quality and accessible day care are just not compatible.

What is urgently needed in Canada is a *publicly funded, universally accessible, quality–ensured* day care system. A national, shared–cost program, funded and delivered in the same way as the existing programs in health and education, could be jointly administered by provincial agencies to set and enforce standards, to distribute funds, and to provide program support services and a local, parent–elected board at each centre to hire the staff and to supervise day–to–day operations. A network of centres established in existing schools could also provide before and after–school care for school–age children. There would also be more convenient access for the parents, since their children's care would be in the neighbourhood.

In other words, the day care system would become the logical extension of our existing public and separate school systems. In the nineteenth century, we opted for a universally accessible, publicly funded school system for all children. Now the same arguments can be made to extend that system to all children of working parents. With good programming, such a system will produce more independent and happier kids. And it will provide immense practical and psychological comfort to their parents.

Further, the occupation of day care worker needs to be professionalized. Day care training programs, and more early childhood education programs, could be established and become a prerequisite for those who wish to pursue careers as day care educators. And day care work could become a career, much like teaching, with a decent income, a future, security, recognition and prestige. Day care work today is characterized by low wages, few benefits, little prestige, and no future. Even well–educated and competent people attracted to day care work can rarely afford to stay very long, even when the work is a source of much satisfaction.

Ideally, the program might be entirely publicly funded, while making some provision for degrees of accessibility for non–working mothers in traditional families. An alternative could be to establish a transitional system funded primarily by federal and provincial money, plus a reasonable user fee based on income. The problems of freedom of choice could be initially resolved by continuing the day care tax deduction for those who want an alternative to the public system. But that problem would quickly disappear as the public system proved itself and gained wide acceptance.

The benefits of such public day care cannot be overstated. The anxieties of working parents, especially single parents and working mothers, would be alleviated. The problems associated with the poor supervision of many of the children of working parents would be resolved. The negative psychological consequences for children of poor quality care would become things of the past. Most importantly, such a system would systematically grant women, as a recognized community sanctioned public right, degrees of freedom during significant portions of the day from primary parenting responsibilities. And the decision to have children would be less profound in its consequences for both parents. Assured access to quality day care would make the decision to have a child rendered somewhat less fraught with difficulty.

Maternity, Paternity, and Parental Leave

Canada's maternity leave program, administered through the unemployment insurance system, has filled an obvious need. In 1987 four of every 100 working women took maternity leaves.[3] Over nine in 10 of these were compensated leaves, and most of these (72 per cent) derived benefits from unemployment insurance funds. Another one in five women on maternity leave received full or partial compensation for lost pay from employers or group insurance plans. Federal and provincial labour laws currently grant women the legal right to 17 or 18 weeks of unpaid maternity leave. The UIC program guarantees a working woman a compensated maternity leave of 15 weeks at 60 per cent of her wage to a maximum in 1989 of $363 weekly. There is a two–week waiting period before benefits begin, and the woman must have worked at least 20 weeks in the previous 12 months. Quebec has the best system of maternity leave and has promised to extend it further.[4]

While our current system is much better than that prevailing in the U.S., Canada lags far behind most other industrialized nations, which provide 90 to 100 per cent compensation for lost wages, with a variable cap, for periods extending up to a year and more.[5] For example, West Germany provides six months at full pay, while Italy provides a more modest five months at 80 per cent of pay. Sweden is probably best — 12 months at 90 per cent of pay, slated to increase to 15 months this year and 18 months next year.[6] Such benefits are often available to either parent. Currently in Canada biological fathers are not eligible for the benefits, but adoptive fathers are. Ottawa has moved to remove that anomaly by adding on 10 weeks of paid parental leave to the existing 15 weeks and allowing the parents to decide whether the father or the mother will take the leave.[7] How soon these extra benefits will be available to all Canadians will depend on how quickly the provinces amend their labour laws to give statutory effect to Ottawa's program.

Canada needs to go further. Why not entitle women to a full year of maternity leave at 100 per cent of their foregone pay, with a maximum based at least on the average full–time industrial wage? The waiting period could be eliminated. But lost wages are only one of the economic penalties women face. There are also negative consequences in terms of normal salary increments, merit pay, and promotions. Therefore, federal and provincial labour laws could provide a statutory prohibition of any employer's use of a pregnancy–related absence to deny a woman job

advancement and salary increments. Furthermore, women returning from maternity leave, which they had taken as a legal right
despite an employer's displeasure, sometimes find themselves
dismissed from the job very soon after. Quebec currently forbids
the dismissal of a woman returning from maternity leave during
the first 20 weeks back on the job. Why not extend this protection
to a year and provide it to women across Canada?

The move to a full year of maternity/parental benefits would
go some distance in resolving the controversy regarding paid
paternity leave. Although Gallup reported in 1986 that a majority
of Canadians — 52 per cent — opposed paid paternity leave,[8]
court decisions have made it clear that it is discriminatory to deny
men some form of paid leave. One typical initial response was the
proposal by MP Sheila Copps to allow the mother and father to
decide who would take what portion of the 15 weeks available.
This was criticized by many as granting men something by taking
it away from women. Majorie Cohen called it "equality with a
vengeance."[9] Ottawa's response of adding 10 weeks of paid leave
that can be shared, while retaining the initial 15 weeks for the
mother, was an effort to find some middle ground. Extending the
period of paid pregnancy–related parental leave to a full year,
while perhaps stipulating that at least the first four or five months
must go to the mother, could enable couples more easily to negotiate how the rest of the leave might be shared.

Canada's working parents require another kind of parental
leave relating to ongoing child care responsibilities. Currently
when a parent misses work for a family–related reason, most feel
compelled to use sick leave days or holiday time to avoid a loss
of pay. What has been called "family responsibility leave" is
extremely rare in Canada.[10] Most federal civil servants, and public
employees in some provinces, have been able to negotiate paid
"personal leave" clauses into their contracts, ranging from two to
10 days a year. Few unions in the private sector have been as
successful, and the business lobby — like the Canadian Manufacturers' Association and the Canadian Federation of Independent
Business — is stridently opposed to such benefits. Again, Quebec
has led the way, granting employees the statutory right to five
days parental responsibility leave each year, including two with

pay. Quebec also provides parents a degree of protection when job obligations might conflict with family obligations — employees with children must be given at least 12 hours notice by an employer requesting overtime. Federal and provincial labour laws could be amended granting parents up to 10 days of paid family responsibility leave each year. Further, parents should be provided with the statutory right to refuse, without penalty, unusual job demands — like overtime or work–related travel — that interfere with their family obligations.

The general objective of such policies is clear. If we want parents, particularly mothers, to work; if we want to ensure that parents, especially women, do not pay economic penalties as a result of bearing and rearing children; if we want to establish conditions that ease the decision to have children for working parents; and if we want to ease the stress faced by working parents carrying the double burden, then work ought to stop being organized in ways which assume that family obligations do not exist. We already know that family obligations are not easy to reconcile with work obligations, again, more particularly for working women. Work therefore must become more reconcilable with family obligations.

Family Breakdown, Mediation, and Counselling

Though the grounds have been eased, divorce remains largely adversarial, especially over the division of property and child custody. There has been progress on the property question with the presumption of the joint contribution to marital property and its more or less equal division. But child custody battles frequently continue to be very bitter. The notion of no–fault divorce and the realization that at some point it is best for all concerned to end a troubled marriage have both gained wide acceptance. Given that divorce is no longer an exceptional event, perhaps it is time to refer questions of separation, divorce, property division, and child custody to a system of non–adversarial family courts with *exclusive jurisdiction*. Guided by the principles of natural justice and sexual equality, such a system could minimize the suffering that is frequently inflicted by our present system.

More extensive family counselling services are urgently required, not just to help those going through the divorce process, but also those in troubled marriages who might avoid divorce. More adequate preparation for marriage could ensure more realistic decisions.[11] Studies have also shown the diminishing satisfaction with marriage among new parents and the effect of intervention and counselling on marital adjustment to a first child.[12] The counselled couples felt more in control and more hopeful, whereas those who did not receive counselling felt "overwhelmed, impotent, hopeless and alienated." Such studies suggest that a wider network of counselling and support services and a deeper commitment to family life education, including marriage and parenting preparation, could help many adjust successfully to marriage and to children who might otherwise fail.

The most important negative impact on children of divorce is the loss of a parent. Studies have shown that frequently even non–custodial fathers have more to do with their children after a divorce than before, that continuing non–conflictful access to both parents is good for children, and that children in joint custody arrangements adjust better than those in sole custody arrangements. Joint custody also tends to reduce relitigation rates between estranged spouses, and other studies have suggested that parents in joint custody arrangements are happier than those in sole custody arrangements. But studies of joint custody have found that children still felt conflicting loyalties and experienced stress as a result of living in two different homes. As well, joint custody creates particular adjustment difficulties for pre–school children and for adolescents. Further, joint custody ought not to be forced, since it puts many women at a grave disadvantage. The question of custody, therefore, might then be determined on a case by case basis. If the divorce process can be made less angry and conflictful, and if both parents recognize the importance to the child of a continuing relationship with both parents, joint custody will become increasingly the arrangement of choice.

Finally, the economic consequences of marriage breakdown for women and their children have to be remembered. Although the 1986 divorce reforms make clear that the principal objective of support payments to formerly dependent spouses (overwhelmingly

women) is to encourage the achievement of economic independence after a reasonable period, most men continue to evade
their economic obligations. Similarly, men often evade paying
child support. The current willingness of most provinces to pursue
men who try to renege on these obligations is to be applauded.
Indeed, enforcement must become more vigorous.

Family Violence

Society has acknowledged the seriousness of family violence, but
women and children who are beaten and otherwise abused need a
more comprehensive network of shelters. The shortage of safe
havens often drives desperate women back to their battering
husbands because they do not have anyone to turn to for help and
protection.[13]

By the time a battered woman calls for help, usually only after
many previous violent episodes, the situation calls for vigorous
action. Police forces and crown prosecutors could establish a
policy that every battering husband will be charged and that the
charge will be laid independent of the wishes of the victim. If
battering men knew with certainty that they would be charged and
tried, they might reflect before the violent event, and certainly
they would be forced publicly to confront what they had done
afterwards. And if battered wives knew that the response to a plea
for help would be prompt, they might be more likely to ask for help.

Courts have to become much less lenient with men who are
convicted. This means that the attitudes of many judges have to
be changed — like that of the Quebec judge who said in court,
"Rules are like women, they are made to be violated."[14] As long
as sexist attitudes exist among the police and the judiciary, violence against women will be taken less than seriously, and men
will continue to believe that they can get away with battering. A
policy of prompt arrest, the laying of charges, and the move to a
speedy trial would send a clear message that the community finds
such behaviour intolerable.

In cases of family violence against children, the problems of
detection are paramount. Children can rarely call for help, and if
they do they are unlikely to be taken seriously. All provinces

should strengthen and more vigorously enforce existing laws that place a clear obligation on those who regularly come into contact with children to report suspected cases of abuse or neglect. Effective education and propaganda campaigns among such groups of professionals could teach them how to detect, and to deal with, suspected cases. Child protection agencies need more social workers and a clearer mandate to intervene to protect abused children. And the foster homes and other facilities where children are placed for their protection cry out for improvement and more close supervision.

The message must be clear and unmistakeable. No institution — not even the family — is so sacred and private that the community will take no action to protect victims of violence.

Family Poverty and Child Hunger

Family policy alone cannot solve the problems of economic injustice. But we could eliminate child hunger easily. And we could eliminate child poverty. Hot breakfast and lunch programs in schools and community centres in targeted areas afflicted by child hunger are an obvious and vital first step. The overwhelming majority of Canadians would agree that no child in this country should suffer from hunger and would therefore support the measures necessary to feed children. More controversial, and more costly, would be a policy commitment to end child poverty. If we indeed believe that the impact of poverty on children in their formative years is unacceptable, and if we realize that the long–term emotional and economic costs of child poverty are incalculably high, then a commitment to end child poverty is not beyond our grasp.

Back in the optimistic sixties there was a lot of talk about the guaranteed annual income. The idea was simple. Abolish all programs involving government income transfers to individuals and families and substitute a comprehensive guaranteed annual income to ensure that all Canadians enjoy income levels sufficient to live a reasonable life. The idea was suffocated by the economic difficulties of the 1970s and 1980s, but every now and then the idea is reproposed by a politician or an interest group. Canadians do believe that everyone should be guaranteed a tolerable level of material existence, and they are willing to consider new ideas of how that might be best achieved as long as such "new" ideas do not camouflage a hidden agenda to dismantle some of the social security gains made over the years. But such ideas raise anxieties about means tests, criteria for cut–offs, and the threat to universality.

Canadians might therefore support the idea of a guaranteed annual income, fixed at the Statistics Canada poverty line (or at a more generous one, like the Senate's or CCSD's), *for all families with dependent children.* Such an income would not be great, and poverty, in the real rather than the official sense, would not disappear. But it would be an important step in the elimination of some of the more extreme forms of deprivation faced daily by a million Canadian children.

Well–Family Clinics

Schools are an expensive public infrastructure that exists from coast to coast and to which all who have school–age children are daily linked. When one reflects on how to deliver many of the family programs proposed, the task seems complex and expensive. But school buildings need not just be used for educational and recreational purposes. Schools could become important neighbourhood centres where programs are established and delivered to improve family life. The day care program could be delivered in existing schools. Schools, and perhaps targeted community centres, are probably the best places to deliver breakfast and lunch programs. And it is the teachers, more than any single group, who will be most likely first to notice evidence of possible child abuse and/or neglect.

Schools, or at least selected schools, would also be a logical place to establish a network of Well–Family Clinics, staffed by family physicians, nurses, and counsellors. Such clinics could run family life educational programs, provide sexual and birth control counselling for adolescents, and help troubled families, as well as deliver primary health care. Schools could become, then, centres of support for family life in the neighbourhood. For children, schools could become places of protection and nurturance in times of trouble and conflict.

A fantasy? Perhaps. But let us not forget that our very recent ancestors went through the disruptions and horrors of the Industrial Revolution, many political revolutions, two World Wars, and a devastating depression, leaving us with one of the most advanced, prosperous and caring countries in the world. Comparatively, building a network of family support programs, and centres to house them, to help us through the present crisis of the family seems an eminently modest proposal.

More Government Funding for NGO Advocacy and Service Goups

Many of the supports the family in transition requires cannot be directly provided by government bureaucracies. Indeed, government agencies may be the least efficient and acceptable means of delivering many programs. Therefore, more public funds could be made available to non–government organizations (NGOs) involved in family–related and women–related advocacy and service activities. Programs involving family life education, abortion and birth control counselling, and early marriage preparation are probably best left to groups like Planned Parenthood, with the active co–operation of federal, provincial, and local government agencies. Counselling groups for battering males might best be established by men's groups that include former batterers as counsellors. Troubled families might more readily seek help from family counselling services that are clearly independent of government, perhaps established by the social agencies of churches or groups of professionals organized in community–controlled practices. Shelters for battered women are probably best run by sympathetic women's groups or voluntary community organizations, whose staff would include former victims. But such efforts need government funds, organizational help, and some degree of inspection and regulation. Perhaps a line should be drawn at services for abused, neglected, and disturbed children. The record of private agencies has not been very reassuring. Child welfare and protection programs would be best run by government agencies with clear policies and regular inspection to ensure that the interests of the children in care are always paramount.

Although the service function of NGOs is clearly important, of perhaps more general importance is their advocacy function through education and propaganda efforts. Women's groups, pro–women men's groups, non–government service organizations, and the reproductive choice movement can all go much further in advocacy and in alerting the public to family and women–related problem areas than government agencies are typically willing or allowed to go. A great many of the problems of adjustment to the new realities are attitudinal. We should not therefore underestimate the effectiveness of education and propaganda not only in convincing people to accept the changes, but also in helping them to come to terms with them in their minds, hearts, and personal lives.

All these policy proposals imply a profound shift in our attitude to the family. Community supports and interventions amount to a recognition that sustaining the family is a shared social responsibility. The desire to resist the intrusion of public policy into the family is understandable. But surely there is no basic contradiction between our individual right to a private family life and our collective obligation to provide supports essential to helping the new emerging family forms survive and flourish.

15 / Proposed Directions in Feminist Policy

Family policies developed in isolation from policies designed to deliver justice to women cannot hope to succeed. The fact is women's struggle for justice has moved forward in tandem with emerging family forms. Any policy mix to deal with the family's crisis must also come to grips with the central issues on the feminist agenda today.

Reproductive Choice

Women's reproductive choice, including the unfettered access to abortion services, is *not* a family issue. It is an issue of women's rights and freedoms. Indeed, it is arguably one of the most profound issues of women's rights at the present time in Canada.[1] Forced pregnancy was a central feature of the traditional patriarchal family. Until 1969 women were legally proscribed from abortion under any circumstances; indeed birth control measures were illegal if practised for birth control rather than for an acceptable "medical" reason — to prevent venereal disease or to deal with problems of menstrual regularity. After 1969, birth control was legal, but women seeking abortions had to go through the degrading process of seeking the permission of a therapeutic abortion committee at "an accredited or approved hospital" for medical reasons. Many women routinely got around the effort at control with the help of sympathetic doctors and abortion committees, but access was limited and uncertain. Anti–choice activists harassed doctors and hospitals and launched court actions to deny access to abortion.

Dr. Henry Morgentaler symbolized the crusade for women's right to reproductive choice by establishing free–standing abortion clinics and openly defying the law. In 1970, he was charged with two counts of conspiracy to perform an abortion. In 1973, a Montreal jury acquitted him. In 1974, the Quebec Court of Appeals quashed the acquittal, and Morgentaler was sentenced to 18 months in jail. He was acquitted of similar charges in 1975 and 1976, whereupon the Quebec attorney–general ordered a stop to prosecutions against him. In 1983 Morgentaler and seven others were charged with procuring abortions in Winnipeg, and he and two others were charged in Toronto. In 1984 Morgentaler lost his challenge to the abortion law under the Charter in the Ontario Supreme Court. That same year a Toronto jury again acquitted him, but in 1985 the Ontario Court of Appeal overturned the jury's decision and ordered a new trial. In 1986 Morgentaler appealed to the Supreme Court of Canada, alleging that the abortion law violated women's rights under the Charter. In January 1988 he was completely vindicated — the Supreme Court restored the original jury acquittals in the 1984 Toronto case and ruled, five to two, that the federal abortion law was unconstitutional. In the majority decision, Chief Justice Brian Dickson and Justice Antonio Lamer said:

Forcing a woman, by threat of criminal sanction, to carry a fetus to term unless she meets certain criteria unrelated to her own priorities and aspirations, is a profound interference with a woman's body and thus an infringement of security of the person.

But Justice Bertha Wilson went further

The right to liberty contained in section 7 guarantees to every individual a degree of personal autonomy over important decisions intimately affecting his or her private life. Liberty in a free and democratic society does not require the state to approve such decisions, but it does require the state to respect them.

A woman's decision to terminate her pregnancy falls within this class of protected decisions. It is one that will have profound psychological, economic and social consequences for her ... It is not just a medical decision; it is a profound social and ethical one as well.

The Supreme Court decision did leave the door open to some future possible legislation to protect a potentially viable fetus in the advanced stages of pregnancy, but it made it clear that any interference in a woman's abortion decision during the early stages of a pregnancy would violate her rights.

Subsequently, Canadians have been subjected to a spectacle of indecision, political cowardice, and irresponsibility as the government and the House of Commons scrambled to respond to the Court's decision. The outcome is a new proposed abortion law that has pleased no one and continues to violate women's rights and freedoms. The law puts abortion back in the Criminal Code, making it illegal unless a woman's health, very broadly and liberally defined, is threatened. A doctor performing an abortion is liable to imprisonment if he or she performs an abortion for reasons other than a threat to physical or mental health.

Although an improvement on the old law, the new law neither guarantees access nor forces provinces to cover the procedure under medicare. Further, a woman who wants an abortion will have to shop around for a willing doctor, and the old degrading charade will have to recommence; women who aren't mentally or physically threatened by the pregnancy will have to pretend to be so. And doctors performing the service will be constantly looking over their shoulders, fearing lawsuits from anti–choice groups and estranged biological fathers. A mature, healthy, emotionally stable woman can be legally denied an abortion, and a physician who respects her right to make the decision faces two years in prison. This renders the new law as constitutionally invalid as the old and for the very same reasons. The law will ultimately be struck down by the Supreme Court.

Why put women through another period of uncertainty while the issue is again fought through the courts? What will the state do when Morgentaler, or some other physician, courageously declares publicly that he or she has performed a number of abortions just because the women wanted to terminate the pregnancies?

The "rights of the unborn" are a matter for theology, not for the state and the law. They concern personal religious conscience. Some believe that human life starts at conception, others at "quickening," others at birth. The right to unfettered reproductive choice for women would not mean that a woman who believed that human life started at conception would be forced to have an abortion. The fact that the Supreme Court did recognize the possibility of fetal rights of some sort in the later stages of pregnancy — presumably when a fetus is theoretically viable — does not enunciate a legal principle of the right to life of the unborn. It simply says that the state *may* have a reasonable and arguable case for deliberately violating a woman's rights in such circumstances.

The best situation would be to have the criminal law remain silent. Those opposed to abortions could decline to have them and even continue their aggressive proselytizing efforts to win others to their views. But those women who wanted abortions could obtain them.

In important ways this new abortion law is one of the last gasps of the legally constituted patriarchal family. It seeks to control women. It seeks to make them something less than full legal persons. It seeks to intervene in their personal lives in ways that men would never tolerate. It is probably true that most women who want abortions — assuming fair geographical access and medicare funding — will be able to get them under this new law. Yet to do so they will have to present themselves as flawed, troubled, and less than whole persons before the throne of legal patriarchy.

Economic Equality

The reasons for women's persisting economic inequality are complex. Partly it has to do with women's recent entry into the labour force and the legacy of inferior education and training. Partly it has to do with the ghettoization of women into low paying jobs. Partly it has to do with women's own lower labour market aspirations. Partly it has to do with women's primary responsibility for home and family. And finally, it has to do with outright sexual discrimination. Taken together, these reasons reinforce a structure of sexual discrimination in the economy. Equality before the law and laws demanding equal pay for equal work have proven inadequate to ensure women economic equality.

As a result, the argument that the only way forward was through programs of pay equity and affirmative action was accepted. Equal pay for the same work will only protect those women who manage to break into traditional male occupations. Women in traditional female occupations will continue to suffer pay discrimination. The solution is pay equity — or equal pay for work of equal value. Affirmative action programs would help women to obtain access to traditional male occupations and to advance within them. Taken together these two policies could begin to attack the structures of sexual discrimination in the job market. But pay equity and affirmative action programs require real structural changes, cost real dollars, and take away real male privileges.

As recently as 1980, the Retail Council of Canada, representing most of the country's largest retailers and comprising one of the most notoriously underpaid female job ghettos, complained that pay equity for women would hurt the economy by driving labour costs up.[2] In 1982 Ontario's Labour Minister explained that he opposed a pay equity law because it would close businesses and drive people out of work.[3] In 1984 the Canadian Chamber of Commerce declared its opposition to equal pay for work of equal value.[4]

The campaign against pay equity and affirmative action suffered a serious blow after the release of Judge Abella's report of her Royal Commission on Equality in Employment.[5] Although it focussed on four structurally disadvantaged groups — women, native people, the disabled, and visible minorities — by far the greatest significance of the report was its impact on the debate about pay equity and affirmative action programs as necessary means to achieve equality for women. The judge insisted that only tough interventionist measures could successfully combat discrimination in the work world. Women particularly needed barriers removed by means of programs involving day care, affirmative action, equal pay for work of equal value, and educational leave. She argued forcefully that only positive action would remove the barriers and that not to act to remove them was to "tolerate prejudice and discrimination." She concluded,

> It is not that individuals in the designated groups are inherently unable to achieve equality on their own, it is that the obstacles in their way are so formidable and self–perpetuating that they cannot be overcome without intervention.[6]

The MacDonald commission on the economy nevertheless advocated that programs of equal pay for work of equal value be shelved until further research could be done on their long–term economic consequences.[7] But the tide had already turned. In the 1984 election campaign, the leaders of all three major federal parties publicly declared themselves committed to affirmative action and pay equity programs.

By 1985, Ottawa, Quebec, Ontario, Manitoba, the Northwest Territories, and the Yukon Territory either had put in place, were committed to putting in place, or were seriously studying programs of equal pay for work of equal value. By and large, these were directed at the public sector. But Ottawa's law was directed at corporations in federal jurisdiction, and provinces like Manitoba and Ontario indicated that programs in the private sector would follow very quickly on the heels of programs in the public sector, if not simultaneously. The business lobby and its friends became very uneasy. The Canadian Manufacturers' Association declared such programs would close down businesses. The Canadian Federation of Independent Business said, "Equal pay can only have a negative impact on employment. For small business the concept is totally unworkable."

In 1987 Ontario led the way in Canada with comprehensive pay equity legislation affecting both the public and private sectors.[8] Employers in the provincial public sector were enjoined to formulate pay equity plans within two years. Improvements in women's salaries were to start at that time. Full pay equity is to be achieved five years after the plans are in place. Theoretically, then, the sex–related pay gap in the Ontario public sector should disappear by 1994 or 1995. The requirements for the private sector are somewhat less stringent, based upon the size of the firm. Though it excludes the estimated 238,000 women employed in enterprises with fewer than 10 employees, it covers 87 per cent of the 1.7 million working women in Ontario. The improvements in pay are to come from a fund to be established by each employer of 1 per cent of the total payroll. At the expiration of the time period allowed for developing a plan and beginning its implementation, employees will have the right to seek redress through Ontario's Pay Equity Commission, and employers will be obliged to demonstrate that they have achieved pay equity. The fulminations of the small business lobby leading up to the bill's passage had obviously been effective: smaller employers were given more time to implement the policy, and those with fewer than 10 employees were exempted.

In the aftermath of the adoption of the law, the opposition of Ontario's business lobby became very much louder, condemning pay equity "as costly, ineffective ... a threat to women's jobs" and "a massive intrusion in the free market."[9] The president of the Ontario Chamber of Commerce argued that the legislation would actually hurt women:

> Once you raise the salaries, it forces employers to look at those jobs which were paying $15,000 a year and ask if they still need them at $20,000 a year ... There will be fewer jobs — because employers will eliminate them ... The guy working under the truck in the cold may now decide he would rather be inside answering the telephone. He will compete for a job once held by a woman.

Employers expressed worries about the Pay Equity Commission, arguing that it will be costly to administer and jeopardize Ontario's competitiveness with the U.S.

Business protest notwithstanding, by 1988 pay equity programs had become well–established across Canada.[10] All provinces, with the predictable exceptions of Alberta and Saskatchewan, and the federal government now either have in place, or have promised quickly to put in place, pay equity programs for the public service. Ontario is the only province to have extended the program to the private sector. Now the debates are increasingly about how to determine and compare the value of jobs to an employer and just how much of the sex pay gap is clearly the result of sexual discrimination. Ontario's program established four criteria for assessing the value of jobs: skills, effort, responsibility, and working conditions. The government also provides advice on assessment procedures. Disputes will ultimately be settled by the Pay Equity Commission. Time, research, experience, and continuing argument will allow that issue to work itself out.

The question of how much of the pay gap between men and women specifically results from sex discrimination is potentially controversial. Phillips and Phillips argued that studies generally suggest that about one–half of the sex pay gap results from forms of sexual discrimination, the other half from women's inferior training and experience.[11] In 1988 Ontario's Pay Equity Commissioner presented a much more modest figure, arguing that about one–third of Ontario's 36 per cent sex pay gap is the result of "genuine male–female wage discrimination ... the rest can be attributed to experience, education and non–gender–based employment equity issues."[12] Feminists and their supporters will argue for a much wider conception of sex discrimination. Government and business will tend to argue for a very narrow one. To what extent is a woman's lack of training and experience a result of forms of sex discrimination? Does a woman's required absence from the labour market to bear and raise children, and the subsequent negative economic consequences of that, constitute sex discrimination? For the first time, as a society, we are legally committed to a close scrutiny of job value and sexual discrimination in pay.

Pay equity programs are easier to assess more or less objectively than affirmative action programs. In matters of value of work, clear criteria can be established, jobs compared, and pay levels codified. Effective affirmative action programs are more difficult to put in place and to monitor. Gaining access for women to traditional male occupations is difficult, because the gatekeepers jealously and zealously guard the portals and have endless good reasons for their choices. A university hiring committee will always have good, sound academic reasons for why they chose the man over the woman. Even in cases where, on paper, the woman is manifestly superior, defensible if vague reasons can always be found. Reasons for hiring and promoting people are notoriously subjective, and most of them have to do with the biases of those making the initial recommendation or decision. That is why the board and administration of a corporation, or a university, or a civil service bureaucracy can elaborate the most elegant and impressive sounding affirmative action plan for women and find later that it isn't working. Voluntary affirmative action programs have been around for almost two decades, yet they have made very little overall difference in the occupational discrimination women face.

In response to that reality, in June 1986 Ottawa passed the Employment Equity Act, and in October 1986 established the Federal Contractors' Program.[13] The act applied to federal crown corporations and corporations operating in areas of federal jurisdiction. They were given two years to come up with an affirmative action plan to eliminate discriminatory employment barriers against women, native people, the disabled, and visible minorities. The plan had to provide positive opportunities for employment, and for advancement. The Contractors' Program imposed similar requirements on all companies doing business with, or having contracts with, the federal government or its agencies exceeding $200,000. Strict reporting requirements were also put in place to allow the monitoring of achievement of the stated goals. Such corporations had to sign an undertaking to adhere to the program in order to continue to be eligible for government business.

The legislation sounded good on paper. But a 1990 report declared that the employment equity law was failing miserably.[14] An assessment of the reports of 372 affected corporations and companies, employing over 600,000 workers, found that women had made few gains — the pay gap between men and women in the companies had closed by only one–half of 1 cent over a year, and promotions going to women had not increased significantly. There are no clear enforcement mechanisms, nor a clear set of sanctions to be applied against those who do not comply. Granted Ottawa can refuse contracts, but that has only been used against those who fail to sign up; it has not been suggested that such sanctions will be applied against those companies which go through the motions, continue to claim to be trying, and promise to try harder. Nor are there any clear sanctions to ensure that federal agencies, crown corporations, departments, or companies active in federally regulated sectors will comply seriously.

The only clear sanctions are via the federal Human Rights Commission. The Commission does indeed have the authority to impose strict affirmative action requirements, including hiring quotas, on offenders. In the famous CN case the Commission ruled that CN would have to hire women in one in four job vacancies until women had 13 per cent of the total jobs, a percentage equal to the average of blue collar jobs held by Canadian women at that time. But this puts the onus for enforcing the affirmative action law on women — or the other disadvantaged groups — rather than on the federal government. And when enforcement depends not just on a victim's complaint, but on a victim's having the willingness and resources to mount an effective prosecution, then enforcement becomes a bad joke. Voluntary affirmative action programs are now widely seen as scandalously ineffective. The necessity for mandatory affirmative action programs is now widely accepted, and even embodied in a federal law, however inadequately. What is now needed is the will to make mandatory affirmative action programs effective through diligent enforcement and the establishment of precise and compulsory objectives.

What is clearly happening in the struggle for women's economic equality is that, as a society, we are now trying to make the painful structural transition from words to action. In the 1960s and the 1970s rhetoric on women's economic equality was codified into impressive policies and laws designed to grant women economic justice. They did not work, or at least failed to work as quickly as expected for as many women as hoped. But the words and laws symbolized a move to a deepening political acceptance that the injustices faced by women had to be rectified. The words and laws tracked a reshaping of the society's political will and the establishment of a new consensus. Having committed ourselves to the words of equality, we could not forever avoid the required actions. The 1980s witnessed the commencement of the process, which will accelerate in the 1990s, of translating those words into action. Systems of privilege are rarely easy to dismantle, and the system of male economic privilege will not be an exception. If we succeed we will emerge in a better place to live as men and women.

Afterword:
A Joyous Funeral

The human species invented the family somewhere in its dark pre–history. It proved the secret of our evolutionary success as a species. But like all human inventions, the family has had to be continuously reinvented.

During the Neolithic Revolution, some ten or fifteen thousand years ago, the human family went through a major reinvention as it developed agriculture and learned how to domesticate animals. The old hunting and gathering family, in which the two sexes enjoyed rough equality as a result of mutual economic interdependence, was replaced by patriarchal family forms. Women were enslaved and consigned to the home and hearth under the control of men. The simple and complementary sexual division of labour was replaced by a separation of human life into the public economic sphere, dominated by men, and the domestic sphere, where women were subordinated.

During the Industrial Revolution, two to three hundred years ago, the human family had to be reinvented again in fundamental ways. The patriarchal family form was reinforced, and the separation between the public sphere and the private domestic sphere increased. Initially women were more deeply enslaved and became more deeply dependent. But the Industrial Revolution also set the stage for the increasing liberation of women, both politically and economically. As women achieved more recognition of their rights as persons, conceptions of the family changed. The modern industrial nuclear family emerged based on a new family ideology in which men and women married for love and carried out their obligations to each other and to their children as wives and husbands. Woman's place was in the home. Man's place was outside the home in the public economic sphere where he earned the family's daily bread. But even as women continued to win legal recognition as persons and more complete civil and political rights, their economic dependence on men in the patriarchal nuclear family still enslaved them. But this reality was cloaked by the happy myth of the nuclear family where men and women lovingly lived out their ordained roles.

After World War II, and particularly since the 1960s, the reality of the family again changed fundamentally. As women moved into the labour force, achieving unprecedented degrees of economic independence, the structural hold of patriarchy on women began to erode. As women successfully demanded relief from forms of sexual oppression, it was inevitable that the traditional patriarchal family would have to change radically. Throughout the 1960s, 1970s, and 1980s, the speed of change in the family was so rapid and so fundamental that people found themselves swept up into a crisis of the family, and new family forms emerged. Old certainties were replaced by new uncertainties. Children, women, and men were confronted with the always difficult need to adapt to a major structural change. Traditional notions of masculinity and feminity were increasingly out of step, and new notions had not yet fully developed. Old core sexual identities found little confirmation in the new reality, and new core sexual identities were only tentatively evolving. The costs, economically and emotionally, were great, but the rewards of the changes were potentially enormous.

In retrospect it is now clear that patriarchy, and the traditional male–dominated family it rested on, was in final decline. As women struggled against patriarchal privilege, it became clear that the foundation of male privilege was rooted in women's economic dependence. Increasingly it became clear that women could achieve their fullest liberation only as the patriarchal family declined. And it has. But it has not been easy. And the crisis is not yet over.

Today, therefore, we are in the final stages of yet another major reinvention of the family. This time we are striving to create a family based on true equality between men and women, a family form that neither requires nor insists on the oppression of women.

There is no doubt that the new human family will emerge stronger and happier than its predecessors. But it will be a very different family than those of the past. Men, women and children, together, should openly celebrate its birth, while joining together in the burial of the remnants of the traditional patriarchal family. That will be a joyous funeral.

ENDNOTES

Preface

1 In 1986 the marriage rate was 6.9 per 1000 population. The divorce rate was 3.1 per 1000 population. These are the latest figures, and the divorce rate has been growing dramatically in recent years. Therefore, in 1990 the divorce rate will have come close to one-half the marriage rate (Statistics Canada, *Canadian Social Trends* [Winter 1988]: 31).

2 Owen Adams, "Divorce Rates in Canada," Statistics Canada, *Canadian Social Trends* (Winter 1988): 18-19. In 1969 the median duration of marriage before divorce was 15 years. In 1986 it was just over nine years.

3 "Changes in Living Arrangements," Statistics Canada, *Canadian Social Trends* (Spring 1989): 27-29.

4 Regina *Leader Post*, 19 August 1988.

5 *Globe and Mail*, 19 August 1988.

6 Ibid., 14 January 1987.

7 Regina *Leader Post*, 13 May 1988.

8 *Globe and Mail*, 19 February 1989.

9 Ibid., 1 June 1987.

10 Regina *Leader Post*, 14 December 1986.

11 Robert S. Lynd, *Knowledge for What?* (New York: Grove Press, 1964 [1939]).

12 C. Wright Mills, *The Sociological Imagination* (New York: Oxford University Press, 1959).

Part I: The Changing Nature of the Family
Chapter 1: Families Past

1 See S. Freud, *Totem and Taboo* (New York: Standard Edition, vol. 13, 1950 [1913]), and S. Freud, *Moses and Monotheism* (New York: Standard Edition, vol. 23, 1939).

2 S. Freud, *Civilization and Its Discontents* (London: Lewis, 1963 [1930]).

3 F. Engels, *The Origin of the Family, Private Property and the State* (New York: International, 1972 [1884]).

4 Marshall D. Sahlins, "The Origin of Society," *Scientific American* 203, no. 31 (1960): 76–86.

5 Jane B. Lancaster and Phillip Whitten, "Family Matters," *Sciences* (January 1980): 10–15.

6 Ibid., p. 14.

7 Kathleen Gough, "The Origin of the Family," in *Toward an Anthropology of Women*, ed. R. Reiter Rayna (New York: Monthly Review, 1975), p. 52.

8 Ibid., p. 53.

[9] Karen L. Anderson, "Historical Perspectives on the Family," in *Family Matters*, ed. Karen L. Anderson et al. (Toronto: Methuen, 1987), pp. 21–39.

[10] Paul Phillips and Erin Phillips, *Women and Work* (Toronto: Lorimer, 1983), pp. 35–36.

[11] All statistics quoted are taken from the Census of the year indicated, unless otherwise noted.

[12] Pat Armstrong and Hugh Armstrong, *The Double Ghetto* (Toronto: McClelland and Stewart, 1984), pp. 19, 21.

[13] F.H. Leacy, ed., *Historical Statistics of Canada* . (Ottawa: Statistics Canada, 1983), Series D8–85. [Hereafter cited as HSC.]

[14] HSC, Series E60–68.

[15] *Gallup Report*, 23 March 1987.

[16] HSC, Series B1–14.

[17] HSC, Series B51–58.

[18] Simone de Beauvoir, *The Second Sex* (New York: Bantam, 1961).

[19] Betty Friedan, *The Feminine Mystique* (New York: Norton, 1963).

[20] *Report of the Royal Commission on the Status of Women in Canada* (Ottawa: Information Canada, 1970).

[21] Phillips and Phillips, *Women and Work*, p. viii.

[22] HSC, Series A110–24.

[23] Owen Adams, "Divorce Rates in Canada," Statistics Canada, *Canadian Social Trends* (Winter 1988): 18–19.

[24] HSC, Series D431–48.

[25] *Gallup Report*, 23 March 1987.

[26] Statistics Canada, *Women in Canada: A Statistical Report* (Ottawa, 1984), composed from tables through the publication.

[27] Maureen Moore, "Women Parenting Alone," Statistics Canada, *Canadian Social Trends* (Winter 1987): 31–46.

[28] Margrit Eichler, *Families in Canada Today* (Toronto: Gage, 1983), p. 236.

Chapter 2: Families Present

[1] "Changes in Living Arrangements," Statistics Canada, *Canadian Social Trends* (Spring 1989): 27–29.

[2] Maureen Moore, "Dual–Earner Families: The New Norm," Statistics Canada, *Canadian Social Trends* (Spring 1989): 24–26.

[3] Jo–Anne B. Parliament, "Women Employed outside the Home," Statistics Canada, *Canadian Social Trends* (Summer 1989): 3–6.

[4] In 1988, the average real family income was lower than in 1980 (*Globe and Mail*, 13 February 1988). The purchasing power of all women declined between 1982 and 1987 (*Financial Post*, 4 January 1988).

[5] Colin Lindsay, "The Decline of Real Family Income, 1980 to 1984," Statistics Canada, *Canadian Social Trends* (Winter 1986): 15–17.

[6] Betty Jane Wylie, *All in the Family: A Survival Guide for Family Living and Loving in a Changing World* (Toronto: Key Porter, 1988).

[7] Colin Lindsay "The Decline in Employment among Men Aged 55–64, 1975–1985," Statistics Canada, *Canadian Social Trends* (Spring 1987): 12–15.

[8] Colin Lindsay and Craig McKie, "Annual Review of Labour Force Trends," Statistics Canada, *Canadian Social Trends* (Autumn 1986): 2–6.

[9] Maureen Moore, "Women Parenting Alone," Statistics Canada, *Canadian Social Trends* (Winter 1987): 31–46.

[10] Regina *Leader Post*, 11 June 1983.

[11] *Globe and Mail*, 8 March 1983.

[12] *Regina Leader Post*, 1 February 1983 and 20 February 1980.

[13] *Globe and Mail*, 23 May 1985.

[14] Brigitta Arnoti, "Children in Low–income Families," Statistics Canada, *Canadian Social Trends* (Winter 1986): 18–20.

[15] Maureen Moore, "Female Lone Parenthood: The Duration of Episodes," Statistics Canada, *Canadian Social Trends* (Autumn 1988): 40–42.

[16] Holly Johnson, "Wife Abuse," Statistics Canada, *Canadian Social Trends* (Spring 1988): 17–20.

[17] Emily M. Nett, *Canadian Families: Past and Present* (Toronto: Butterworths, 1988), p. 147.

[18] *Globe and Mail*, 8 March 1983.

[19] Monica Boyd, "Canadian Family Forms: Issues for Women," in *Reconstructing the Canadian Family: Feminist Perspectives*, eds. Nancy Mandell and Ann Duffy (Toronto: Butterworths, 1988), pp. 85–109.

[20] Suzanne Methot, "Low Income in Canada," Statistics Canada, *Canadian Social Trends* (Spring 1987): 2–7.

[21] Robert A. Stebbins, "Men, Husbands and Fathers: Beyond Patriarchal Relations," in *Reconstructing the Canadian Family*, eds. Mandell and Duffy, pp. 27–47.

[22] Craig McKie, "Common–Law: Living Together as Husband and Wife without Marriage," Statistics Canada, *Canadian Social Trends*, (Autumn 1986): 39–41; and Pierre Turcotte, "Common–Law Unions: Nearly Half a Million in 1986," Statistics Canada, *Canadian Social Trends* (Autumn 1988): 35–39.

[23] *Globe and Mail*, 27 and 28 July 1989.

[24] Ibid., 27 December 1984.

[25] Ibid., 11 January 1989.

[26] Boyd, "Canadian Family Forms," p. 89.

[27] Margrit Eichler, *Families in Canada Today* (Toronto: Gage, 1983), p. 236.

[28] Angela Clubb Neuman, *Love in the Blended Family* (Toronto: NC Press, 1988).

[29] Nett, *Canadian Families*, p. 161; Eichler, *Families in Canada*, p. 235; C. James Richardson, "Children of Divorce," in *Family Matters*, eds. Karen L. Anderson et al. (Toronto: Methuen, 1987), p. 193; and Anne–Marie Ambert and Maureen Baker, "Marriage Dissolution," in *Family*

Bonds and Gender Divisions, ed. B. Fox (Toronto: Canadian Scholar's Press, 1988), pp. 453–75, 469.
30 Ambert and Baker, "Marriage Dissolution," p. 475.
31 Regina *Leader Post*, 26 August 1985.
32 Ibid., 8 June 1988.
33 *Globe and Mail*, 18 May 1988.
34 Regina *Leader Post*, 5 April 1989.
35 The parliament of Denmark recently legalized homosexual marriages granting them the same rights enjoyed by married heterosexual couples. Sweden also passed a similar law in 1988 (Regina *Leader Post*, 26 May 1989). New York's highest state court recently ruled that a partner of a long–term gay relationship can retain the lease on an apartment when the holder of a lease dies. The court found that the legal definition of "family members" should include adults who show long–term financial and emotional commitment.

Chapter 3: Families Future

1 *Globe and Mail*, 8 March 1983.
2 Brenda Rabkin, *Loving and Leaving: Why Women Are Walking out of Marriage* (Toronto: McClelland and Stewart, 1985).
3 Barbara Ehrenrich, *Hearts of Men: American Dreams and the Flight from Commitment* (Garden City, N.Y.: Anchor, 1983).
4 Yehudi A. Cohen, *Social Structure and Personality* (New York: Holt, 1961), pp. 459ff.
5 See Cohen, *Social Structure*, pp. 457ff; John J. Schwab and Mary E. Schwab, *Sociocultural Roots of Mental Illness: An Epidemiological Survey* (New York: Plenum, 1978); M. Harvey Brenner, *Mental Illness and the Economy* (Cambridge, Mass.: Harvard University Press, 1973); George W. Brown and Tirril Harris, *Social Origins of Depression: A Study of Psychiatric Disorder in Women* (London: Tavistock, 1978); A.B. Hollingshead and F.C. Redlich, *Social Class and Mental Illness* (New York: Wiley, 1958); L. Srole, T.S. Langer et al., *Mental Health in the Metropolis: The Midtown Manhattan Study* (New York: Harper, 1975; A.H. Leighton, *My Name Is Legion*, vol. I, Stirling Country Study (New York: Basic, 1959); C.C. Huges et al., *People of Cove and Woodlot*, vol. II, Stirling County Study (New York: Basic, 1960); D.C. Leighton et al., *The Character of Danger*, vol., III, Stirling County Study (New York: Basic, 1963); Bernard J. Gallagher, *The Sociology of Mental Illness* (Englewood Cliffs, N.J.: Prentice–Hall, 1987), pp. 266ff.
6 Regina *Leader Post*, 24 March 1986.
7 Regina *Leader Post*, 29 October 1979.
8 M.C. Mahood, "Depression in Women," unpublished paper, 1986.
8 Brenner, *Mental Illness and the Economy*.
9 R. Julian Hafner, *Marriage and Mental Illness: A Sex–Roles Perspective* (New York: Guilford, 1986).
11 *Toronto Star*, 26 February 1987.

Part II: Victims of the Crisis: Children
Introduction: Who Cares for the Children?

[1] *U.N. Declaration of the Rights of the Child* (New York: United Nations, 1960); *The Universal Declaration of Human Rights* (New York: United Nations, 1949).

[2] See S. Brody and S. Axelrod, *Mothers, Fathers and Children: Explorations in the Formation of Character in the First Seven Years* (New York: International University Press, 1978); M.S. Maher, F. Pine, and A. Bergman, *The Psychological Birth of the Human Infant* (New York: Basic, 1975); R.A. Spitz, *The First Year of Life* (New York: International University Press, 1968); and G.H. Mead, *Mind, Self and Society* (Chicago: University of Chicago Press, 1973 [1934]).

[3] A. Leibowitz, "Home Investments in Children," *Journal of Political Economy* (March/April 1974): 111–31; and A. Leibowitz, "Parental Inputs and Children's Achievement," *Journal of Human Resources* (Spring 1977): 242–51, both cited in Osberg, *Economic Inequality*, p. 84.

[4] Nancy Mandell, "The Child Question: Links between Women and Children in the Family," in *Reconstructing the Canadian Family: Feminist Perspectives*, eds. N. Mandell and A. Duffy (Toronto: Butterworths, 1988), p. 51.

[5] *Globe and Mail*, 29 April 1989.

[6] Ibid., 31 July 1985; Regina *Leader Post*, 6 April 1988.

[7] Gallup Report, 14 August 1989.

[8] Regina *Leader Post*, 2 March 1983.

[9] *Globe and Mail, Report on Business*, 29 December 1986.

[10] Regina *Leader Post*, 15 April 1989.

[11] Statistics Canada, *Canadian Social Trends*, (Summer 1986): 19.

[12] House of Commons, *Sharing the Responsibility: Report of the Special Committee on Childcare* (Ottawa: Queen's Printer, 1987), pp. 8, 34, 35, 36, 44, 151, 155.

[13] *Globe and Mail*, 14 January 1987.

[14] Ibid., 15 January 1987.

[15] *Globe and Mail, Report on Business*, 2 December 1988.

[16] Catherine E. Ross and John Mirowsky, "Child Care and Emotional Adjustment to Wives' Employment," *Journal of Health and Social Behaviour* 29, no. 2 (June 1988): 127–38.

[17] Mandell, "The Child Question," pp. 75–76.

Chapter 4: The Economic Insecurity of Children

[1] Statistics Canada, *Charting Canadian Incomes, 1951–81* (Ottawa: Supply and Services, 1984).

[2] David P. Ross, *The Canadian Fact Book on Poverty — 1983* (Toronto: Lorimer, 1983), pp. 1–8.

[3] National Council of Welfare, *Poverty Profile: 1988* (Ottawa: Supply and Services, 1988), p. 4. All data on poverty are taken from this source unless otherwise noted.

[4] *Globe and Mail*, 11 July 1985.

[5] Regina *Leader Post*, 5 May 1988.

[6] National Council of Welfare, *1988 Poverty Lines* (Ottawa: Supply and Services, 1988), p. 6.

[7] Regina *Leader Post*, 28 October 1988.

[8] *Globe and Mail, Report on Business*, 12 January 1985.

[9] Cited in Richard H. de Lone, *Small Futures: Children, Inequality and the Limits of Liberal Reform* (New York: Harcourt Brace Jovanovich, 1979), p. 20.

[10] National Council of Welfare, *Poor Kids* (Ottawa: National Council of Welfare, 1975) p. 1.

[11] Ian Adams et al., *The Real Poverty Report* (Edmonton: Hurtig, 1971), p. 22.

[12] *Globe and Mail*, 16 June 1989.

[13] Ibid., 28 March 1985.

[14] Regina *Leader Post*, 17 November 1988.

[15] *Globe and Mail*, 15 June 1989.

[16] Ibid., 22 July 1987.

[17] Ibid., 2 August 1987.

[18] Regina *Leader Post*, 4 November 1986.

[19] *Globe and Mail*, 8 April 1987.

[20] Ibid., 3 October 1987.

[21] Ibid., 22 December 1983 and 30 October 1987.

[22] Ibid., 24 May 1988.

[23] Graham Riches, *Food Banks and the Welfare Crisis*. (Ottawa: Canadian Council on Social Development, 1986).

[24] *Globe and Mail*, 13 May 1988.

[25] *Financial Post*, 14 April 1984.

[26] *Globe and Mail*, 15 September 1987.

[27] Ibid., 16 December 1983.

[28] National Council of Welfare, *Poor Kids*.

[29] *Globe and Mail*, 16 June 1989.

[30] Ibid., 25 July 1989.

[31] Ibid., 16 October 1987.

[32] These estimates of poor children for whom marriage breakdown was a significant factor in precipitating a fall below the poverty line were arrived at by multiplying the total number of poor children in single parent categories by the percentage of such families resulting from separation or divorce.

[33] Ross, *Fact Book on Poverty*, pp. 60–61.

[34] Greg J. Duncan et al., *Years of Poverty, Years of Plenty* (Ann Arbor: University of Michigan Press, 1984), ch. 2, "The Dynamics of Poverty," pp. 33ff.

[35] Regina *Leader Post*, 5 May 1986.

[36] *Globe and Mail*, 4 and 22 July 1980 and 21 April 1980.

[37] Y. Lamontagne et al., "Les jeunes itinérants de Montréal: une enquête transversale," *Canadian Journal of Psychiatry* 33, no. 8 (November 1988): 716–22.

[38] *Globe and Mail*, 14 July 1984 and 11 July 1985.

[39] Regina *Leader Post*, 5 April 1983.

[40] Thomas S. Parish and Gary K. Nunn, "The Importance of the Family in Forming Life Values and Personal Values," *Journal of Psychology* 122, no. 5 (September 1988): 519–21.

[41] Javad H. Kashani et al., "Characteristics of Well–Adjusted Adolescents," *Canadian Journal of Psychiatry* 32, no. 6 (August 1987): 418–22.

Chapter 5: The Emotional Insecurity of Children

[1] For reviews of some of the sociological literature, see the following: Anne–Marie Ambert and Maureen Baker, "Marriage Dissolution," in *Family Bonds and Genders Divisions*, ed. Bonnie Fox (Toronto: Canadian Scholars' Press, 1988), pp. 453ff; Margrit Eichler, *Families in Canada Today* (Toronto: Gage, 1983), chs. 7 to 9, pp. 201ff; Emily M. Nett, *Canadian Families: Past and Present* (Toronto: Butterworths, 1988), pp. 160–61, 260–61; and C. James Richardson, "Children of Divorce," in *Family Matters*, eds. Karen L. Anderson et al. (Toronto: Methuen, 1987), pp. 163ff.

[2] Eichler, *Families in Canada*, pp. 216, 218, emphasis added.

[3] Ambert and Baker, "Marriage Dissolution," pp. 466–67.

[4] See Richardson, "Children of Divorce"; and John F. Peter, "Changing Perspectives on Divorce," in *Family Matters*, ed. Anderson, pp. 141ff.

[5] Richardson, "Children of Divorce," p. 166.

[6] Regina *Leader Post*, 11 June 1983.

[7] Richardson, "Children of Divorce," p. 165.

[8] Regina *Leader Post*, 29 October 1979.

[9] Ralph Sutherland and M. Jane Fulton, *Health Care in Canada* (Ottawa: Health Group, 1988), pp. 16–18, 30.

[10] *Globe and Mail*, 15 October 1982.

[11] G. Caplan, *Support Systems and Community Mental Health* (New York: Behavioural Publications, 1974); and M. Greenblatt et al., "Social Networks and Mental Health: An Overview," *American Journal of Psychiatry* 139 (1982): 977–84.

[12] *Globe and Mail*, 15 October 1982.

[13] Ibid., 24 March 1986.

[14] Stuart Fine, "Children in Divorce, Custody and Accesss Situations: An Update," *Journal of Child Psychology and Psychiatry* 28, no. 3 (May 1987): 361–64; and B.E. Robson, "The Impact of Divorce and Separation on Children," *Contemporary Paediatrics* 2 (1986): 6–21.

[15] Alan Breier et al., "Early Parental Loss and Development of Adult Psychopathology," *Archives of General Psychiatry* 45 (November 1988): 987–93.

[16] Q. Rae–Grant and G. Awad, "The Effects of Marital Breakdown," in *Psychological Problems of the Child in the Family*, eds. P.D. Steinhauer and Q. Rae–Grant (New York: Basic, 1983).

[17] S. McLanahan and L. Bumpass, "Intergenerational Consequences of Family Disruption," *American Journal of Sociology* 94, no. 1, (June 1988): 130–52.

[18] Regina *Leader Post*, 25 February 1989.

[19] E. Papthomopoulos et al., "Suicidal Attempts by Ingestion of Various Substances in 2050 Children and Adolescents in Greece," *Canadian Journal of Psychiatry* 34, no .3 (April 1989): 205–10.

[20] B.D. Garfinkel, "Suicidal Behaviour in a Pediatric Population," *Proceedings*, Congress for Suicide Prevention and Crisis Intervention, Ottawa, 1979.

[21] H.S. Merskey and G.T. Swart, "Family Background and Physical Health of Adolescents Admitted to an Impatient Psychiatric Unit, I: Principal Caregivers," *Canadian Journal of Psychiatry* 34, no. 2 (March 1989): 79–83.

[22] B.J. Fidler and E.B. Saunders, "Children's Adjustment during Custody/Access Disputes: Relation to Custody Arrangement, Gender and Age of Child," *Canadian Journal of Psychiatry* 33, no. 6 (August 1988): 517–23.

[23] E.M. Hetherington et al., "The Aftermath of Divorce," in *Mother–child/Father–child Relations*, eds. J.H. Stevens and M. Matthews (Washington: National Association for the Education of Children, 1978); E.M. Hetherington et al., "Family Interactions and the Social, Emotional and Cognitive Development of Children Following Divorce," in *The Family: Setting Priorities*, eds. J.C. Vaughan and J.B. Brazelton (New York: Science and Medicine Publishers, 1979); E.M. Hetherington, "Play and Social Interaction in Children Following Divorce," *Journal of Social Issues* 35, no. 4 (1979): 26–49; and E.M. Hetherington, et al., "Long–Term Effects of Divorce and Re–marriage on the Adjustment of Children," *Journal of the American Academy of Child Psychiatry* 24 (1985): 518–30.

[24] For a brief review of this literature, see Q. Rae–Grant and B. Robson, "Moderating the Morbidity of Divorce," *Canadian Journal of Psychiatry* 33, no. 6, (August 1988): 443–52.

[25] B. Robson, "Changing Family Patterns: Developmental Impacts on Children" *Journal of Counselling and Human Development* 19, no. 6 (1987): 2–12; T.M. Cooney et al., "Parental Divorce in Young Adulthood: Some Preliminary Findings," *American Journal of Orthopsychiatry* 56 (1986): 470–77; J.S. Wallerstein, "Children of Divorce: Stress and Developmental Tasks," in *Stress, Coping and Development in Children*, eds. N. Garmenzy and M. Rutter (New York: McGraw–Hill, 1983); B. Robson, "Marriage Concepts of Older Adolescents," *Canadian Journal of Psychiatry* 28, no. 8 (1983): 646–49; and J.S. Wallerstein and J.B. Kelly, *Surviving the Breakup: How Children and Parents Cope with Divorce* (New York: Basic, 1980).

[26] Regina *Leader Post*, 10 August 1983.

[27] J. Saucier and A. Ambert, "Adolescents' Perception of Self and of Immediate Environment by Parental Marital Status: A Controlled Study," *Canadian Journal of Psychiatry* 31, no. 6 (1986): pp. 505–12.

[28] Rae–Grant and Robson, "Moderating the Morbidity of Divorce," p. 446.

[29] Richardson,"Children of Divorce," p. 171.

Chapter 6: The Physical Insecurity of Children

[1] *Globe and Mail*, 8 June 1987.

[2] CTV News Report, 29 September 1989.

[3] *Globe and Mail*, 4 March 1988.

[4] When the word "more" is used, it is understood to mean a larger proportion of children rather than necessarily more in absolute numbers.

[5] *Globe and Mail*, 20 June 1980.

[6] Regina *Leader Post*, 5 September 1980.

[7] *Globe and Mail*, 8 July 1988.

[8] L. Lapierre and H. Aylwin, *Canadian Youth: Perspectives on Their Health* . (Ottawa: Supply and Services, 1985), pp. 80–81.

[9] *Toronto Star*, 9 September 1989.

[10] R. Beneteau, "Trends in Suicide," Statistics Canada, *Canadian Social Trends* (Winter 1988): 22–24.

[11] According to psychiatrist and suicide specialist Barry Garfinkel, *Globe and Mail*, 15 October 1982.

[12] All data on mortality are taken from the following: Dominion Bureau of Statistics, *Vital Statistics, 1966*, Catalogue 84–202, (Ottawa, 1966); Vital Statistics, vol. III, *Deaths* (Ottawa: Information Canada, 1974); Vital Statistics, vol. III, *Mortality: Summary List of Causes* (Ottawa: Supply and Services, 1983); and Statistics Canada, *Mortality: Summary List of Causes* (Ottawa: Supply and Services, 1988).

[13] See C.R. Pfeffer, *The Suicidal Child* (New York: Guilford, 1986).

[14] B. Rabkin, *Growing Up Dead: A Hard Look at Why Adolescents Commit Suicide* (Toronto: McClelland and Stewart, 1978), p. 13.

[15] B.D. Garfinkel, "Suicidal Behaviour in a Pediatric Population," *Proceedings*, Congress for Suicide Prevention and Crisis Intervention, Ottawa, 1979; B.D. Garfinkel and H. Golombek, "Suicidal Behaviour in Adolescents," in *The Adolescent and Mood Disturbance*, eds. B.D. Garfinkel and H. Golombek (New York: International University, 1983): 189–217; H.M. Hoberman and B.D. Garfinkel, "Completed Suicide in Youth," *Canadian Journal of Psychiatry* 33, no. 6 (August 1988): 494–502; G.F.G. Moens et al., "Epidemiological Aspects of Suicide among the Young in Selected European Countries," *Journal of Epidemiology and Community Health* 42 (1988): 279–85; F. Nelson et al., "Youth Suicide in California: A Comparative Study of Perceived Causes and Interventions," *Community Mental Health Journal* 24, no. 1 (1988): 31–42; J. Pettifor et al., "Risk Factors Predicting Childhood and Adolescent Suicides," *Journal of Child Care* 1 (1983): 17–49; D.J. Poteet, "Adolescent Suicide," *American Journal of Forensic Medical Pathology* 8 (1987):

12–17; D. Shaffer and P. Fisher, "The Epidemiology of Suicide in Children and Young Adolescents," *Journal of the American Academy of Child Psychiatry* 20 (1981): 545–65; N. Shaffi et al., "Psychological Autopsy of Completed Suicide in Children and Adolescents," *American Journal of Psychiatry* 142 (1985): 1061–64; H.S. Sudak et al., "Adolescent Suicide: An Overview," *American Journal of Psychotherapy* (1984): 350–63; and T.R. Thompson, "Childhood and Adolescent Suicide in Manitoba," *Canadian Journal of Psychiatry* 32, no. 4 (1987): 264–69.

[16] Thompson, "Childhood and Adolescent Suicide in Manitoba," pp. 265, 267.

[17] *Globe and Mail* 10 and 11 November 1982.

[18] E. Bass and L. Thornton, eds., *I Never Told Anyone: Writings by Women Survivors of Child Sexual Abuse* (New York: Harper and Row, 1983); S. Cole, "Child Battery," in *No Safe Place: Violence against Women and Children*, eds. C. Guberman and M. Wolfe (Toronto: Women's Press, 1985) (also in *Family Bonds and Gender Divisons*, ed. B. Fox) (Toronto: Canadian Scholars' Press, 1988); J. Drakich and C. Guberman, "Violence in the Family," in *Family Matters*, ed. K. Anderson et al. (Toronto: Methuen, 1987); R. Finkelhor et al., eds., *The Dark Side of Families: Current Family Violence Research* (Beverly Hills: Sage, 1983); M.A.B. Gammon, ed., *Violence in Canada* (Toronto: Methuen, 1978); G. Gerbner et al., eds., *Child Abuse* (New York: Oxford, 1980); R. Helfner, ed., *The Battered Child* (Chicago: University of Chicago Press, 1980); B. Pressman, *Family Violence: Origins and Treatment* (Guelph: University of Guelph, 1984); *Report of the Committee on Sexual Offences against Children and Youth* (Ottawa: Supply and Services, 1984) (Badgley Report); Senate of Canada, *Child at Risk* (Ottawa: Supply and Services, 1980); Social Development Standing Committee, Ontario Legislature, *Second Report on Family Violence: Child Abuse* (Toronto: Government of Ontario, 1983); N. Von Stolk, *The Battered Child in Canada* (Toronto: McClelland and Stewart, 1978).

[19] Regina *Leader Post*, 18 September 1989.

[20] *Gallup Report*, 13 October 1988.

[21] *Globe and Mail*, 10 March 1983.

[22] L. MacLeod, *Battered but Not Beaten ... Preventing Wife Battering in Canada* (Ottawa: Canadian Advisory Council on the Status of Women, 1987), pp. 32–33.

[23] A.E. Waller et al., "Childhood Injury Deaths: National Analysis and Geographic Variations," *American Journal of Public Health* 79, no. 3 (March 1989): 310–15. The quotation is from the *Globe and Mail*, 1 March 1989.

[24] P. Resnick, "Murder of the Newborn: A Psychiatric Review of Neonaticide," *American Journal of Psychiatry* 126, no. 10 (1970): 1414–20.

[25] E. Cherland and P.C. Matthews, "Attempted Murder of a Newborn: A Case History," *Canadian Journal of Psychiatry* 34, no. 4 (May 1989): 337–39.

26 H. Johnson and P. Chisholm, "Family Homicide," Statistics Canada, *Canadian Social Trends* (Autumn 1989): 17–18.

27 H. Johnson, "Homicide in Canada," Statistics Canada, *Canadian Social Trends* (Winter 1987): 2–6.

28 Regina *Leader Post*, 23 May 1989.

29 National Council of Welfare, *In the Best Interests of the Child* (Ottawa, 1979). A recent *Globe and Mail* article estimated the number of children in care in Canada at 50,000 (30 September 1989). This report estimated 80,000 in 1979.

30 Ibid., p. 22.

31 Interview with Trevor Williams, Family Service of Canada, Ottawa, 9 October 1989.

32 John H. Maher, *Report In The Matter of a Royal Commission Appointed By the Lieutenant Governor of the Province of Saskatchewan Under the Public Inquiries Act to Inquire into the Wilderness Challenge Camps as Proposed and Operated by the Ranch Ehrlo Society*, Regina, Saskatchewan, 1977.

33 *Globe and Mail*, 8 March 1980.

34 Ibid., 30 September 1989.

35 D. Tickell, *The Protection of Children: The Rights of Children: The Urgent Need to Improve a System in Crisis* (Regina: Saskatchewan Ombudsman, 1986).

36 Montreal *Gazette*, 20 October 1986.

Part III: Victims of the Crisis: Women
Introduction: The Oppression of Women

1 *Globe and Mail, Report on Business*, 6 December 1988.

2 Ibid., 12 August 1985.

3 Ibid., 7 July 1989.

4 Regina *Leader Post*, 20 January 1986.

5 *Globe and Mail*, 17 March and 23 May 1985.

6 See Pat Armstrong and Hugh Armstrong, *A Working Majority: What Women Must Do for Pay* (Ottawa: Canadian Advisory Council on the Status of Women, 1983); and *The Double Ghetto: Canadian Women and Their Segregated Work* (Toronto: McClelland and Stewart, 1984); A. Duffy et al., *Few Choices: Women, Work and Family* (Toronto: Garamond, 1989); Jane Lewis, ed., *Labour and Love: Women's Experience of Home and Family* (London: Blackwell, 1986); M. Luxton, *More Than a Labour of Love: Three Generations of Women's Work in the Home* (Toronto: Women's Press, 1980); N. Mandell and A. Duffy, *Reconstructing the Canadian Family: Feminist Perspectives* (Toronto: Butterworths 1988); M. Meissner et al., "No Exit for Wives: Sexual Division of Labour and the Cumulation of Household Demands," *Canadian Review of Sociology and Anthropology* 12, no. 4 (November 1975): 424–39; and A. Oakley, *The Sociology of Housework* (New York: Pantheon, 1974).

7 Dorothy Dinnerstein, *The Mermaid and The Minotaur: Sexual Arrangements and Human Malaise* (New York: Harper and Row, 1976).

[8] Sylvia Hewlett, *A Lesser Life: The Myth of Women's Liberation in America* (New York: Morrow, 1986).

[9] Regina *Leader Post*, 4 April 1985.

[10] *Globe and Mail*, 28 September 1985.

[11] Ibid., 8 September 1989.

[12] *Gallup Report*, 16 October 1989.

[13] *Globe and Mail*, 19 August 1987. The report is called *The More Things Change, the More They Stay the Same* . The authors of the report refused to recommend a single one of 12 readers approved by the Ontario Ministry of Education. The following is based on a summary by the *Globe and Mail* 's Margaret Polanyi.

[14] Maureen Baker, *What Will Tomorrow Bring? ... A Study of the Aspirations of Adolescent Women* (Ottawa: Canadian Advisory Council on the Status of Women, 1985). In addition to reporting on data collected in 1983 and 1984, Baker also provides a review of earlier studies on the question. For a more impressionistic and personal account, based on interviews with "fifty or so" adolescent girls, see Myrna Kostash, *No Kidding: Inside the World of Teenage Girls* (Toronto: McClelland and Stewart, 1987).

[15] Baker, *What Will Tomorrow Bring?* p. 3.

[16] Ibid., pp. 3–4.

[17] Ibid., pp. 113–114.

[18] Regina *Leader Post*, 27 December 1988.

[19] Harry MacKay and Catherine Austin, *Single Adolescent Mothers in Ontario* (Ottawa: Canadian Council on Social Development, 1983). The 17,000 figure is taken from this report, p. vii.

[20] Rex E. Culp et al., "Adolescent and Older Mothers: Comparison between Prenatal Maternal Variables and Newborn Interaction Measures," *Infant Behaviour and Development* 11, no. 3 (1987): 353–62.

[21] S. Freud, *Civilization and Its Discontents* (London: Hogarth, 1972 [1930]), p. 61.

[22] Susan Brownmiller, *Femininity* (New York: Simon and Schuster, 1984), pp. 14, 236.

Chapter 7: The Double Burden

[1] For much of what follows and a good review of the literature, see P. Armstrong and H. Armstrong, *The Double Ghetto* (Toronto: McClelland and Stewart, 1984), pp. 64ff.

[2] Armstrong and Armstrong, *The Double Ghetto*, p. 69.

[3] "The Value of Household Work in Canada," Statistics Canada, *Canadian Social Trends* (Autumn 1986): 42. For the complete explanation of the calculations, see J.L. Swinamen, "The Value of Household Work in Canada, 1981," Statistics Canada, *Canadian Statistical Review*, Catalogue 11–003E, vol. 60, no. 3.

[4] M.S. Devereaux, "New Necessities: Popular Household Appliances," Statistics Canada, *Canadian Social Trends* (Autumn 1988): 31–34.

[5] L. Robbins, "Eating Out," Statistics Canada, *Canadian Social Trends* (Summer 1989): 7–9.

[6] Regina *Leader Post*, 1 November 1989.

[7] Ibid., 2 November 1989.

[8] R.A. Stebbins, "Men, Husbands and Fathers: Beyond Patriarchal Relations," in *Reconstructing the Canadian Family*, eds. N. Mandell and A. Duffy (Toronto: Butterworths, 1988) p. 31.

[9] Regina *Leader Post*, 7 November 1985.

[10] *Globe and Mail*, 2 April 1988.

[11] A. Hochschild and A. Machung, *The Second Shift: Inside the Two–Job Marriage* (New York: Penguin, 1989).

[12] Armstrong and Armstrong, *The Double Ghetto*, p. 93.

[13] S.N. Lewis and C.L. Cooper, "The Transition to Parenthood in Dual–earner Couples," *Psychological Medicine* 18, no. 12 (May 1988): 477–86.

[14] C.E. Ross and J. Mirowsky, "Child Care and Emotional Adjustment to Wives' Employment," *Journal of Health and Social Behaviour* 29, no. 2 (June 1988): 127–38.

[15] *Globe and Mail, Report on Business*, 2 December 1988.

[16] Regina *Leader Post*, 14 July 1989.

[17] Ibid., 23 September 1989.

[18] *Globe and Mail*, 8 March 1989.

[19] Ibid., 15 August 1989; Regina *Leader Post*, 3 August 1989.

[20] P.L. Kotler, *Having It All: Multiple Roles and Mortality* (New York: Columbia University Press, 1989).

[21] *Globe and Mail*, 8 June 1989.

[22] The following statements are taken from A. Duffy et al., *Few Choices: Women, Work and Family* (Toronto: Garamond, 1989), pp. 32, 39; and P. Armstrong and H. Armstrong, *A Working Majority* (Ottawa: Canadian Advisory Council on the Status of Women, 1983), pp. 203ff; and *Globe and Mail*, 7 January 1989.

Chapter 8: Women's Economic Oppression

[1] P. Phillips and E. Phillips, *Women and Work: Inequality in the Labour Market* (Toronto: Lorimer, 1983), p. ix.

[2] Regina *Leader Post*, 20 March 1987.

[3] *Globe and Mail*, 11 March 1989.

[4] Ibid., 18 June 1988.

[5] J–A. Boule and L. Lavallée, *The Changing Economic Status of Women* (Ottawa: Supply and Services, 1984), pp. 27ff.

[6] All figures are taken from data in the 1980s and percentages are rounded. See P. Armstrong and H. Armstrong *The Double Ghetto* (Toronto: McClelland and Stewart, 1984); K. Kendall, *Profiling Women in the Saskatchewan Economy* (Saskatoon: Community Educators for Women, 1989); Statistics Canada, *Women in Canada: A Statistical Report* (Ottawa: Supply and Services, 1985); Boule and Lavallée, *Changing Economic Status of Women* ; *Globe and Mail*, 22 March 1985; 13 and

20 March 1987; Regina *Leader Post*, 23 January 1989; *Globe and Mail*, 11 March 1989.

[7] Phillips and Phillips, *Women and Work*, p. ix.

[8] Armstrong and Armstrong, *The Double Ghetto*, pp. 33–36.

[9] *Globe and Mail, Report on Business*, 18 August 1988.

[10] Armstrong and Armstrong, *The Double Ghetto*, p. 43.

[11] *Globe and Mail*, 17 May 1989.

[12] Ibid., 18 May 1989.

[13] Phillips and Phillips, *Women and Work*, pp. 57–58.

[14] Cited in ibid., p. 58.

[15] Regina *Leader Post*, 16 February 1987.

[16] *Globe and Mail, Report on Business*, 3 October 1985.

[17] K. Marshall, "Women in Male–Dominated Professions," Statistics Canada, *Canadian Social Trends* (Winter 1987): 7–10, and "Women in Professional Occupations: Progress in the 1980s," ibid. (Spring 1989): 13–16.

[18] C. McKie, "The Law: A Changing Profession," ibid. (Summer 1986): 28–34.

[19] *Globe and Mail*, 11 August 1988.

[20] Kim Zarzour, "Women in Medicine: Making Healthy Gains in the Medical World," Toronto *Star*, 13 November 1987. The figures below are largely from this source, which used data from the Association of Canadian Medical Colleges and the Canadian Medical Association.

[21] J. Hollands, "Women Teaching at Canadian Universities," Statistics Canada, *Canadian Social Trends* (Summer 1988): 5–7.

[22] G. Wheeler, "Employment of Humanities and Sciences Graduates," Statistics Canada, *Canadian Social Trends* (Summer 1989): 28–30.

[23] *Globe and Mail*, 19 September 1980.

[24] Ibid., 20 August 1988.

[25] Ibid., 11 September 1987.

[26] Ibid., *Report on Business*, 7 November 1989.

[27] Ibid., 11 August 1988.

[28] A.I. Dagg and P. Thompson, *MisEducation, Women and Canadian Universities* (Toronto: OISE Press, 1988).

[29] *Globe and Mail*, 2 May 1988.

[30] Ibid., 18 June 1988.

[31] Ibid., 22 October 1988.

[32] Ibid., *Report on Business*, 17 November 1988.

[33] National Council of Welfare, *Poverty Profile: 1988* (Ottawa: Supply and Services, 1988), pp. 66–74; and D.P. Ross and R. Shillington, *The Canadian Fact Book on Poverty* (Ottawa: Canadian Council on Social Development, 1989).

[34] Phillips and Phillips, *Women and Work*, p. 37ff.

[35] *Globe and Mail, Report on Business*, 5 December 1989.

[36] Ibid., 21 April 1986.

[37] J-A. B. Parliament, "Women Employed outside the Home," Statistics Canada, *Canadian Social Trends* (Summer 1989): 3–6; and M.A. Burke,

ENDNOTES* 241*

"The Growth of Part–Time Work," Statistics Canada, *Canadian Social Trends* (Autumn 1986): 9–14.

[38] M. Boyd et al., *Ascription and Achievement: Studies in Mobility and Status Attainment in Canada* (Ottawa: Carleton University Press, 1985): 516–17.

[39] Regina *Leader Post*, 16 February 1987.

[40] Boyd, *Ascription and Achievement*, p. 519.

[41] *Globe and Mail*, 11 March 1989.

[42] K. Marshall, "Women in Male–Dominated Professions," p. 11; see also K. Marshall, "Women in Professional Occupations: Progress in the 1980s."

[43] *Globe and Mail*, 11 August 1988.

[44] *Financial Post*, 13 October 1979.

[45] E. Gilson (with S. Kane), *Unnecessary Choices: The Hidden Life of the Executive Woman* (Toronto: Macmillan, 1987).

[46] Margot Gibb–Clark, "Sex Differences Show in Behaviour at the Workplace," *Globe and Mail, Report on Business*, 8 August 1987.

[47] *Globe and Mail*, 5 April 1989.

[48] Rosalie S. Abella, *Report of the Commission on Equality in Employment* (Ottawa: Supply and Services; 1984). The report examined the employment problems faced by women, native people, disabled persons, and visible minorities.

[49] Regina *Leader Post*, 16 November 1988.

[50] Parliament, "Women Employed outside the Home," p. 4.

[51] Regina *Leader Post*, 14 March 1986.

[52] Ibid., 27 March 1981.

[53] Ibid., 5 May 1986.

[54] *Globe and Mail*, 21 November 1989.

[55] National Council of Welfare, *Poverty Profile: 1988* (Ottawa: Supply and Services, 1988), p. 31.

Chapter 9: Women's Emotional Oppression

[1] See P. Armstrong and H. Armstrong, *The Double Ghetto* (Toronto: McClelland and Stewart, 1984), pp. 100ff for this and what follows.

[2] C. Degler, *At Odds: Women and the Family in America from the Revolution to the Present* (New York: Oxford, 1980). See also P. Armstrong, *Labour Pains: Women's Work in Crisis* (Toronto: Women's Press, 1984); B. Fox, ed., *Hidden in the Household* (Toronto: Women's Press, 1980); P. Kome, *Somebody Has to Do It* (Toronto: McClelland and Stewart, 1982); M. Luxton, *More Than a Labour of Love* (Toronto: Women's Press, 1980); A. Oakley, *The Sociology of Housework* (New York: Pantheon, 1974).

[3] J.M. Lewis et al., *No Single Thread: Psychological Health in Family Systems* (New York: Brunner and Mazel, 1976).

[4] D.A. Luepnitz, *The Family Interpreted: Feminist Theory in Clincial Practice* (New York: Basic, 1988).

[5] C.M. Anderson and D.P. Holder, "Women and Serious Mental Disorders," in *Women in Families: A Framework for Family Therapy*, eds. M. McGoldrick et al. (New York: Norton, 1989).

[6] *Globe and Mail*, 7 November, 1987.

[7] P.S. Penfold, "Family Therapy: Critique from a Feminist Perspective," *Canadian Journal of Psychiatry* 34, no. 4 (May 1989): 311–15.

[8] J.H. Gold and E. Gold, "The Belittled Wife: Social, Legal and Psycho-therapeutic Considerations," *Canadian Journal of Psychiatry* 26, no. 6 (October 1981): 402–5.

[9] P. Caplan and I. Hall–McCorquodale, "Mother–Blaming in Major Clinical Journals," *American Journal of Orthopsychiatry* 55 (1985): 345–53.

[10] K. Chernin, *The Obsession: Reflections on the Tyranny of Slenderness* (New York: Harper and Row, 1981).

[11] Luepnitz, *The Family Interpreted*, pp. 13–17, 144.

[12] For this and what follows see: J. Bernard, *The Future of Marriage* (New York: Bantam, 1972); S. Bothwell and M.M. Weissman, "Social Impairments Four Years after an Acute Depressive Episode," *American Journal of Orthopsychiatry* 47 (1977): 231–37; G.W. Brown and M.W. Brolchain, "Social Class and Psychiatric Disturbance among Women in an Urban Population," *Sociology* 9 (1975): 225–54; G.E. Brown and T. Harris, *Social Origins of Depression* (London: Tavistock, 1978); C. Chamberlain et al., "The Role of Intimacy in Psychiatric Help–Seeking," *Canadian Journal of Psychiatry* 34, no. 1 (February 1989): 1–7; P. Chesler, *Women and Madness* (Garden City, N.Y.: Doubleday, 1972); B.J. Gallagher, *The Sociology of Mental Illness* (Englewood Cliffs, N.J.: Prentice–Hall, 1987); W.R. Gove, "The Relationship between Sex Roles, Marital Status and Mental Illness," *Social Forces* 51 (1972): 34–44; W.R. Gove and J.F. Tudor, "Adult Sex Roles and Mental Illness," *American Journal of Sociology* 78 (1973): 812–35; R.J. Hafner, *Marriage and Mental Illness* (New York: Guilford, 1986); M. Kaplan, "A Woman's View of DSM–III," *American Psychologist* (July 1983): 786–814; K.R. Merikangas et al., "Marital Adjustment in Major Depression," *Journal of Affective Disorders* 9 (1985): 5–11; S. Penfold and G. Walker, *Women and the Psychiatric Paradox* (Toronto: Eden, 1983); L.S. Radloff, "Depression and the Empty Nest," *Sex Roles* 6 (1980): 775–81; A. Rich, *Of Woman Born: Motherhood as Experience and Institution* (New York: Norton, 1976); C.E. Ross and J. Mirowsky, "Child Care and Emotional Adjustment to Wives' Employment," *Journal of Health and Social Behaviour* 29, no. 2 (June 1988): 127–38; C. Tennant et al., "Female Vulnerability to Neurosis: The Influence of Social Roles," *Australian and New Zealand Journal of Psychiatry* 16 (1982): 135–40; M.M. Wiseman and E.S. Paykel, *The Depressed Woman: A Study of Social Relationships* (Chicago: University of Chicago Press, 1974).

[13] Anderson and Holder, "Women and Serious Mental Disorders," p. 389.

[14] Regina *Leader Post*, 7 May 1980 and 7 March 1983; *Globe and Mail*, 1 and 15 November 1985 and 7 November 1987.

[15] Regina *Leader Post*, 15 November 1985.

[16] *Globe and Mail*, 8 July 1989.

[17] *Gallup Report*, 11 February 1989.

[18] See the studies noted in footnotes 14 to 24, inclusive, in Chapter 5. A good summary of the literature up to 1988 is provided in Q. Rae–Grant and B.E. Robson, "Moderating the Morbidity of Divorce," *Canadian Journal of Psychiatry* 33, no. 6 (August 1988): 443–52.

[19] Rae–Grant and Robson, ibid., p. 445.

[20] A. D'Ercole, "Single Mothers: Stress, Coping and Social Support," *Journal of Community Psychology* 16, no. 1 (January 1988): 41–54.

[21] J. Essen, "Living in One–Parent Families: Attainment at School," *Child: Care, Health and Development* 5, no. 3 (1979): 189–200; C. Hobart and D. Brown, "Effects of Prior Marriage Children on Adjustment in Re–Marriage: A Canadian Study," *Journal of Comparative Family Studies* 19. no. 3 (Fall 1988): 381–96; K. Morrison and A. Thompson–Guppy, *Stepmothers: Exploring the Myth* (Ottawa: Canadian Council on Social Development, 1985); A.M. Morton and P.S. Glick, "Marital Instability in America," in *Divorce and Separation*, eds. G. Levingen and O.C. Moles (New York: Basic, 1979).

Chapter 10: The Physical and Sexual Oppression of Women

[1] John Boswell, *The Kindness of Strangers: The Abandonment of Children in Western Europe from Late Antiquity to the Renaissance* (New York: Pantheon, 1988) pp. 4–5.

[2] *Globe and Mail*, 16 February 1985.

[3] Ibid., 11 October 1989.

[4] Regina *Leader Post*, 13 August 1987.

[5] "Family Violence," Solicitor General of Canada, *Liaison* 15, no. 3 (March 1989): 4–13.

[6] H. Johnson, "Wife Abuse," Statistics Canada, *Canadian Social Trends* (Spring 1988): 17–22.

[7] *Globe and Mail*, 23 October 1980.

[8] Ibid., 30 June 1988.

[9] *Gallup Report*, 3 November 1988.

[10] *Globe and Mail*, 30 June 1988.

[11] Ibid., 16 February 1985.

[12] Ibid., 12 August 1985.

[13] Ibid., 13 August 1985 and for some of what follows.

[14] Ibid., 13 January 1988.

[15] Ibid., 19 August 1989.

[16] Ibid., 3 September and 20 January 1989.

[17] Regina *Leader Post*, 23 September 1985.

[18] *Globe and Mail*, 3 May 1988.

[19] Ibid., *Report on Business*, 16 March 1987.

[20] Ibid., 6 December 1988.

[21] For the examples below see: *Globe and Mail*, 30 July 1987; ibid., *Report on Business*, 6 December 1988; ibid., 11 August 1988; ibid., *Report on*

Business, 16 March 1987; ibid., 12 August 1989; ibid., 16 January 1988; ibid., 8 November 1989; Montreal *Gazette*, 22 October 1989.

[22] *Globe and Mail*, 8 November 1989.

[23] Ibid., 16 June 1988.

[24] Ibid., 11 October 1985.

[25] Ibid., 11 October 1989.

[26] Regina *Leader Post*, 23 September 1980.

[27] *Globe and Mail*, 23 October 1980.

[28] Regina *Leader Post*, 26 December 1989.

[29] See *Globe and Mail* and Regina *Leader Post*, 7 to 11 December 1989; *Maclean's*, 18 December 1989; *CAUT Bulletin* 37, no. 1 (January 1990); and *Le Devoir*, 7 to 12 December 1989.

[30] Letter to editor, Regina *Leader Post*, 18 January 1990.

[31] For an overview and background to wife battering, see T. Davidson, *Conjugal Crime: Understanding and Changing the Wife Beating Pattern* (New York: Hawthorn, 1970); J.M. Eekelaar and S.N. Katz, eds., *Family Violence* (Toronto: Butterworths, 1978); D. Finkelhor et al., eds., *The Dark Side of Families* (Beverly Hills: Sage, 1983); R.J. Gelles, *The Violent Home* (Beverly Hills: Sage, 1972); J.P. Martin, ed., *Violence and the Family* (New York: Wiley, 1978); M. Roy, *The Abusive Partner* (New York: Van Nostrand Reinhold, 1982); W.A. Stacey and A. Shupe, *The Family Secret* (Boston: Beacon, 1983); S.K. Steinmetz, *The Cycle of Violence* (New York: Praeger, 1977); M.A. Straus and G.T. Hotaling, eds., *The Social Causes of Husband–Wife Violence* (Minneapolis: University of Minnesota Press, 1980); L.E. Walker, *The Battered Woman* (New York: Harper and Row, 1979); and L.E. Walker, *The Battered Woman Syndrome* (New York: Spring, 1984). See also footnote 16 in Chapter 6. For an excellent, selective review of both feminist and non–feminist approaches to wife battering, see D. Scott, "Theoretical Approaches to the Problem of Wife Assault: A Critique and Modest Reformulation" (M.A. thesis, Social Studies, University of Regina, 1988), chs. 2 and 3, pp. 9ff.

[32] L. MacLeod, *Wife Battering in Canada: The Vicious Circle* (Ottawa: Canadian Advisory Council on the Status of Women, 1980); and *Battered but Not Beaten* .

[33] H. Johnson, "Wife Abuse."

[34] E. Lupri, "Male Violence in the Home," Statistics Canada, *Canadian Social Trends* (Autumn 1989): 19–21.

[35] L. MacLeod, *Battered but Not Beaten ... Preventing Wife Battering in Canada* (Ottawa: Canadian Advisory Council on the Status of Women, 1987), p. 16.

[36] H. Johnson, "Homicide in Canada," Statistics Canada, *Canadian Social Trends* (Winter 1987): 2–6; H. Johnson and P. Chisholm, "Family Homicide," ibid. (Autumn 1989); Statistics Canada, *Homicide in Canada: A Statistical Perspective*, Catalogue 85–209 (Ottawa: Supply and Services, 1989); Regina *Leader Post*, 23 May 1989.

[37] Regina *Leader Post*, 20 April 1989.

[38] Ibid., 7 October 1988.

[39] F. McNulty, *The Burning Bed: The True Story of an Abused Wife* (New York: Avon, 1980).

[40] Ibid., pp. 279, 283.

[41] B. Vallée, *Life with Billy* (Toronto: McClelland and Stewart, 1986).

[42] MacLeod, *Battered but Not Beaten*, pp. 19ff.

[43] MacLeod, *Wife Battering in Canada*, p. 14.

[44] Regina *Leader Post*, 13 August 1987.

[45] Johnson, "Wife Abuse," pp. 17–18.

[46] Lupri, "Male Violence in the Home," pp. 20–21.

[47] *Globe and Mail*, 10 December 1988.

[48] Statistics Canada, *Homicide in Canada*, pp. 17, 55, 67.

[49] *Globe and Mail*, 4 November 1982.

[50] Regina *Leader Post*, 26 December 1989.

[51] Ibid., 19 September 1989.

[52] Scott, *Theoretical Approaches to the Problem of Wife Assault*, ch. 5, pp. 116–38.

[53] Ibid., pp. 136–37.

[54] This was confirmed in a study of 99 identified men who abused their wives. Eighty–seven were found to exhibit evidence of a serious personality disorder including: "Schizoidal/borderline," "narcissistic/anti–social," and "passive dependent/compulsive." Reasonably serious psychopathology and wife abuse seem to go together. See L.K. Hamberger and J.E. Hastings, "Personality Correlates of Men Who Abuse Their Partners: A Cross–Validation Study," *Journal of Family Violence* 1, no. 4 (1986): 323–41.

Part IV: Victims of the Crisis: Men
Introduction: Elusive Masculinity and Patriarchy

[1] Simone de Beauvoir, *The Second Sex* (New York: Bantam, 1961 [1949]), p. 678.

[2] Ibid., p. 645.

[3] See N. Chodorow, *The Reproduction of Mothering* (Berkeley: University of California Press, 1978); D. Dinnerstein, *The Mermaid and the Minotaur* (New York: Harper and Row, 1976); and B. Easlea, *Science and Sexual Oppression: Patriarchy's Confrontation with Women and Nature* (London: Weidenfeld and Nicolson, 1981).

[4] S. Oberson, *Finding Our Fathers* (New York: Free Press, 1986).

[5] R.T. Hare–Mustin, "The Problem of Gender in Family Therapy Theory," in *Women in Families: A Framework for Family Therapy*, ed. N. McGoldrick et al. (London: Norton, 1989): 70–71.

[6] R.M. Eisler and J.R. Skidmore, "Masculine Gender Role Stress: Scale Development and Component Factors in the Appraisal of Stressful Situations," *Behaviour Modification* 11, no. 2 (April 1987): 123–36.

[7] W.E. Snell et al., "The Masculine Role as a Moderator of Stress–Distress Relationships," *Sex Roles* 15, nos. 7–8 (1986): 359–66.

[8] R.M. Counts and K. Reid, "A Comparison of Men Who Are Divorce Prone with Those Who Are Marriage Phobic," *Journal of Divorce* 10, nos. 1–2 (Fall/Winter 1986): 69–86.

[9] *Globe and Mail*, 24 December 1986.

[10] S. Blotnick, *Ambitious Men: Their Drives, Dreams and Delusions* (New York: Penguin, 1988).

[11] M.E. Snow et al., "Sex–of–child Differences in Father–child Interactions at One Year of Age," *Child Development* 54 (1983): 227–32.

[12] K. Millett, *Sexual Politics* (New York: Avon, 1969), p. 33.

[13] de Beauvoir, *Second Sex*, p. 679.

[14] Millett, *Sexual Politics*, p. 40.

[15] de Beauvoir, *Second Sex*, pp. 639, 641.

Chapter 11: Men and Economic Stress

[1] M. Moore, "Dual–Earner Families: The New Norm," Statistics Canada, *Canadian Social Trends* (Spring 1989): 24–26.

[2] *Globe and Mail, Report on Business*, 5 December 1989.

[3] National Council of Welfare, *Poverty Profile: 1988* (Ottawa: Supply and Services, 1988).

[4] G.I. Bowen and D.K. Orthner, "Sex–role Congruency and Marital Quality," *Journal of Marriage and the Family* 45 (1983): 223–33; T. Garland, "The Better Half: The Male in the Dual–Career Professional Family," in *Toward a Sociology of Women*, ed. C. Safilios–Rothschild (Lexington: Xerox College Publishing, 1972): 199–215; L.A. Gilbert, *Men in Dual–Career Families: Current Realities and Future Prospects* (Hillsdale, N.J.: Lawrence Erlbaum, 1985), ch. 3, "The Husband–Wife Relationship," pp. 22ff; B. Gray–Little and N. Burks, "Power and Satisfaction in Marriage," *Psychological Bulletin* 93 (1983): 513–38; S. Hardesty and N. Betz, "The Relationship of Career Salience, Attitudes toward Women, and Demographic and Family Characteristics to Marital Adjustment in Dual–Career Couples," *Journal of Vocational Behaviour* 17 (1980): 242–50; and E. Nettles and J. Lovinger, "Sex Role Expectations and Ego Level in Relation to Problem Marriages," *Journal of Personality and Social Psychology* 45 (1983): 676–87.

Chapter 12: Men and Emotional Stress

[1] M. Komarovsky, *Dilemmas of Masculinity* (New York: Norton, 1976), pp. 252–53.

[2] *Globe and Mail*, 21 April 1987.

[3] Ibid., 25 August 1984.

[4] See G.I. Bowen and D.K. Orthner, "Sex–role Congruency and Marital Quality," *Journal of Marriage and the Family* 45 (1983): 223–33. Bowen and Orthner found "low marriage quality" in relationships between traditional men and liberated women. Marriage quality was best in relationships where the sex–role attitudes of the men and the women were congruent.

[5] B. Yeh and D. Lester, "Statewide Divorce Rates and Wives' Participation in the Labour Market," *Journal of Divorce* 11, no. 1 (Fall 1987): 107–14.

[6] Regina *Leader Post*, 16 September 1980. H. Goldberg, *The New Male* (New York: New American Library, 1980).

[7] See the sources cited in footnotes 11 to 16 in Chapter 9 and footnotes 4, 5, and 9 in Chapter 3.

[8] *Globe and Mail*, 23 October 1989. An unpublished study by Statistics Canada and the Canadian Institute for Advanced Research, based on Canada Pension Plan data for 500,000 men who turned 65 on 1 September 1979, reports that unmarried men of age 65 experienced a 50 per cent greater chance of dying before the age of 70 than those who were married. The study also found an extremely direct positive correlation between the amount of income earned in the last 20 years of a man's working life and life expectancy. Men in the bottom 5 per cent income group faced twice the probability of death by the age of 70 as men in the top 5 per cent income group.

[9] J. Kiecolt–Glaser et al., "Marital Discord and Immunity in Males," *Psychosomatic Medicine* 50, no. 3 (1988): 213–29.

[10] A. Zeiss et al., "Sex Differences in Initiation of and Adjustment to Divorce," *Journal of Divorce* 4 (1980): 21–33.

[11] D.S. Huntington, "Fathers: The Forgotten Figures in Divorce," in *Divorce and Fatherhood*, ed. J. Jacobs (Washington, D.C.: American Psychiatric Association, 1986), pp. 53–83, 63–64 (my emphasis). Cited in Q. Rae–Grant and B. Robson, "Moderating the Morbidity of Divorce," *Canadian Journal of Psychiatry* 33, no. 6 (August 1988): 443–52.

[12] E. Goffman, *The Presentation of Self in Everyday Life* (New York: Anchor, 1959).

[13] F. Travato, "A Longitudinal Analysis of Divorce and Suicide in Canada," *Journal of Marriage and the Family* 49, no. 1 (1987): 193–203.

[14] O. Adams, "Divorce Rates in Canada," Statistics Canada, *Canadian Social Trends* (Winter 1988): 18–19.

[15] E. Durkheim, *Suicide* (New York: Free Press, 1966 [Paris, 1897]), ch. 3, "Egoistic Suicide," pp. 171ff, and ch. 5, "Anomic Suicide," pp. 241ff.

[16] Ibid., pp. 275–76.

[17] Regina *Leader Post*, 20 October 1984.

[18] Ibid., 12 January 1990.

[19] *Globe and Mail*, 28 November 1980.

[20] For the following on anti–and pro–women men's groups see the following: *Globe and Mail*, 11 March 1988; 25 February, 15 July, 2 August, and 17 October 1989.

[21] Komarovsky, *Dilemmas of Masculinity*, p. 257.

[22] de Beauvoir, *The Second Sex*, p. 689.

[23] Ehrenreich, B. *The Hearts of Men*, p. 182.

[24] Millett, K. *Sexual Politics* (New York: Avon, 1969), p. 363.

Chapter 13: The Double Burden: Men's Version

[1] M. Eichler, *Families in Canada Today* (Toronto: Gage, 1983), pp. 75ff.

2 J.–A. B. Parliament, "How Canadians Spend Their Day," Statistics Canada, *Canadian Social Trends* (Winter 1989): 23–27.

3 A. Hochschild and A. Machung, *The Second Shift: Inside the Two–Job Marriage* (New York: Penguin, 1989).

4 Regina *Leader Post*, 16 September 1980.

5 For what follows, see L. Haas, "Role–sharing in Couples: A Study of Egalitarian Marriages," *Family Relations* 29 (1980): 289–96; L. Haas, "Domestic Role–sharing in Sweden," *Journal of Marriage and the Family* 43 (1981): 957–68; S. Model, "Housework by Husbands," in *Two Paychecks: Life in Dual–Career Families*, ed. J. Aldous (Beverly Hills: Sage, 1982); J. Scanzoni, *Sex Roles, Women's Work and Marital Conflict* (Lexington: Heath, 1978); K. Weingarten, "The Employment Pattern of Professional Couples and the Distribution of Involvement in the Family," *Psychology of Women Quarterly* 3 (1978): 43–53; and S. Yogev, "Do Professional Women Have Egalitarian Marital Relationships?" *Journal of Marriage and the Family* 43 (1981): 865–71.

6 L.A. Gilbert, *Men in Dual–Career Families: Current Realities and Future Prospects* (Hillsdale, N.J.: Lawrence Erlbaum, 1985). In this excellent book Gilbert not only reports the results of her study, but also provides a first–rate review of much of the pertinent literature to which much of this section on men is indebted.

7 *Globe and Mail, Report on Business*, 2 December 1988.

8 Ibid., 7 January 1989.

9 S. Feinman, "Why is Cross–Sex Role Behaviour More Approved for Girls than for Boys?" *Sex Roles* 7 (1981): 289–300.

10 Cited in R. Maynard, "The New Executive Father," *Report on Business Magazine*, March 1989, p. 46.

11 Ibid., p. 48.

12 Gilbert, *Men in Dual–Career Families*, pp. 115ff.

13 Ibid., p. 115.

14 D.H. Bell, "About Men," *New York Times Magazine*, 31 July 1983, cited in Gilbert, *Men in Dual–Career Families*, pp. 3, 47.

15 C. Avery–Clark, "Sexual Dysfunction and Disorder Patterns of Husbands of Working and Nonworking Women," *Journal of Sex and Marital Therapy* 12, no. 4 (1986): 282–96.

16 Gilbert, *Men in Dual–Career Families*, pp. 115ff.

17 Ibid., pp. 85 ff.

Part V: Conclusion: Easing the Crisis
Introduction: Toward a New Family Policy

1 House of Commons, *Sharing the Responsibility: Report of the Special Committee on Child Care* (Ottawa: Queen's Printer, 1987).

2 M. Eichler, *Families in Canada Today: Recent Changes and Their Policy Consequences* (Toronto: Gage, 1983), ch. 9, "Legal Policies," pp. 272ff., and ch. 10, "Governmental Policies," pp. 306ff., especially pp. 320ff.

3 Ibid., p. 329.

4 Ibid., pp. 330–331.

Chapter 14: Proposed Directions in Family Policy

[1] *Gallup Report*, 14 August 1989.

[2] *Globe and Mail*, 3 February 1989.

[3] J. Moloney, "Maternity Leave," Statistics Canada, *Canadian Social Trends* (Autumn 1989): 30–34.

[4] *Globe and Mail*, 14 September 1989. See also ibid., 27 December 1984, 13 April 1988, and 1 November 1989.

[5] Ibid., 29 February 1989.

[6] Ibid., 11 January 1989.

[7] Ibid., 13 April 1989.

[8] *Gallup Report*, 4 December 1986.

[9] M. Cohen, "Giving Fathers an Even Break," *Globe and Mail*, 29 February 1989.

[10] *Globe and Mail, Report on Business*, 7 January 1989.

[11] Q. Rae–Grant and B.E. Robson, "Moderating the Morbidity of Divorce," *Canadian Journal of Psychiatry* 33, no. 6 (August 1988): 443–52.

[12] N. Rae–Grant, "Primary Prevention: Implications for the Child Psychiatrist," *Canadian Journal of Psychiatry* 33, no. 6 (August 1988): 433–42.

[13] Regina *Leader Post*, 1 April 1989.

[14] *Globe and Mail*, 13 February 1990.

Chapter 15: Proposed Directions in Feminist Policy

[1] For what follows, see: *Globe and Mail*, 23 and 29 January, 17 and 21 May, 27 July, 8 and 22 August 1988; 19 and 25 July, 5 August 1989, 4, 6 and 23 November 1989.

[2] Regina *Leader Post*, 17 January 1980.

[3] *Globe and Mail*, 28 August 1982.

[4] Ibid., 31 July 1989.

[5] Rosalie S. Abella, *Report of the Commission on Equality in Employment* (Ottawa: Supply and Services, 1984).

[6] Ibid., p. 254.

[7] *Globe and Mail*, 7 September 1989.

[8] Ibid., 16 June 1987.

[9] *Financial Post*, 22 June 1987.

[10] Ibid., 30 May 1988.

[11] P. Phillips and E. Phillips, *Women and Work* (Toronto: Lorimer, 1983), pp. 57–58.

[12] *Financial Post*, 30 May 1988.

[13] Ibid., 9 May 1988.

[14] *Globe and Mail*, 17 January 1990.

Index